1

Introduction

IN July 1950 a most extraordinary event in the history of broadcasting took place. In the UK, the British Broadcasting Corporation (BBC) broadcast a series of television programmes, entitled *Andy Pandy*, aimed at children under 5 years of age. Two years later it was joined by *The Flowerpot Men* and both programmes were scheduled under the heading *Watch with Mother*.[1] Later in the 1950s *Rag, Tag and Bobtail*, *Picture Book* and *The Woodentops* were introduced into the series.[2] Even though the BBC had been making children's radio programmes for nearly thirty years, it had not set aside a regular time of the day for children under 5. Until this moment the 'very young child' audience had not been 'completely neglected', but it could not, as Derek McCulloch, London Organizer and, later, Controller of *Children's Hour* Radio, stated in 1942, be 'catered for deliberately'.[3] He imagined that this audience could only enjoy a 'twinkly tune or certain sound effects, particularly domestic animals and everyday noises normally associated with the home'. It was not that, in hindsight, this small audience did not have the capacity to enjoy radio, but rather for McCulloch, and much of the *Children Hour* staff at the time, this audience was seen to come 'into no real category at all'.[4]

In 1967, as a small child myself, I remember sitting in a small suburban sitting room watching the black-and-white images of Andy Pandy and his friends. My mother, sometimes in the room with me

---

1 The BBC dropped the title in 1980. Anna Home, Head of Children's Programmes, says that the main reason for dropping the title 'was that large numbers of children at that time were not watching with Mother but were on their own or in groups' (Home 1993: 77).

2 *Rag, Tag and Bobtail* first started in 1953 and *Picture Book* and *The Woodentops* started in 1955. In 1955 they were scheduled within *Watch with Mother*: *Picture Book* on Monday, *Andy Pandy* on Tuesday, *The Flowerpot Men* on Wednesday, *Rag, Tag and Bobtail* on Thursday, and *The Woodentops* on Friday. The series finally finished in 1980 when it was replaced by a new pre-school programme, *See-Saw*.

3 See also McCulloch 1946: 230.

4 McCulloch, in a document on *Children's Hour* policy, distinguished between the 'individual listener' ('quite a common category for the modern child'), the 'group listener' ('who listens to most things') and the 'younger listener' ('who is able to glean a certain amount from most of our programmes'). He stated that very young listeners, the three to five year olds, 'are much in the minority and cannot, I think, be catered for deliberately in the limited time at our disposal' (McCulloch, July 1942, WAC R11/51/2).

and sometimes in the kitchen with the dishes, was a constant presence. My father, out working in a world I neither knew nor, at that age, cared about, would not return until near my bedtime in the early hours of the evening. He would return home, put on the daily news and I would retire to a world away from the television screen. Our home at the time was a recently built post-war modern house. In the sitting room, with sleek furniture and all-in-one hi-fi/drinks cabinet, sat a large bulky upright television set with a small screen. As I grew from pre-school to primary school, my television viewing was rationed to a couple of hours of children's programmes on weekdays and the odd programme at the weekend. If I was naughty or if I bit my finger-nails, my mother would exert strict control: 'No television today!' In my mid-childhood years, in the 1970s, the old television set was removed and a new streamlined silver-grey set with spindly legs took its place. My viewing was less restricted, but increasingly my fascination with its stories and facts took second place to playing outside with my friends.

In 1991, while conducting research for this book, my first child would sit with me watching the old black-and-white images of the same old programmes now transferred from film to video tape. We lived in a small flat, with little space, and the second television set was placed in the parental bedroom/study. The positioning of the supplementary television was a conscious decision to disperse the three children (two older children from my partner's previous marriage) across the home. Conflicts over viewing were equally displaced. As I took notes for my research, my daughter would sit and watch. The programmes played, one after the other, a single week's worth now condensed into a couple of hours. She would look up to me and call, 'Again', as the tape ended and began to rewind. My good fortune of having the BBC release these old nostalgic memories, ones which were not peculiar to myself, was harvested in the pleasures reaped by my 3-year-old daughter.

The repetition of pleasures across the three generations of audiences—audiences quite distinct in time and place—were made possible by the wilful and deliberate attempts of a small group of individuals who took a chance and decided to cater for an audience who, in hindsight, had been so wilfully neglected. This small and apparently insignificant event—the making of a series of programmes for the under-5 audience in 1950—exemplifies and foregrounds a basic fact of television, and the media more generally, that audiences are invented, but also that the conditions of their invention and reproduction are not controlled by a single agency, technology or regime. In this book I look at how a television audience is literally made through discursive and non-discursive elements. I look at how broadcasters, audience researchers, journalists, social scientists,

OXFORD TELEVISION STUDIES

General Editors **Charlotte Brunsdon**
John Caughie

Television, Childhood, and the Home

Feminist Television Criticism
A Reader
edited by Charlotte Brunsdon, Julie D'Acci, and Lynn Spigel

The Feminist, the Housewife, and the Soap Opera
Charlotte Brunsdon

British Television
A Reader
edited by Edward Buscombe

Television Drama
Realism, Modernism, and British Culture
John Caughie

Critical Ideas in Television Studies
John Corner

The Intimate Screen
Early British Television Drama
Jason Jacobs

British Youth Television
Cynicism and Enchantment
Karen Lury

Television and New Media Audiences
Ellen Seiter

Television, Childhood, and the Home

A History of the Making of the Child Television Audience in Britain

David Oswell

CLARENDON PRESS · OXFORD

OXFORD
UNIVERSITY PRESS

Great Clarendon Street, Oxford OX2 6DP
Oxford University Press is a department of the University of Oxford.
It furthers the University's objective of excellence in research, scholarship,
and education by publishing worldwide in

Oxford New York
Auckland Bangkok Buenos Aires Cape Town Chennai
Dar es Salaam Delhi Hong Kong Istanbul Karachi Kolkata
Kuala Lumpur Madrid Melbourne Mexico City Mumbai Nairobi
São Paulo Shanghai Singapore Taipei Tokyo Toronto
with an associated company in Berlin

Oxford is a registered trade mark of Oxford University Press
in the UK and in certain other countries

Published in the United States
By Oxford University Press Inc., New York

British Library Cataloguing in Publication Data
Data available

Library of Congress Cataloging in Publication Data
Data available

ISBN 0–19–874260–6

1 3 5 7 9 10 8 6 4 2

Typeset in Minion
by Graphicraft Ltd,
Hong Kong
Printed in Great Britain
on acid-free paper by
T.J. International Ltd,
Padstow, Cornwall

Oxford Television Studies

General Editors
Charlotte Brunsdon and **John Caughie**

OXFORD TELEVISION STUDIES offers international authors—both established and emerging—an opportunity to reflect on particular problems of history, theory, and criticism which are specific to television and which are central to its critical understanding. The perspective of the series will be international, while respecting the peculiarities of the national; it will be historical, without proposing simple histories; and it will be grounded in the analysis of programmes and genres. The series is intended to be foundational without being introductory or routine, facilitating clearly focused critical reflection and engaging a range of debates, topics, and approaches which will offer a basis for the development of television studies.

Acknowledgements

THIS project has been a long time in the waiting. It was started as a piece of Ph.D. research in 1989 and completed in 1995. Some of the material has appeared in various articles including: 'Making Room for Other Views: Some Problems with TV Literacy', in H. Domby and M. Robinson (eds.), *Literacy for the Twenty-First Century*, Brighton: Literacy Centre, 1992; 'All in the Family: Television in the Postwar Period', *The Media Education Journal*, no. 17, Winter 1994; 'Watching with Mother', in Cary Bazalgette and David Buckingham (eds.), *In Front of the Children*, London: BFI, 1995; 'A Question of Belonging: Television, Youth and the Domestic', in Tracey Skelton and Gill Valentine (eds.), *Cool Places: Geographies of Youth Cultures*, London: Routledge, 1997; 'Early Children's Broadcasting in Britain, 1922–1964: Programming for a Liberal Democracy', *Historical Journal of Film, Radio and Television*, 18(3), 1998; 'And What Might Our Children Become? Future Visions, Governance and the Child Television Audience in Postwar Britain', *Screen* 40(1), 1999.

My thanks go to various colleagues working in the field including Maire Messenger Davies, Sonia Livingstone, David Buckingham, Cary Bazalgette, Lewis Rudd, and Andrea Millwood Hargrave. To my students on the *Childhood, Technology, Culture* module. To Peter from Compendium Bookshop (who while I was a student always provided me with books on the cheap and who I would have liked to have seen this finished product). To Sean, Wendy, Bella, Ollie, Beatrix and Matilda (who, at three, talked about the 'ghosts in the television set'), Pat, Eric, Joyce, Sue, and Mike—family and friends. I don't need to say how supportive you've been! A very special thanks to Maria who read through and corrected various versions of this research.

Thanks also to Jacqueline Kavanagh and her staff at the BBC Written Archives, Caversham, UK. And to librarians and archivists at the British Library Newspaper Division, the Independent Television Commission, the Design Museum, the Architectural Association, the British Film Institute, the National Film and Television Archive, and the Fawcett Library.

My final thanks go to my Ph.D. supervisors, Valerie Walkerdine and James Donald. Both were and continue to be a great inspiration (intellectual and otherwise). And also to Stuart Hall who encouraged me to continue the project when I was about to give it all up, who has been a tremendous intellectual inspiration and extremely supportive.

Contents

government, and parents talk about the relation between children and television. But I also look at how this talk is mobilized in relation to programmes and programme schedules, television sets, domestic architectures, and imagined public communities. I look at the emergence of a particular arrangement of these symbolic and material elements in order to show how a child television audience was able to become addressed through forms of programming, made visible in the home as a problem needing supervision, constructed as an object of knowledge, and made available as the site of broad public discussion, argument, and organization. These arrangements are analysed in terms of their contingent, but also residual nature. I focus my attention on one particular historical instance concerning the making of the child television audience in the 1940s, 1950s, and early 1960s in the UK and in conclusion draw out its specificity by examining the present state of affairs.

The child television audience is still a site of heated public discussion and debate. It is caught up in arguments about how adults' television viewing should be regulated and in concerns about the appropriate forms of programming and viewing conditions for the child. In the US, Canada, UK, Australia, and elsewhere, there has been much discussion about the V-chip and the forms of content regulation it encodes. Jyotsna Kapur argues that the V-chip 'positions parents, particularly mothers, as their children's enemy or drill sergeant, who must carry out the orders of the experts in order to control children and protect them from television' (1999: 122). And Heather Hendershot argues that the development and implementation of the V-chip is closely tied to the interests of corporate power:

> The v-chip, a small part of the Telecommunications Act of
> 1996, will enable parents to block out programs they do not
> want their kids to see. Meanwhile, the rest of the act allows
> virtually unlimited media conglomeration. By focusing only
> on the act's import for child viewers, we lose sight of its
> important, broader implications. (1998: 218)

Children's television is not preserved from accusations of public decadence. A US-produced and globally distributed programme such as *Barney* is as likely to presage debates about public violence as about domestic attachments between mother and child. In the mid-1990s, the US suffered a spate of 'Barney bashings'. One such bashing took the form of a college student in Worcester, Massachusetts, jumping from a car and hitting a woman dressed as Barney, the purple dinosaur. Others took the form of Internet on-line hate talk about Barney (cited in Blair Hilty 1997: 72). Similarly, the UK-produced and globally distributed pre-school programme *Teletubbies* has inspired discussion from children's linguistic, cognitive and social development to gay rights issues. In the US Jerry Falwell, the fundamentalist Christian minister, attacked the show on the basis that one of its characters, Tinky Winky, was assumed to carry the connotations of gayness. He was a male character who carried a handbag. And in the UK, *The Guardian*, a daily national newspaper, carried a cartoon of Bill Clinton, the US President at the time, dressed up as a teletubby with cigar and 'Red Hot Dutch' (the satellite pornography channel) displayed on his tummy-screen. In the background, Monica Lewinsky was represented as the teletubby hoover. The copy ran: 'Clinty Winty comes clean'. The phallic connotations were clear.

However, instead of ranging across a loose assemblage of public and popular discourses about children's television and the figuring of the child in regulatory initiatives, my focus in this book is much more localized and specific. In looking at the making of the child television audience in the 1940s, 1950s, and early 1960s in the UK, we can begin to see how this focus of concern—namely, 'the child television audience' which is the addressee of particular cultural forms and which is represented in regulatory debates as a collective needing protection—was itself constituted as a distinct, separate, and substantive entity. In focusing on the UK and on one particular period, we can see in detail how an audience is both invented and substantiated. The child television audience is literally brought into being and given substance in this period. And it is only by looking at the detailed relations between particular social actors, particular discourses, and particular institutional arrangements that such a history of this coming into being of the child television audience can be made visible as a rich texture of social, cultural, and technical relations. Thus, this case study is able to provide both a point of comparison with the present (as detailed in the conclusion) and with other national contexts and configurations.

| Making Child Television Audiences | This book is primarily historical in the tone and form of its argumentation. Or, to put it another way, the theoretical import of my argument will be made using historical resources, rather than drawing upon a series of theories developed within social theory and media, communications, and cultural studies. That said, here I make visible, in a provisional manner, some of the significant theoretical ground upon which my argument rests. |

Making Child Television Audiences

■ **Social Studies of Audience-Making**

This book is primarily historical in the tone and form of its argumentation. Or, to put it another way, the theoretical import of my argument will be made using historical resources, rather than drawing upon a series of theories developed within social theory and media, communications, and cultural studies. That said, here I make visible, in a provisional manner, some of the significant theoretical ground upon which my argument rests.

Research on the invention and construction of audiences is a relatively under-explored field. It has focused on the economic construction of audiences as measured and marketized. Dallas Smythe, in his analysis of the audience as a commodity, classically stated that it was not programmes delivered to audiences, but audiences delivered to advertisers that counted (1977). In this model of analysis the audience is constructed as a 'coin of exchange'. Smythe's focus is not on individual viewers or their contexts of reception, but on a political economy of the television°audience (as a collective identity). Webster and Phalen identify three key aspects of this model:

1. Audiences have an economic value that is expressed in measurements of their size and composition.
2. Commercial media must be allowed to create and sell audiences if the media are to exist.
3. The public interest is served by preserving the system of advertising supported media. (1994: 30)

Of importance to us here is the notion that the commodification of the audience is dependent upon the production of scientific knowledge of the numerical size and demographics of that audience. Ien Ang has argued that:

Ratings discourse transforms the audience from a notion that loosely represents an unknown and unseen reality, a *terra incognita*, into a known and knowable taxonomic category, a discrete entity that can be empirically described in numerical terms. (1991: 56)

Other writers, such as Barnes and Thomson, have argued that audience measurement technologies 'play a vital role in sustaining the media whose audiences they measure' (1991: 92). Thus shifts from mass to niche audiences are reliant on corresponding shifts in audience measurement technologies (at the levels of data collection, analysis and legitimation).

Research on the relations between audience measurement techniques, ratings and the television industry has not only added substance to Smythe's basic thesis (that the audience is an economic entity), but also provided an agenda, posed forcefully by Ang (1991) and Morley (1990), for television studies to construe ethnography as the critical alternative. Ang, for example, argues that '[t]he importance of ethnographic discourse, in short, lies in its capacity to go beyond the impression of "false necessity" (Unger 1987) as prompted by the abstracted empiricism of taxonomized audience information' (Ang 1991: 169). In doing so, ethnography is given a privileged epistemological status in its understanding of the being of actual audiences. The ethnographic project of understanding the everyday cultures of broadcasting audiences has precedents in earlier research. For example, Hilda Jennings and Winifred Gill's use of interview and observational techniques allowed them to document the rich texture of radio cultures in a working-class neighbourhood in Bristol (1939).

Although, as Shaun Moores (1993) notes, the 'rather exaggerated comparison' between an earlier moment before radio and the 1930s with radio demonstrates a particular middle-class orientation to the data, the documenting of everyday cultures cannot be construed as having a privileged epistemological status external to the wranglings and negotiations of broadcasting institutional power. The research was sponsored by the BBC and accorded closely to its underlying philosophy at the time. Nevertheless, it would be too crude simply to locate such concerns within the extension of an overarching institutional apparatus, which constructs the audience as an imagined community (cf. Hartley 1987), in a way that erases any epistemological difference or critical distance between academic critical ethnography and industry-oriented audience research. But it is precisely this kind of argument that is made by the critic John Hartley.

In the work of Hartley audience measurement and market technologies play a central role in the way in which audiences are constructed and regulated as childlike. Hartley's argument is perceived as at the extreme wing of audience construction analysis inasmuch as the audience is theorized as if it were only ever a representation. For Hartley, the audience is an imagined community produced by an institutionalized regime. The audience has no external reality. And, although Hartley acknowledges that academic research is institutionally distinct from industry-motivated audience measurement, both forms of knowledge production are collapsed into a single regime through which audiences are imagined and regulated. There is no epistemological escape to ethnography, to a form of knowledge distanced from industry research, critical of it and with a situated affinity to the audience studied.

Understandably, a number of audience researchers, such as David Morley and David Buckingham, have been critical of some of the more extreme points of Hartley's argument. Buckingham rightly reads Hartley's analysis as one which allows no place for empirical (let alone empiricist) audience research. But rather weakly Buckingham argues that '[i]f audiences are just constituted in discourse, there would seem to be little point in bothering to find out about them' (1993a: 274). However, the issue is not that our investment in audience research (in the crude sense of what makes us get out of bed to do it) is dependent on the ontological status of the audience. Clearly many audience researchers, whether located in industry or academia, have little interest in explicit questions concerning the ontology or epistemology of the audience. The central issues are that Hartley, in construing the audience as an effect of the television institution, conceives of the discursive relations that construct the audience as monologic, presumes that the institution has an absolute agency and authority over the audience, and reproduces institution/audience relations within a binary logic. His approach raises serious questions, then, regarding the relations of agency, authority, and knowledge.

Michael Billig, in his argument for a more interactive notion of discourse to be taken up in media analysis (one derived in part from Bakhtin's analysis of discourse), argues that Hartley 'makes no attempt to situate these comments [by television producers and regulators] in order to examine the contexts of their utterance' (1997: 222). Hartley merely treats these utterances as symptomatic of a unitary regime of 'paedocratisation'. He fails to account for the dialogic, interactional, and dynamic way in which utterances about audiences are utterances, not statements: namely, they are addressed to others, with reference to external 'worlds' and in the context of a field of intertextual and dialogic relations (cf. Volosinov 1973). Thus as Buckingham also argues, 'Hartley's argument would seem to lead to audiences being silenced yet further, in favour of the "truly" critical voice of the analyst' (1993a: 274).

Buckingham has typified audience research within media and cultural studies as 'caught in an uneasy tension between perspectives that proclaim "the power of the reader" and those that insist on "the power of the text" ' (1993b: 14). Hartley's analysis seems to be caught in just such a binary, not between reader and text, but between audience and institution. However, Hartley's critics tend to reproduce the same problems. We can frame these problems in terms of the relations between agency and authority. First, these analyses of audience-making assume, *a priori*, that there are two primary categories 'audience' and 'institution'. Second, authority and agency are either located on one side of the binary or negotiated between the two positions. And third, questions of ontology are reproduced across this binary divide.

In this book, I methodologically put in brackets such a divide between 'institution' and 'audience' and instead look at the relations of agency and authority which both support and govern this division. Although I start by looking at a group of children's broadcasters, I make no assumptions about their identity or about their relations to others. I put on hold any notion that those who make the programmes have a distinct and separate identity from those who listen to the programmes and that the programmes are made for an 'audience'. I argue that we need greater complexity in the analysis of cultural production: namely an understanding of cultural production as a form of organization involving a network of agencies, each of which is specific to that particular cultural form. Children's television and the child television audience are brought into being through broadcasters, educationalists, psychologists, parents, and children in relation to specific sets of problems about the visibility of the child in the home, the disruption caused by television to other routines and forms of conduct, the appropriate forms of television programming, and the harm to the mental well-being of the child. Other cultural forms bring into play different actors and problems. What is important here is not an abstracted agent, such as the 'State', the 'Market' or 'Television', but the detailed singularity and form of the network. In this sense, I pursue a more micro-sociological analysis of the construction of (and divisions between) 'audience' and 'institution' as the outcome of mobilizations of networks of actors, action, and authority. The contrast between the 1950s and 1960s and the present makes clear the shifts in the arrangement of socio-technical actors. The child television audience is understood, examined, assessed, addressed, supervised, and regulated increasingly as an economic entity. The earlier actors, and the discourses that shape and arrange them, do not simply disappear; they become reconfigured. The psychologist, the broadcaster, and the parent, for example, still talk about the care and welfare of the developing child, but the child television viewer is now increasingly differentiated, studied, and governed within the context of the economic status of the child television audience. Authority and agency are not placed on one side or other of the divide between audience and institution nor are they internal to one or the other of these categories; rather, relations of agency and authority are both internal and external to these categories inasmuch as they both support and govern that division. Children's broadcasters, in building a sense of their audience and providing programmes for them, draw on and negotiate with agencies (such as experts, parents, and government) external to the television institution proper. Moreover, these agencies cannot, as Hartley argues, be analytically constructed as a single entity 'the television institution' (the paedocratic regime) which then constructs its audience as a representation. Rather the audience makes itself visible, not simply through its representation (such as in mechanisms of audience research), but through its ability to be multiply aligned and translated across audience researchers, audience measurement companies, lobby and pressure groups, government, consumer associations, parents, and children themselves. The 'audience' is not other to these agencies (just as the 'institution' cannot name its collective identity). Despite Hartley's emphasis that television institutions 'need not only to represent audiences but to enter into *relations* with them' (1987: 127), he reduces these relations to the divide between audience and institution.

It is only in the context of such an *a priori* divide that debate concerning the ontology of audiences becomes intelligible. Much of this debate has focused on the discursive nature of audiences: namely to what extent are 'audiences' simply representations? For example, Morley claims that Hartley confuses epistemology with ontology—in the sense that 'it is possible to recognize the necessarily constructivist dimensions of any research process without claiming that audiences only exist discursively' (1997: 135). Although Morley accepts that 'any empirical knowledge which we may generate of television audiences will be constructed through particular discursive practices and the categories and questions present and absent in those discourses will determine the nature of the knowledge we can generate', he argues, contra Hartley, that 'audiences do in fact exist outside the terms of these discourses' (1997: 135). In doing so, Morley reproduces (although inversely) the distinction between discourse and reality in terms of a binary divide between audience and institution. Of course audiences exist outside of any specific discursive/knowledge formation, but their existence is only knowable as existence through other discursive formations. Any attempt to reveal the being of an audience is always negotiated in relation to other authorities who reveal that being as different. The problem with Hartley's account, as with other work on the social construction of audiences, is that agency and authority are collapsed into a rather simplistic binary opposition.

Nevertheless, Hartley's work has been important for thinking about the social construction of the child television audience inasmuch as it shows how the social construction of childhood (although Hartley does not analyse 'childhood' *per se*) has played a significant role in the governance of television and in the way audiences are imagined.[5] In looking at the figuring of the 'child' in audience construction and regulation, this work has also shown how 'social research' (whether produced by academics, government, or industry) is, in some circumstances, closely interrelated with 'industry research' into ratings. The mass audience is, according to Hartley, a childlike audience and is governed accordingly. And yet historically, the child television audience, as opposed to an infantilized family or trans-generational audience, has been predominantly constructed and problematized as a *social* and *psychological* phenomenon. Or rather its status as an economic entity, as governed by measurement techniques and ratings, has always been secondary to its social and psychological status. The child television audience has normally only been visible as an economic entity within the purview and authoritative supervision of those experts who have in their interests the welfare of the child. In this sense, the economic status of the child has never been pure. It has always been socially inflected. But the extent to which this is still the case is made clear in the contrast between the 1950s and 1960s and the present. In providing such a perspective, we can identify the main ground of negotiation and mobilization.

Carmen Luke's history of US discourses on children and television provides an important account of how the child television audience

---

5 See also Richard Paterson 1987.

has been constructed as a social and psychological problem within the context of academic production of scientific knowledge (1990). She shows how scientific knowledge of the child television viewer is socially constructed and historically specific. She provides an account not of myths of childhood innocence, but of the socially situated production of truth. Truths about the child viewer, she argues, are constructed within specific discursive rules and relations 'which regulate, make possible, and yet delimit who can speak, under what conditions, about what kinds of problems'. She continues '[t]hese rules and relations constitute discursively formalized knowledges which, in turn, construct historical versions of the human subject' (1990: 5). For Luke, the production of truth about the child television viewer has both a sociology and a history, but one which is limited by a select group of experts authorized to speak about the child viewer within specific institutional settings and in relation to specific discursive rules and relations. She argues that:

> concepts, theories, and data about TV and children came
> from those institutional sites and authorities 'authorized'
> to speak about children: from field and laboratory
> experiments conducted by some educationalists, but mostly
> by psychologists and sociologists. The scientific knowledges
> imposed on TV-viewer relationships, situated predominantly
> in the private domain of family and household, came from those
> disciplinary authorities, sites, and perspectives that claimed
> privileged knowledges about children. (Luke 1990: 15)

Luke claims that such knowledge is derived from 'school-associated sites, rather than at the site and in the context of the home viewing situation' (1990: 16). For Luke, the authorities who have been able to speak, scientifically and authoritatively, about the child viewer 'were predominantly academics employed in universities, from whence their institutional authority and status derived' (1990: 16). Moreover, 'public and government reactions to findings exposed and authorized by academic expertise can also be read as a "knowledge effect" of prevailing theory and research which frames the TV/youth debate' (1990: 13). This statement by Luke presumes, in the first instance, a certain understanding of knowledge and expertise. It is one that would preclude knowledge and expertise produced by children's broadcasters, government committees, and so on. And in the second instance, it presumes that policy is simply symptomatic of academic knowledge. Luke's approach is problematic on both counts.

In Luke's account, academic scientific knowledge has a primacy with regard to wider social relations and actor-networks within which the child television audience is encoded. The discourses that shape the contours of parental supervision in the home or those that feed into the practices of making television programmes for children or those that circulate in the press as a mix of expertise and opinion are all conceived as secondary, in Luke's analysis, to the academic production of scientific truth. Notwithstanding the importance of academic knowledge, I will argue that the child audience is also constituted through other forms of authority and discourse. Broadcasters, policy makers, government, the press, and parents, for example, might align themselves with academic authority and knowledge, but their actions, thoughts, and decisions, with regard to the child audience, are not reducible to such academic authority. I will show how a range of authorities are aligned or misaligned in an emergent formation of the child television audience in the immediate post-war period in the UK.

■ **Historical Reception**   Much of the work on the social construction of media audiences has (as I've already mentioned), looked at the institutional production of knowledge about audiences. Therefore, particular forms of institutional organization have been foregrounded: namely, audience research departments, marketing, planning and strategy departments, and academic research. Some of this research has, exceptionally, considered creative production (cf. Cantor 1987 and 1994; Tunstall 1993; Wartella 1994), but mainly in terms of what producers think about or how they talk about their creative products and the relation between them and other organizational factors (e.g. the economics and regulation of the industry). Accordingly, much of this research has had little to say about media texts (i.e. films, television programmes, and so on) or their relation to viewers, spectators, or readers. Much of this research has paid little attention to the aesthetic strategies visible in the texts themselves or to the way in which the textuality of, for example, television programmes positions and configures historically specific forms of subjectivity (whether or not these positions or configurations are taken up by 'actual' viewers). Work within historical reception studies has responded to these limitations and, although problematic, such studies help us to understand the complex dialogic relations across the traditional boundaries of 'institution' and 'audience'. Most notably, historical reception study provides leverage for introducing important questions regarding the specificity and singularity of the cultural forms of children's television and the modes of address to imagined viewers at home.

Thus, whereas studies of audience-making have worked mainly from a sociological perspective, studies of historical reception have been more concerned with a literary and historical analysis of the contingent, but possible, interpretative strategies deployed at a given socio-historical moment in relation to historically specific textual forms. Much of this work has emerged from a dissatisfaction with a-historical and universalist psychoanalytic accounts of text/subject relations within cinema studies (cf. Mayne 1993). In an early formulation of its object of study, Janet Staiger condenses its problematic in the following manner:

> What we are interested in, then, is not a so-called correct reading of a particular film but the range of possible readings and reading processes at historical moments and their relation or lack of relation to groups of historical spectators. (Staiger 1986: 20)

Although writers such as Brunsdon (1981) and Kuhn (1984) had made a distinction between textually-inscribed spectators (or viewers in our case) and social audiences, Staiger, in her discussion, interestingly shifts between both terms while focusing mainly on the subjective and subjectivity. Thus work like this in historical reception studies has a different methodological focus to that of sociological studies of audience-making. Such work is more textualist in its orientation; it tends to be centred on understanding historically the range of possible meanings regarding particular media texts (i.e. a single film or television programme); and it tends to analytically foreground the relation between text and subject in terms of the process of *reading*. This is the case despite attempts, by critics such as Tony Bennett and Janet Woollacott (Bennett 1982; Bennett 1987; and Bennett and Woollacott 1987), to broaden the analytical objects of study from texts to intertextual relations. Bennett and Woollacott, for example, use the notion of 'reading formation' to understand the socially specific intertextual relations through which particular readings are made possible.

Robert Allen offers a broader understanding of the legitimate areas and objects of study for historical reception analysis. Taking his lead from Philip Corrigan's (1983) argument that 'the problem of the audience in film history could usefully be recast within the rubric of cultural studies' (Allen 1998: 15), Allen presents four components of such a study: (*a*) *exhibition* refers to 'the institutional and economic dimensions of reception' (ibid.); (*b*) *audience* refers to the discursive construction of spectators within a collective such that '[i]ndividuals are not only solicited but constructed as audience members through industry attempts at marketing research, advertising, promotions, the decor of movie theatres, and so on' (1998: 17); (*c*) *performance* includes 'the immediate social, sensory, performative context of reception' (1998: 18); and (*d*) *activation* refers to 'what realists would call the "generative mechanisms" that operate variably and uneven force in producing the myriad readings of individual texts among viewers and over time' (1998: 19). Allen provides a framework for including both a more textualist account of particular filmic readings and a sociologically-oriented analysis of audience construction. This analysis thus moves beyond the hermeneutic boundaries of historical reception study established by Staiger, and helps to construct a space in which historical relations across institutions and audiences, texts and subjects can be made intelligible. Similarly, Janet Thumin, in her discussion of methodology with regard to historical television reception study, suggests 'two different routes towards an understanding of the historical television audience . . . neither is wholly satisfactory but used in conjunction they might lead somewhere into this almost effaced landscape of the 1950s' (1995: 53). She argues that one route involves a textual analysis of spectator positioning and the other analysis of 'other types of "audience" data', such as programme reviews, programme notes and 'a range of examples of the ways in which television programmes, audiences, viewing practices and so on were being discussed' (1995: 54). Whereas social studies of audience-making have tended to conceive of audiences as institutional constructions, they have paid little, or no, attention to the socially and historically specific relations between institutional discourses and conditions of reception.

Staiger usefully reminds us that there can be no recourse to an idealist notion of the spectator or viewer as 'individual' (1986: 20), as it is precisely the subject that is historicized. The subject is caught up in historical texts through a common constitutive bond of language. The subject, in this sense, is not outside of history. Equally though, there can be no recourse to an historicist move of 'binding meaning to a temporal point of an object's appearance' (ibid.). Instead, we should attempt to reconstruct from historical data (texts and discourses) the ' "horizons of expectation" for any given text' (1986: 22). But Staiger's analysis founders on the organizing metaphor of 'reading'. The meanings of particular texts and subjective interpretations of them are historicized, contextualized, and made contingent, but the relation between text and subject is reduced to a process of reading, such that texts are only ever made intelligible inasmuch as they are read and such that 'reading' constitutes a historical constant, the basis of a structural relation between text and subject. Despite attempts to historicize the relations between text and subject through a hermeneutic understanding of intertextuality as the horizon of expectation, the categories of 'text' and 'subject' (or spectator, viewer or reader) remain intact. For Staiger the relation between text and subject constitutes a distinct analytic object of study, structurally similar to that of the relation between institution and audience.

In this book, although historical reception studies underpin my attempt to loop back conditions of reception within questions of audience-making, the text/subject relation remains fundamentally problematic as it, *a priori*, presupposes a form of relationship that is precisely my object of enquiry: not simply how is the relation between television institution and child audience constructed and governed, but how is the relation between children's text and child subject made possible as a site of constant innovation? How is children's television programming constituted as a distinct, albeit complex, cultural form? How does it emerge in the form that it does? How do the differences between different forms of children's television emerge? How do the programmes themselves and talk about the programmes relate to, imagine, and address a child audience at home? How does the division between the child viewer at home and the adult producer in the studio (or on location) emerge as an almost natural and inevitable one? In the deliberations of children's television broadcasters (in terms of what to present before the child and in terms of how they imagine the context of the child's viewing), but also in the pronouncements of regulators (whose adjudications mark the limits of children's television, family television and adult television), the child television audience circulates as a virtual figuring. This is meant not in the sense that child viewers or parental subjects at home interpret television through the horizons set by those others (as if the relay of power between broadcaster, regulator, parent, and child were transparent and immediate), but in the sense that the actions and authorities of those others help to establish the conditions of possibility of the child television audience itself. What is striking in our genealogy is that the metaphors deployed to account for the relation between children's television programmes and child viewer are plentiful and do not simply reduce to that of 'reading'. Parents, social scientists, broadcasters, government, and others speak of the behavioural effects of television, of children's cognitive competencies, of domestic habits and manners and of emotions. To reduce these categories to 'meaning' and 'reading' would be to reduce our understanding of the contingent dynamics at play in this history.[6]

■ Childhood The third line of thinking that informs this book concerns the problematic of the child and childhood. To put the problem starkly, the child is so easily imagined within the structural relations of institution/audience and text/viewer because it is so easily imagined as being devoid of the competencies of production. The child can only be imagined as 'viewer' or 'audience'. How else could it be imagined and acted upon? By and large, historically this has been the case. Broadcasting cannot simply invent the child as a producer, a decision-maker, an author of texts. It cannot simply invent the child as an authority, given the baggage that this entity carries with it, through the weight of earlier and co-temporaneous histories. Nevertheless, the moment under investigation in this book (roughly 1940 to 1960)

6 Ang makes a similar point (1991:13).

is significant because at this time broadcasters did make attempts
to involve children in television production and to understand them
as participating in television broadcasting. Moreover, the relations
of audience knowledge and expertise at this time were fragile and
precarious. In the archives of broadcasting policy, journalistic com-
mentaries, and academic research we can see how children were literally made into an audience and, correspondingly, how authorities
and forms of expertise were established to watch over (to know and
protect) this fledgling entity.

Despite the growing academic interest in television and cultural
constructions of childhood, much of my study implicitly connects to
a longer history and analytic investigation of childhood. The sociology
and social history of childhood has pieced together a well-documented
field of research which makes visible the emergence of modern forms
of childhood, the relations of intimacy between child and parents,
and the growth of expertise which surrounds the child. Most notably,
the social historian Philippe Ariès has argued that childhood was a
social invention that began to emerge in the late seventeenth century.
Aries boldly states that '[i]n medieval society the idea of childhood
did not exist' (1962: 125). Despite his numerous critics, Ariès contends
that it was the *idea* of childhood, not actual children, that was brought
into existence at this time. Ariès focused primarily on the institution
of childhood through the apparatus of schooling and much subsequent research has looked at childhood as a temporal period which
is divided into developmental stages and governed accordingly (cf. Rose
1989; Walkerdine 1984). However, these dividing practices within
the school (and between school, family and public life) are now also
analysed in terms of their spatial characteristics. The discipline of the
classroom, whether in nineteenth-century monitorial schools or
child-centred schools of the 1970s onwards, is spatially orchestrated
in terms of the arrangement of desks, the relation between pupils and
the relation of pupils to teachers (cf. Foucault 1979; Walkerdine 1984;
Donald 1992).

There is, as mentioned above, a growing field of study that looks
at media representations of childhood (cf. Kinder 1999; Bazalgette
and Buckingham 1995; Holland 1992). In these writings childhood is
primarily analysed in terms of its textual inscription. For example,
Lynn Spigel, in her wonderful analysis of the US cartoon strip *Peanuts*,
draws on expert and institutional discourses (e.g. child psychology)
not in order to say something specific about those institutions, but as
resources to detail the manner in which a specific imaging of childhood was accomplished (1999). Her work focuses on the textuality of
children's media culture, but there is also a wealth of research within
media and cultural studies and sociology which considers the figuring of the child and childhood across institutional sites such that both

adult and child are regulated—most notably Donzelot's analysis of nineteenth-century governance and policing of families (1979). The sustained work on moral panics (which takes the circulation of media images of childhood innocence as a sign of, and precursor to, censorship) pursues research in this vein, but somewhat differently to that of Donzelot's analysis (cf. Barker 1984; Barker and Petley 1997).

The imaging, spatialization, and temporalization of childhood finds its most singular expression in the figure of the child. Instead of posing childhood against the child, in terms of image/reality, myth/truth and society/nature, work within the sociology of childhood has begun to unpick the reality, truth and nature of the child itself. Much of this work has provided a deconstruction of the ideas of the developmental psychologist Jean Piaget. Valerie Walkerdine's research on developmental psychology and schooling precisely details the methodological minutiae through which psychologists are able to make claims concerning the truth of cognitive development, not simply for one child, but for all children (Walkerdine 1984 and 1988). Alan Prout and Allison James neatly summarise one aspect of this type of argument:

> The singularity of 'the child' . . . is constructed around the
> twin assumptions of the naturalness and universality of
> childhood. Children do not have to appear: 'the child', as the
> bodily manifestation of cognitive development from infancy
> to adulthood, can represent all children. (1990: 11–12)

The 'child viewer' is predicated on this singular, universal, and natural image of the child. The child viewer is not simply a particular child, but an instance of an universal subject: the child. The child television viewer, whether in the form present in the discussions of broadcasters regarding the addressee of their programmes or in the expert languages of social scientists, discloses particular children within the purview of a universal category. Moreover, those children who for whatever reason do not fit the mould are thus also made visible as anomalies, as different, to be worked on or excluded in the various manifestations of power and knowledge.

In contrast, it is 'children' who become bearers of the experiential, the actual, the ordinary, and the everyday. However, despite many reservations about the category of 'children' inasmuch as it emerges, in much academic writings, as a counter to (and point of criticism of) institutional arrangements of power and inasmuch as it reproduces a model of structure and agency, 'children' are the limit case of my analysis. For methodological reasons, my historical knowledge of real children watching television in the 1940s, 1950s, and 1960s is primarily gained through the accounts of adults, through their research, their reports in the press, policy documents or, secondarily, through their memory (cf. O'Sullivan 1991). As Staiger perceptively noted:

'evidence of marginalized readings may be unavailable simply because of their marginalization . . . [a]nd much of what may be available may be severely warped by that which is missing. Thus, a constant dialogue between theory and "evidence" is necessary' (1986: 21–2).

My intention in this book is not to pose the child television audience in terms of any one of these categories of child, children, and childhood. The child television audience is neither simply the aggregate of actual children watching television nor is it a composite of the child television viewer (with variations from the norm) nor is it simply a socially constructed discursive category. The child television audience is constituted through the relations between these different categories of childhood, but also problematizes them. In this sense, my argument is not reducible to a crude notion that institutional arrangements have an 'effect' on the subjectivities of actual viewers at home.

Historical Methodologies	One of the reasons for this rather elusive analytical definition of the historical child television audience is that it cuts across different registers. My investigation of the child television audience as a historical object of study thus involves analysis of the following: the analysis of the conditions of reception within which the child television viewer was seen to be located; the discourses of programme makers in their attempts to address the child; the textual features, forms of address and discourses of childhood encoded in children's programmes; the veridical discourses of academic and industry researchers who research actual children, assemble them in a taxonomic collective and divide them on the basis of normative (and normalizing) models of the child viewer; and the policy documentation and press accounts which circulate publicly available discourses of childhood.

However, another reason for the elusiveness of the historically inscribed child television audience (at least in the context of my study) is that it accommodates the analysis and documentation of this entity's conditions of emergence: namely at the moment it becomes visible as a distinct and separate entity. My book is based on extensive primary research on children's broadcasting in the UK. It initiates an excavation of the field in such a way that particular problems at particular moments in time are invoked and investigated according to the plentifulness of surviving historical documentation and inasmuch as these problems have a resonance and significance for a contemporary understanding of the relations between television, childhood, and historical reception. Given these qualifications, my book tells a story— a genealogy—of a small group of dedicated individuals who have an interest in, but no necessary control over, the processes in which they have an interest: namely, domestic reception, programming, knowledge of the audience, national identity and the market.[7] This group of individuals is bound together through a common ethical investment in serving the child, but also changes and transforms across time and space. We can see a common lineage between children's television broadcasters now and radio broadcasters from the 1920s and 1930s, but there are also clearly differences and discontinuities. Moreover, this group, in order to pursue its interests, necessarily assembles with other actors (both human and non-human). There are clear shifts in terms of the relations between different assemblages of actors (parents, experts, technologies, children, spaces, and so on) at different, for want of a better phrase, epistemic moments.

In conducting my research, I initially went through various files containing policy statements, departmental memos, personal memos, letters of complaint and praise, audience research, programme notes, press cuttings and various other documents at the BBC Written Archives in Caversham, Reading, UK. I looked at documents from the earliest days of *Children's Hour* radio in the 1920s to those concerning children's television programmes in the 1960s. Likewise, I went through documentation held by the Independent Broadcasting Authority (now the Independent Television Commission). In addition, I looked at the surviving children's programmes, which the BBC had recorded and not destroyed, from the National Film and Television Archive and was able to take full advantage of the release on video of many of the recorded pre-school programmes from the 1950s to the present. This archive of programmes enabled me to provide an analysis of the relationship between programme material and wider policy debates.

From this initial starting point, I followed the leads 'upwards' to various government reports of the broadcasting and educational committees from the 1920s to the 1960s and then 'downwards' to various articles in newspapers, journals, and magazines held at the British Library Newspaper Division at Colindale, North London, UK. In my analysis of women's magazines, for example, I looked at the weekly magazine *Woman* from 1937 to 1939 in its entirety and I looked at the monthly magazines (*Ideal Home, Home and Garden, Woman and Home,* and *Everywoman*) and the weekly magazines (*Woman* and *Woman's Own*) between 1946 to 1965 in their entirety. As with Spigel, my intention was to look at how television was represented in popular discourses, to see how it was imagined in the home and to see whether, at this level, the child was figured as an object of concern. Given these magazines' interest in the design and architecture of television in the home, I moved 'upwards' again to a series of government reports concerning domestic architecture and design. A constant pursual of

---

7 They have no control, but they clearly have an impact.

leads, a constant following of actors and references: neither inductive nor deductive, but encyclopaedic in motivation.

This book explores, then, how the child television audience as a whole (albeit divided and separated) has been constructed and how programmes have been specifically designed for it. Forms of living, which now seem so ordinary and taken for granted, are investigated in the conditions of their emergence. How, and why, have children's broadcasters been so concerned about the child audience? How have these concerns been constructed as a central element in the figuring of an ethical practice (most visible in public service broadcasting)? How have these concerns been aligned with knowledge produced by audience researchers in the broadcasting institutions and by social scientists (statisticians, psychologists, and educationalists) in the academy? How have parents, predominantly mothers, and the domestic spaces and times they watch over been incorporated and reconstructed in relation to pleasures and problems associated with children watching television? How has the press represented these concerns?

The book is organized into a further six chapters which, in turn, address a set of specific issues concerning the formation of the child television audience. In Chapter 2, I return to children's radio broadcasting in the 1920s and 1930s in order to mark out the child television audience's prehistory. Any difference is not shaped simply by the difference in technology, but by the way the technology is assembled within a different series of authorities, practices, and discourses. In this period we see the emergence of an ethical relation between the children's broadcaster and their audience. Seventy years ago the audience was shaped within a whole set of concerns about democracy and about making the culture of broadcasting commensurate with the cultures of the everyday population of radio listeners. Notably in this period there was no conception of a distinct child audience, but rather the child listener was always addressed in the context of a familial and domestic audience. In the following chapters I look at the formation of the child television audience in the post-war period. In Chapter 3 I look at how children's television broadcasters addressed their audience and attempted to involve children as participants in broadcasting culture. The child audience was both addressed as a distinct audience and differentiated according to age and developmental factors. In Chapter 4 I look at how television was accepted into the home, at its design within the home and at the forms of supervision developed in order to accommodate children's television viewing. In Chapter 5 I consider the way in which a series of expert discourses came into play, shaping the child television audience as an entity quantified through audience measurement technologies and one normalized and pathologized through psychological knowledge. In

Chapter 6, I look at how concerns about the child television audience were circulated across broadcasting institutions, press, and government policy. Finally, to conclude, I look at some contemporary issues regarding the child television audience. Most notably, I consider the changing shape of the audience with regard to the globalization, segmentation, and hybridization of audiences in order to make visible the degree to which the discourses and practices of the 1950s have a pertinence in the present.

2
The Early Years:
Ethics and the Public Good

PERHAPS unlike other forms of broadcasting, children's broadcasting has required that those who make the programmes have a responsibility to their audience over and above the money that might be made from transmission or the entertainment of the children watching. Even those at the hard edge of market competitiveness feel compelled to justify the worth of their programmes for children in terms other than those of profit or pleasure maximization. In contemporary discourse, even the most commercial and market-oriented companies legitimate and conceptualize their children's programmes through claims of 'education' and a sense of care for the developing child. How seriously we want to take such claims is another question.

Despite some important discursive and institutional changes in later years (which I discuss in later chapters in the book), notions of the public good and of the ethical responsibility of the broadcaster were built into the construction of the child audience and its programmes in the early days of children's radio broadcasting. In these early discourses and practices, as now, the distinction between entertainment and education was complex and was not simply analogous to a distinction between commercial and public service broadcasting. Of more importance were questions of how child audience and programme could be construed in relation to the assumed conditions of domestic and national reception and how to shape the child at home and in the community.

The early debates show very clearly how the idea that broadcasting could be constitutive of a modern participative democracy framed the issues of the public good and the ethical duties of the broadcaster. In the 1920s, 1930s, and 1940s children's radio broadcasting was a site of constant innovation. The BBC, better known for its state-sponsored paternalism, was a laboratory of experimental practice in which questions of how to produce programmes for the good of the child were central to the ethical deliberations of the children's broadcasters. At no time before do we encounter such collective deliberations in an institutional setting. The institution of radio was novel in that it brought together committed individuals and provided the space for their collective experimentation. And yet this concern about participative democracy soon fell by the wayside, even if it has been somewhat revived through a burgeoning contemporary debate on children's rights and about the radical potential of digital networked interactive technologies.

Before commencing, I should strike a few notes of caution. First, children's broadcasters conceived and addressed children always in relation to, and within the context of, the family. Children never simply existed as a distinct and separate audience in their own right. Second, the broadcasters demonstrated a keenness in overcoming the gap between themselves and their audience, but despite the inventive solutions devised, this desire was also their shortcoming. The distance between the adult broadcasters (invariably middle class) and children at home was not so easily reconcilable despite attempts at affiliation. As I show later, the difference between broadcaster and audience was made all too clear with new audience research mechanisms which exposed the failings of earlier practices. And yet, in doing so, a fundamental logic of children's broadcasting became instituted: namely the desire for broadcasting to be commensurate with its audience and the invention of mechanisms and knowledges which constantly make visible its failing.

Democracy Made Easy

On 23 December 1922, eight days after the British Broadcasting Company Ltd was formally registered, *Children's Hour* was first broadcast.[1] Reith referred to it as one of the two 'forms of art' (the other being radio drama) which broadcasting was developing 'as specifically its own', which was 'wholly novel', and which 'leaped at once into its permanent place in the scheme of popular life' (Reith 1928: 34). This liminal space between day and night (a twilight zone of magic and fantasy), from its inception, had become conceived as being intimately caught up in the practices of everyday life.

Children's everyday lives were viewed by broadcasters in the 1920s, 1930s, and 1940s within the context of a set of debates about the potential for broadcasting to constitute a democratic space. J. C. W. Reith, Director General of the BBC (1922–38) and powerful shaper of its organizational philosophy and practices, talked about the ethos of giving 'voices to the voiceless':

---

1 *Children's Hour* was usually only 45 minutes long and sometimes only 30 minutes. This space in the day's programmes, between 5 p.m. and 6 p.m., took its name from a poem by Henry Wadsworth Longfellow: 'Between the dusk and the daylight, When the Night is beginning to lower, Comes a pause in the day's occupations, That is known as the Children's Hour.'

One might still have pattered about the benefits to invalids and aged folk; to those whose lot was cast in the loneliness of insularity in space or isolation of spirit. About the amenities of town being carried to the country; about the myriad of voices of nature (nightingale included) being borne to the city street. About the voice of leaders of thought and action coming to the fireside; the news of the world at the ear of the rustic. About the Prime Minister speaking direct to the nation from his room in Downing Street; the King heard by his farthest and most solitary subject; the facts of great issues, hitherto distorted by partisan interpretation, now put directly and clearly before them; a return to the city-state of old. All that and more. (Reith 1949: 100)[2]

For Reith, broadcasting 'could familiarise the public with the central organisation that conducted its business and regulated its inner and outer relations', as well as become 'an index to the community's outlook and personality which the statesman was supposed to read' (1949: 135). Similarly, Derek McCulloch, London Organizer for *Children's Hour* and later Director of *Children's Hour,* in a 1942 policy document argued that the objective of the programme was to 'interest children in *contemporary life*', 'interest them in *their own part of the country*' and 'contribute *to their moral and religious education*' (McCulloch 1942, 2, WAC R11/51/2, my italics).[3] Broadcasting's provision of communicative entitlements was thus to be established, Reith argued, according to the imperative to 'cover more and more of the field of social and cultural life' (1949: 135).

In the US at the time, although there was a desire for radio to reach all of the population, such a desire was less concerned with radio's democratic potential. Instead of imagining radio as making possible the enunciation of a diversity of voices, radio was envisaged as providing a single voice able to unite a nation fragmented by migration: 'A single voice, spoken in Washington but heard throughout the length and breadth of the land, a voice vibrant with emotion, staunch with courage and ringing with authority will summon the nation to action, will wield a hundred million people into a solidarity such as the world has never known before' (A. H. Corwin, March 1923 cited in Boddy 1994: 109).

In the UK, the concepts of 'mixed programming' and the 'general public', deployed in order to integrate diverse publics, to allow the

---

2 Reith was originally General Manager while the British Broadcasting Company was a private monopoly, but his title changed to Director General once the British Broadcasting Corporation had become a public body in 1927.

3 I use the standard notation for files kept at the BBC Written Archives Caversham (WAC).

exhibition of different cultural forms within a shared common culture and to make the population visible to government in all its complexity, were central to the shaping of *Children's Hour*, as they were to BBC programme policy generally (cf. Scannell and Cardiff 1982). McCulloch referred to *Children's Hour* as

> a miniature of broadcasting as a whole, covering a wide field representing drama, music, talks, stories and dialogue stories, outside broadcasts, variety features, topicalities, competitions, quiz features, religious services and regular prayers, and programmes by young artists. We produce a miniature, or microcosm of broadcasting because we cover almost every type of broadcast material under those headings. (McCulloch 1946: 229)

Children's programming was designed, not merely to present material of interest to listeners nor simply to provide a space for children's voices, but to represent the life of the child population to government: namely, to make children visible within broadcasting and to invent the child audience as an object of government. Surprisingly, though, the broadcasters were far from clear about the nature of the child audience. While the *BBC Handbook* in 1929 stated that the audience consisted of children 'of every age, size, shape and sex' (1929: 253) and J. C. Stobart, a former inspector for the Board of Education and Director of Education at the BBC, stated that *Children's Hour* aimed to address 'the widest range of children having regard to sex, age and social class' (Stobart, 'Children's Hour, Instructions', 1927, 2, WAC R11/27/2), it was equally evident to 'anyone who has had expertise of children that there is a wide gulf between a boy or girl of eight and one of twelve and the adolescent of sixteen' (*BBC Handbook* 1929: 253). Some local stations divided up their programme into different categories of ages. Birmingham, Leeds and Stoke-on-Trent, for example, allotted a quarter of an hour each for 'Tinies', 'Middies' and 'Teens'. Others were very definite that *Children's Hour* was not intended to address the 'very young listener'.[4] The broadcasters also knew that there were 'hosts of other people listening too, thousands of adults among them' and so it conceived of its audience as 'young in years or in mind' (ibid.).[5]

As Simon Frith has stated, BBC radio was constructed as a 'peculiar form of public participation' (Frith 1983: 121). Broadcasting acted as

---

4 Roger Eckersley, Director of Programmes from September 1925, thought it pointless to make programmes for children under eight. He thought that young children were not attentive enough (cf. Hartley 1983: 24; McCulloch 1946: 230).

5 In 1960 adult listeners outnumbered children listening to *Children's Hour*. More children listened to adult programmes on the Light service than listened to *Children's Hour*.

a relay between government and governed, but also constituted the home within that public space: 'the microphone could achieve where print and the philosophic formulation of doctrine had failed . . . Not the printable scheme of government but its living and doing, the bringing of personalities of leading figures to the fireside, which could unite government and governed' (Reith 1949: 135). Radio not only opened up what could be talked about in the public domain, but also provided the basis for public talk within the home. It provided a way, both of constructing the public within the domestic and of imagining the familial as public. Broadcasting, as Sir Ernest Barker stated in the *BBC Quarterly* in 1946, 'enriches the citizen's power of choice' to the extent that 'it already means "Democracy made easy"' (1946: 33).

However, despite Barker's image of broadcasting as extending democracy into the home, such that the citizen 'in his own armchair' could listen to the 'authentic statements of competing ideas' (1946: 33), the hearth far from provided the glue for national community.[6] *Children's Hour*, in terms of the audience it brought into being, posed certain problems. The audience was imagined as including both children and adults within a familial and domestic context. McCulloch stated that: '[t]he *Children's Hour* audience is inevitably a family one by virtue of the content matter of the programme, the design in presentation and the hour of radiation which in general coincides with the time-honoured family institution of five o'clock tea.' The child audience was constituted not as a distinct audience of children but as a family audience and McCulloch argued that: '[i]t is our contention that where family listening exists it can only have good results because parents and children both have common ground for listening and for discussion' (McCulloch 1946: 229–30). There were others, though, who conceived of this domestic space in less than cheery terms. Janet Adam Smith, former literary editor of *The Listener*, writing a year later pictured, in her article 'Children and Wireless' in the *BBC Quarterly*, a very different scenario: 't]he machine turned on full blast, and the baby screaming; the nursery squabbling because two want to hear News from the Zoo and the third can't bear it; banshee wailing as the juvenile experimenter gets to work on the knobs; dinner turned into an anxious misery of scufflings and whisperings because Father wants to hear the one o'clock news' (Adam Smith 1947: 162).

This was an environment in which choice led, not to 'democracy made easy', nor to talk between parent and child, but to familial, and also inter-domestic, disharmony (cf. Moores 1988). For example, 'radio noise' inside and outside the home was conceived as a problem.

6 In contrast to some earlier historical research (cf. Scannell and Cardiff 1991; Frith 1983) I would want to stress the deeply problematic nature of the alignment between hearth and nation.

John May, in an article in *Woman* (May 1937), advised housewives to arrange their rooms so that loudspeakers were away from the walls dividing one's own home and one's neighbours as 'radio vibrations travel very clearly through even thick brick walls, especially the thumping low notes which can be so disturbing'. Likewise he called for listeners not to listen passively and continuously. Honor Croome, in an article entitled 'The Family Listens' in *BBC Quarterly*, talked about the problem of children being addicted to 'noise'. He coined the term 'noise addicts' and suggested that children were particularly susceptible to this form of addiction (Croome 1949).

In this sense, the public sphere of broadcasting, as modelled on the Athenian *polis*, faced certain problems in dealing with the domestic nature of the audience and particularly with children's radio listening. As with Reith, McCulloch conceived of the role of children's broadcasting and the formation of citizenship as constitutive of a form of pastoral care. He formulated the duties of the children's broadcaster in the following manner:

> Our wish is to stimulate their imagination, direct their reading, encourage their various interests, widen their outlook, and inculcate the Christian principles of love of God and their neighbour. It is our desire to try to help to mould the listening tastes of future citizens. There is no smugness in our attitude towards this vital task—only a feeling of great responsibility. (McCulloch 1946: 229)

This responsibility was not simply to the child's radio listening, but to the whole social and cultural life of the child or rather to the cultivation of children as good citizens and 'loyal subjects of the Empire' (McCulloch 1942, 2, WAC R11/51/2). The 'art of broadcasting' for children involved caring for both the soul of the individual child listener and for the morals and manners of the child population as a whole. The governance of *Children's Hour* and of children's radio listening were central to the attempt to realize 'a return to the city-state of old'.

The Ethics of Children's Broadcasting

The art of children's broadcasting was necessarily contradictory and yet organized around a certain relationship between broadcaster and child. The art of broadcasting to children required of the presenters a 'careful training and wide experience', but also an 'innate sympathy with the child-heart'. This 'innate sympathy' was to be found in those who 'maintain living contact with children': youthful adults, parents or genuine aunts and uncles (Davies 1957, 2, WAC R11/51/3). McCulloch stated that:

I would stress the profound necessity for specialised staff who have a real love for, and an understanding of, children in the right sense. I would encourage the appointments of married women where possible as Directors or Organisers. Similarly, their staffs should have youthful interests at heart, and here the employment of single men and women can be satisfactorily visualised. (McCulloch 1944, 4, WAC R34/298)

However, 'innate sympathy' should not, it was argued, lead to 'any excess in the direction of childishness and sentimentality [which] restricts the area of appeal' (Stobart 1927, WAC R11/27/2). The address to the child audience rested upon the ability of the broadcaster to spontaneously express his or her very being to the child listener. This expression was to be honest and profoundly sincere (McCulloch 1946: 230). Major A. Corbett Smith, the first station Director at Cardiff, who moved to London in 1924 to become its Artistic Director and to develop 'features' broadcasting, presented a policy document entitled 'The Children's Corner' which stated that:

A story should never be read, save in very exceptional cases. It should be told as a 'vivid reminiscence' of the teller. It must come spontaneously . . . All art is a projection of personality. The teller must so fuse his own personality with that of the author as to make a perfect art-work . . . Be natural. Do not pose nor 'talk down' to your audience . . . on no account suggest or close with a moral . . . Similarly there must be no suggestion of a hint of education. (Corbett Smith 1924, 3–4, WAC R11/27/1)[7]

The children's broadcaster was not merely someone trained to make programmes, but someone who was formed, and who formed themselves, through a set of ethical practices. These practices required the broadcaster to search within themselves to recognize themselves within their very being: 'the man or woman who can entertain children is a very rare being' (Corbett Smith 1924, 5, WAC R11/27/1). Yet how were these ethical practices elaborated in relation to the problem of addressing a domestic and public audience?

Children's broadcasters needed to address their listeners intimately, as if they were speaking to them individually. Such a mode of address was not limited to *Children's Hour* broadcasters. Reith argued that '[t]here was an intimacy and individuality of appeal in a broadcast talk which made it radically different from those agencies which served for many generations—the oration, press comment, public meeting, club or public discussion' (Reith 1949: 135). Talking to the domestic required a particular discipline. As Hilda Mattheson, who was Head of Talks (1927–31), stated:

---

7 Such ideas about storytelling for children were common at the time (cf. Bryant 1910).

> Early experiments with broadcast talks showed that it was useless to address the microphone as if it were a public meeting, or even to read it essays or leading articles. The person sitting at the other end expected the speaker to address him personally, simply, almost familiarly, as man to man. (Mattheson 1933: 75–6)

Radio talk was not simply an address to the audience at home, but also a way of addressing the microphone physically present before the speaker in the studio. The talk was neither read nor impromptu. It was personal, yet ordered. Manuscripts submitted to the BBC had to be 'translated' into a suitable personal spoken style.[8] Radio talk, to both children and adults, was formed as a way of speaking within the public space of the home and a familiarized public space. For Reith, it was radio talk, as a particular form of address and ethical practice, which offered the possibility of bringing government and governed together through the ether. This was a relationship which according to Reith, as stated earlier, had previously vanished due to the nature of political rule in the West (Reith 1949: 135). As the political franchise was extended in the late nineteenth and early twentieth century and Britain became ever more industrialized and massified, radio seemed to fill the democratic gap (Scannell and Cardiff 1991: 11).

Nevertheless, the form of intimate and individual address to the child presented certain problems for the BBC. Perhaps surprisingly, debates about the construction of children's broadcasters as 'Aunts' and 'Uncles' provide evidence of the difficulties of this form of address. On the one hand, the intimacy of these personalities made possible an affection between listeners and the radio service. Ella Fitzgerald, Central Organiser of *Children's Hour* Programmes (1923–5) stated that: '[f]rom all that I personally have gleaned and opinion I have collected from parents and children it does seem that permanent uncles are the feature of the children's hour that has really won children's affection: they get to know the sort of story a serious uncle reads; the sort of remark a humorous uncle will make; and they build up personalities which are alive and lasting as no casual uncle or aunt can ever become' (Fitzgerald, 'Suggestions for Children's Hour', 1924, 4, WAC R11/27/1). The embeddedness of these personalities within everyday popular discourse is made clear through the use of the closing words of Uncle Mac ('Goodnight children everywhere') and Stephen King-Hall ('Be so good. But not so frightfully good that someone says to you, "Ah! and what mischief are you up to?" So if I were you I should be just fairly good') in Oxo's advertising campaign in women's magazines in 1945.

---

8 Such translation of written script to oral presentation was not peculiar to the BBC. It was, for example, an important radio technique in Nazi Germany (cf. Lacey 1994).

On the other hand, there were those within the BBC who thought that *Children's Hour* should be 'the most strenuous mental and physical work' and that such personalities led to 'relaxation'. Corbett Smith referred to them as 'the most damning evidence of inadequacy' (Corbett Smith, 1924, 6, WAC R11/27/1). Eckersley in a memo to Reith in 1926 stated that he wanted such personalities to be done away with and Stobart, in his 'Children's Hour, Instructions', stated that:

> There is no Headquarters Rule for or against the use of
> these terms, which are traditional in the Children's Hour.
> The purpose is to establish friendly relations and create a
> happy family atmosphere. Experience has shown, however,
> that the excessive use of nicknames and pet names is
> detrimental, especially when applied to senior officials whose
> work lies mainly outside the Hour. Station Directors should
> be careful to see that titles are not abused and that the proper
> informality of the Children's Hour is not allowed to prejudice
> the dignity of the Corporation's work. (Stobart, 1927, 2, WAC
> R11/27/2)

Likewise, Corbett Smith, as early as 1924, also asked whether the success of *Children's Hour* 'is built upon a genuine, worthy, and permanent foundation', to what extent the programme assisted in the 'formation of character' and to what extent it was conducted for the 'entertainment of the "uncles" and "aunts" ' (Corbett Smith, 1924, 6, WAC R11/27/1). In February 1925 Stobart argued at a Programmes Board that there should be a reduction in the 'backchat' of such personalities. By 1936 the Northern Ireland Regional Director stated that he had dropped the use of 'uncles' and 'aunts' and that *Children's Hour* should have full-time permanent staff, with expertise and equal pay (Northern Ireland Director, 1936, WAC R11/27/2). These debates and policy decisions show how the deliberations of children's broadcasters were clearly directed to the reception of radio in the home and yet how problematic it was for broadcasters to 'affiliate to the situation of their audience and align their communicative behaviours with those circumstances' (Scannell 1991: 3): that is, speaking publicly within the home was an ongoing and constant problem.

The domestic nature of this public space equally informed debates concerning the aesthetics of the mode of address. The intimate and yet respectful address to the audience was coupled with one which was neither high- nor low-brow but middle-brow and which was neither simply entertainment, nor education, but entertainment which is 'educative in the best sense' (cf. Frith 1983). Entertainment had been a concern of the BBC as a whole and Reith was at pains to make it clear how the BBC should intervene in this area. In 1924 Reith referred to entertainment in the following way:

entertainment, pure and simple, quickly grows tame; dissatisfaction and boredom result. If hours are to be occupied agreeably, it would be a sad reflection of human intelligence if it were contended that entertainment, in the accepted sense of the term was the only means of doing so. (Reith 1924, quoted in Frith 1983: 108)

However, by 1928, in the *BBC Handbook* of that year, Reith stated:

As to the remaining time given to music and entertainment, let there be no idea that this category is one given grudgingly and under pressure from public and press. It is not so. To provide relaxation is no less positive an element of policy than any other. Mitigation of the strain of a high-pressure life, such as the last generation scarcely knew, is a primary social necessity, and that necessity must be satisfied. (1928: 34)[9]

It might appear that there was a contradiction between the two statements and that Reith had changed his mind as to BBC policy on entertainment. Or it might appear that while the public wanted entertainment in the early 1920s, Reith in 1924 needed to declare his hostility to it in order to present the BBC as an institution worthy of becoming a public corporation and not one pandering to the desires of the masses.[10] Whatever the case, it would be incorrect to assume that Reith simply opposed entertainment and education (cf. Mercer 1986; Frith 1983). There is a distinction to be made between, on the one hand, 'entertainment in the accepted sense' ('entertainment, pure and simple'), which was associated with the 'mass audience' and tainted with the connotations of 'Americanness', and, on the other, 'entertainment which is educative in the best sense'.[11] It should be noted that although Reith typified US radio in terms of 'the chaos of the ether' and attached similarly negative connotations to the commercialism of US radio broadcasting, the crowded nature of much of the airwaves in the US, at least until the Radio Act of 1927, was in fact due to the 'amateur, philanthropic and publicly supported rivals' (Boddy 1985: 128) to the large commercial station operators. Moreover, it was the commercial industry which during the late 1930s and

9 Scannell and Cardiff argue that Reith's defensive tone can be accounted for by the press criticism of the standard of broadcast entertainment in the late 1920s. Newspaper polls showed that audiences preferred vaudeville and variety, which were on short supply from the BBC. The transition from Company to Corporation seemed to many to alter 'the relaxed and friendly relations between broadcasters and listeners' (1991: 225).

10 This may have been so given the fears of Americanization voiced by critics such as F. R. Leavis, Q. D. Leavis, and Denys Thompson. It was important that the BBC set itself apart from other 'mass media' (cf. Donald 1992: 74–5; Frith 1983).

11 The production of entertainment 'in the best sense' allowed broadcasters to address the developmental capacities of the listener (Reith 1949: 145).

1940s, did not want to repeat the chaos of radio broadcasting in the development of television.

Those involved in making programmes for *Children's Hour* stressed that programmes should not be didactic or instructional. Stobart stated that all broadcasting contained the possibility of being 'educative' and that there was a distinction to be made between broadcasting as a 'series of thrills and stunts' and broadcasting as a 'steady supply of enjoyment, entertainment and interest' (cf. Briggs 1985: 69).[12] In June 1927, J. C. Stobart stated in his 'Suggestions for the Conduct of the Children's Hour' that:

> Sound notions on such subjects as fair play, pride of country, personal cleanliness, good manners, thrift, 'safety first', sympathy with animals and birds, tidiness in public places, respect for the aged, self-restraint, etc. should be fostered in the Children's Hour through example in song and story rather than by formal exhortations. (Stobart, 1927, 1, WAC R11/27/2)

Central to this form of address was a recognition of the context of familial and domestic listening. Stobart stated that:

> If the organisers of the Children's Hour keep in mind
> the creation of the atmosphere of a good home and the
> presentation of real beauty in song, story, music and poetry
> on a plane attractive to the young, they will inevitably, without
> self-conscious efforts, raise the standard of culture in their
> young listeners and the result will be educative in the best
> sense. (ibid.)

Although this appears as an idealized projection of the middle-class family, Stobart goes on to argue that the domestic context of listening needs to be understood inasmuch as it is constituted against other institutions which produce children as subjects, namely the school. He states in 'Children's Hour, Instructions' that:

> The Children's Hour is, as its name implies, 'a pause in the day's occupations'. Those in charge of it will bear in mind that their listeners are for the most part children who have had a long day in school already, and very possibly have home lessons still before them. The purpose of the Children's Hour is therefore mainly recreation and not instruction or moral improvement. (Stobart, 1927, 1, WAC R11/27/2)

It is also clear that the distinction between school and home was framed in relation to the spatiality and temporality of children's everyday lives. Although the notion of 'educative in the best sense'

---

12 Stobart also talks about the distinction between broadcasting which 'civilises' and broadcasting which is 'crude' (Stobart, 1927, 1, WAC R11/27/2).

derives from an Arnoldian conception of culture, it functioned not merely as an ideological tool, but as a regulative device for shaping children into citizens in the context of their quotidian temporal and spatial existence. Concerns about education and entertainment were framed within a set of considerations about the address to the domestic audience and the way in which radio listening was embedded within the everyday routines of children.[13] There was a clear demarcation between the requirements of schools broadcasting, which addressed children as 'pupils' and which was instructive, and *Children's Hour* broadcasting, which addressed the child in the home. Programmes for the child audience were thus constituted in relation to specific institutional supports, such as the school and the home. However, although *Children's Hour* broadcasters had to be entertaining in order to distinguish the programme from the institution of schooling and to gather an audience at all, they were caught up within a wider set of debates concerning pedagogy and culture. The BBC needed to distinguish itself from the taint of 'pure entertainment' and to align itself with critics of mass society. Whereas for the Leavisites mass society posed a fundamental problem for democracy, for Reith, and others at the BBC, radio had to be popular in some quantitative sense (or rather it had to make possible through its universality an address to one and all) in order to make radio the condition of possibility for a living democracy.[14] An ethics of the child audience was intimately caught up in a network of concerns about the temporal and spatial location of the child (its routines, habits, activities) as well as a return to the city-state of old.

Family Listening and Forming Future Citizens

In the US, although radio listening was conceived in the early 1920s as an 'active sport', such activity was conceived (as in the UK) as a masculine pastime. Radio sets were large and messy (cf. Spigel 1992; Moores 1988). In the latter part of the 1920s, after the redesigning of radio so that it was now modelled in order to fit neatly with the domestic decor of the living room, in the US there was a recognition that the new female listener took the form of a distracted housewife. In the UK, however, despite similar redesigning of radio sets and the marketing of sets to women at home, such notions of 'distraction' were

---

13 McCulloch stated that: 'We do not then aim primarily at educating our listeners, as is the case in Schools Broadcasting, but we do realise that, for example, good literature and good music are educative in the best sense. We have to remember that the majority of our audience listens to us after a long day in school with a session of homework ahead' (McCulloch 1946: 229).

14 However, it should be clear that it was precisely Reith's aversion to the notion of the mass audience which provided one of the conditions for the conception of the general public and for the need to negotiate between entertainment and education.

taken as the object of concern, something to be removed from the habits of the listening population.

If the ether provided the means of a liveable democracy, the practices of proper listening provided the conditions of good citizenship. Stobart, in 'Suggestions for the Conduct of Children's Hour', argued that 'we grow more fastidious the more good music and good literature we hear and read' (Stobart, 1927, 2, WAC R11/27/2). Likewise, Corbett Smith, in his policy document 'The Children's Corner', stated that:

> Teaching 'how to listen', 'how to appreciate', is of paramount importance. This is, in fact, the keynote of the Hour. It is to send the children to read, listen, or see for themselves and their ever-increasing pleasures and happiness. A child who early learns the loveliness and purity of a Mozart minuet will not in later years be content with 'We have no bananas'. He has learnt the difference between gold and tarnished tinsel. He has won an abiding joy. He will seek to share that joy. His character is a-building. (Corbett Smith, 1924, 5, WAC R11/27/1)

It was through 'good example' that children could listen properly which implied in turn that they engaged in other worthwhile activities. However, although 'culture in itself' provided one of the conditions for proper listening, competency needed to be developed through other techniques of choosing which programmes to listen to and when to turn the radio on and off.

In the early years of the BBC, there was no fixed schedule so that listeners had to consciously choose which programme to turn on. However, during the late 1930s, scheduling began to be introduced and by 1937 there were forty fixed points in the schedule between 6 p.m. and 10.30 p.m. (Scannell and Cardiff 1982: 181). By 1940, after the resignation of Reith, objections to scheduling were seen as evidence of the BBC's aloofness. The *BBC Handbook* stated:

> rightly or wrongly, it was being urged a year or two ago that the BBC was aloof from its listening millions, offering programmes with a complacent air of 'Take it or leave it'. These various experiments in 'Listener participation' with many others are evidence that the ice, if it ever existed, has rapidly melted. New and friendlier contacts have been established on the air. (1940: 83)

Children's Hour, though, had been from its inception regularly broadcast between 5 p.m. and 6 p.m. during the week: a result of the demarcation between school-time and home-time. While scheduling was employed more generally across BBC programme policy, there was still the exhortation to all listeners to look at the *Radio Times* or the daily paper every morning to see what to listen to, when to turn on the radio and when to turn it off. Choosing to turn on the radio was conceived not as a random activity but as an act of 'discrimination'.[15] McCulloch wrote in the *Children's Hour Annual* in 1937:

> We welcome both criticism and appreciation alike, but, it is not fair to criticise unless you have been prompted to do so as the result of selective listening . . . which means taking the weekly edition of Radio Times and making notes about the programmes you really do want to hear. It may be, for example, that on Wednesday you find there is a play you particularly want to hear, but that you have a friend coming to tea—not a quiet friend, but one you must talk the hind leg off a donkey. Have him—or her—to tea, by all means, but cancel your proposed date with the loudspeaker, or of course, cancel the invitation to your friend and arrange another day. (McCulloch 1937, cited in Susan Briggs 1981: 103)

A clear spatial distribution is marked out here, between activities with friends and listening to the radio. The two are conceived as mutually exclusive. Not only did the discourse of proper listening require that one consciously chose whether or not to listen to a programme, but also that radio listening itself become inserted into the fabric of children's everyday lives and become attributed with the importance of everyday decisions. Broadcasting could become intimately connected to the everyday. The act of switching on the radio set was in itself an act of participation: to open oneself to the public. It was a conscious decision to meet the broadcaster some of the way and to 'collaborate' in the programmes (cf. Stowell 1940: 80).

However, as stated above, this concern to make children active and participative listeners was tempered by a conception of the disharmony which radio could bring to the routines of the home and the goals of education. Janet Adam Smith stated that:

> Blackest of all is the threat to concentration. Its most obvious form is interference with homework. There are plenty of homes where preparation is regarded as even more a nuisance by the parents than by the children: schools are expected to relieve the mother of trouble, and not to add to her worries at home by awkward demands for silence and space. And so no effort is made to find a quiet room for a child (this indeed may be a physical impossibility, especially in winter with unheated bedrooms); or even to clear a table, or a corner of a table; and in such homes the

15 John May, in *Woman* magazine, argued that listening to the radio was like going to the theatre. It was an 'appointment with the BBC'. He encouraged listeners to: 'Train yourself and your family (especially the family!) to switch off directly the item that you are listening to is finished. Don't let interest die a lingering death!' (May 1937).

wireless is likely to be kept, if not bawling, at least humming,
while John tries to make sense of *Je suis, tu es.* (1947: 163)

The aim of the broadcasters to encourage proper listening, as a facet
of good citizenship, was caught up in a set of problems concerning the
wider government of domestic and familial space and time. It is clear
that the art of children's broadcasting rested upon the exclusion of
certain types of listening in certain domestic situations which they
knew existed. Reith intended *Children's Hour* to provide 'a happy
alternative to the squalor of the streets and backyards' (quoted in
Frith 1983: 112) and in 1942 McCulloch stated that:

> Inevitably, I think, our programmes are aimed at children of
> elementary and secondary education. Undoubtedly there are
> many poorer class children living in such crowded conditions
> that they cannot really 'listen' in the proper sense of the word.
> I am thinking of the child who spends most of its time running
> errands, minding the baby or, most frequently, playing in the
> street. In these days of better schools and better education I think
> we confront ourselves in the belief that the Children's Hour net
> is spread wide and catches the better majority. (McCulloch, July
> 1942, 3, WAC R11/51/2)

Ien Ang describes such working-class practices, which McCulloch
saw as conducive to improper listening and Reith conceived of as
'obstacles', as the audience's resistance to institutional discipline and
she goes on to say that '[i]n fact, a history of European public service
broadcasting could be written from this perspective: a narrative in
which the resistance of the audience against its objectification in the
name of highminded, national cultural ideals drives the story forward'
(Ang 1991: 101). However, instead of arguing that 'the audience'
somehow pre-existed its formation and that, through its resistance,
it somehow acted as the motor and agent of this particular history,
I want to suggest that these particular 'obstacles' were central to the
ethical deliberations of children's broadcasters. The 'happy alternative' of proper listening within the homes of the 'better majority' (the
goal of those 'highminded ideals') and the obstacles of improper listening within the overcrowded working-class home and the squalor
of the streets and backyards (in Ang's terms, the failure of, and resistance to, those ideals) are clearly presented *within* the discursive formation of the child audience (and *within* the BBC ethos of public service
broadcasting).

The techniques deployed to form proper listening conditions drew
upon the resources of the family. As Croome stated: '[t]he "family"
nature of wireless entertainment does not merely affect the nature of
the programmes themselves; it affects the very nature of listening'

(Croome 1949: 32). For Croome, the responsibility for supervising listening conditions fell upon the parent. Parents needed to accept that children might make choices 'that we ourselves detest', and that, as a result, they, the parents, had some responsibility in providing the conditions for participative and selective listening—even if at a distance.[16] It was not until the 1940s that commentators began to talk in any detail about the responsibilities of the parent (primarily the mother) and then in relation to the general conduct of the family rather than the child listener in particular. At the end of his article, Croome stated that:

> In a sense, the advent of almost universal listening has added something to the responsibilities of parenthood. It is perfectly possible to forestall and check noise-addiction, and that without instituting a tyrannical censorship of listening proper; to establish, among other recognised family rules, the understanding that the wireless shall only be switched on when some freely chosen item is about to begin, and switched off when it ends. Far better an ecstatic concentration on Dick Barton or Much-Binding-in-the-Marsh than a nine-tenths automatic— or enforced—hearing of Bach. (1949: 36)

Croome invokes the responsibility of the mother and housewife, as a relay between the ideals of the broadcasters and everyday life. He says:

> From every aspect, indeed, family listening is what the family makes of it. It is an art, answering to the art of the broadcaster himself; an art by no means easy, comprising both a co-operative technique of programme-building and a skill in harmoniously weaving together this and other elements on family enjoyment. It is in fact part of the art of life in general, and a part capable of being practised in circumstances providing few other facilities;

16 Janet Adam Smith stated: 'How can we foster this active state of mind in the child listening to the wireless? We can begin by not wincing when he chooses what we ourselves detest. Far better that a ten-year-old should turn on "William" because he really likes it than "Camus" because he thinks that it is what you want him to like. The act of choice—which involves studying the programme and being conscious of alternatives—is a necessary and important exercise in keeping the appreciative faculties alert' (Adam Smith 1947: 165). Likewise she continued by stating that: 'That habit of choice established, we can encourage experiment, and prevent too easy discouragement. And above all we can, in our own practice as well as in our explicit advice, insist that there is a two-way traffic in wireless: it brings us music, plays, ideas; it leads us to music, plays, ideas. Here the example of school broadcasts, which always point the way to further activity, is a great influence for good. The parent who encourages his child to listen to string quartets and Sunday evening talks, and never takes him to a concert or suggests a book for him to read, is threatening to make a lazy and passive man of him. For our attitude to listening, and to the arts that we meet through the medium of wireless, helps to determine whether we have an active or passive attitude to life itself' (1947: 165–6). It is clear from the article that it was the mother who was being addressed and it was her responsibility which was being invoked.

amid austerity, restrictions and overwork. And it is an art whose development, in any particular household, falls eminently within the sphere of the housewife, to whom it thus offers indirectly an opportunity far wider than any programme directed specifically to her individual enjoyment or instruction. (ibid.)

Although the broadcaster could not control the way in which radio was used within the home, there was agreement that the 'art of broadcasting' required the broadcaster to 'scan his matter with much of the selective vigilance exercised by a Victorian publisher with his eye on the family reading-aloud circle' (Croome 1949: 32). Broadcasting was used not only to incite the responsibilities of the mother and housewife to care for her children's health and for the home, but also to construct a care for her children's listening among those responsibilities (cf. Moores 1988 and 1993).[17] The techniques of broadcasting provided an instance of, what Donzelot has termed, 'government through the family' (i.e. that the techniques of power and knowledge construct the mother as the State's delegate making her responsible to form, through her care and attention, healthy citizens) (Donzelot 1979). The art of children's broadcasting both constituted the familial and the domestic within its terms and conditions and also offered a solution to the perceived need for *responsibilization* within these given conditions.

However, Adam Smith, at the end of her article in the *BBC Quarterly* asked: 'Do we want conscientious parents to give their children exercises for wireless appreciation, as they do for flat feet and round shoulders?' She went on to answer her question: 'No: for like all the best things in life, listening properly to the wireless will be an instinctive growth, as much the result of unconscious example and never-formulated assumptions as of any conscious plan.' She pictured the 'millions of families' with their individual characteristics unconsciously moving towards family harmony:

How, for instance, are we to harmonise good manners and considerateness in listening with the readiness to experiment that helps to create genuine taste? The answer is that there is no such thing as perfect listening in a perfect family. There are only millions of families, who all want something different in their listening. All family life is an attempt to harmonise varying interests, experiences and emotions: the wireless simply presents us with a new set of tensions that have somehow got to be reconciled to make a harmonious pattern. Each family

---

17 The objectives of broadcasting were aligned with the objectives of those other welfare institutions and practices which were concerned with the health and well-being of the child (cf. Drotner 1988: 192–201).

must resolve them in its own characteristic way . . . (Adam
Smith 1947: 166)

The mapping of the child audience in relation to these manners, habits,
demands, and responsibilities provided not only a way of thinking
about radio in the 'family circle', but also of imagining the child as a
citizen, doing 'good works' in the local community. Here we get a
clear sense of Reith's notion of radio as commensurate with the social
and cultural life of the population. In the early years of *Children's
Hour*, participation was encouraged through the forming of Radio
Circle clubs.[18] In 1923 Birmingham set up the first Radio Circle and
soon afterwards other local stations set up similar clubs.[19] There were
nineteen altogether, linked to the various local stations. They were
known variously as Radio Circles, Radio Sunbeams, Radio Leagues,
Fairy Leagues, and the Fairy League of Animal and Flower Lovers.
The membership ranged from 624 members in Hull to 45,000 members in Cardiff. Although Cardiff had no subscription, most stations
charged 1 shilling. In 1927 all stations were instructed to charge not
more than this amount in order to cover the cost of a badge and
postage. The members, through various activities, developed a
special relationship with their local station. Aberdeen Radio Circle
stated its aims as follows:

> The Radio Circle has the motto 'Truth, Friendship, My Country',
> but the organisation is used mainly to promote a strong bond
> between the listening child and the station. Our general attitude
> is that while we are interested in all children, we are especially
> interested in members of the Radio Circle. Radio Circle members
> have the right to have birthday greetings broadcast, to take part
> in concerts at the studio, receive preferential treatment regarding
> visits to the studio, etc. (Radio Circle, 'Functions of Organisation',
> 1927, WAC R11/58)

Initially *Children's Hour* broadcast birthday greetings for all children
who wrote in. However, after a short while, there were too many re-
quests and they were limited to Radio Circle members only. Likewise
Radio Circle members were invited to visit the station to meet their
favourite personalities and to see how radio broadcasting worked. In
Bournmouth the condition of membership was that 'each member,
loving animals and flowers, promises to cherish them and protect
them from hurt and harm, earnestly to try to spread among children

---

18 *Children's Hour* annuals also played an important part in this respect.

19 These kinds of clubs were not peculiar either to children or to the UK. Although
rather different in organization to the children's radio clubs in the UK, in France
there was a strong tradition of radio clubs made up of amateurs and radio enthusiasts
(cf. Meadel 1994). In the US, Disney initiated a number of clubs for children in the
1930s (cf. de Cordova 1994).

the principles of the Fairy League' (1927). These active citizens held parties and fundraising events and donated their takings to local charities and hospitals. And, although these clubs excluded certain types of listeners, they nevertheless connected broadcasting to the intricate texture and dense network of clubs, churches, hospitals, voluntary societies, and other social institutions of everyday life. These practices helped to connect the child audience not only to the family but also to the community. Proper listening was constructed as an *exemplary* form of citizenship to be shaped within the home in order that its effects could be beneficial to, and performed within, the community.

The Modernization of Children's Broadcasting	The practices which constitute the child audience in the 1920s, 1930s, and 1940s made possible an area of private life which could become accessible to increasing governmental intervention (cf. Hall and Schwarz 1985: 40). The cultural life of the home (its manners and mode of conduct) could become an object of government. However, the discursive formation which I have mapped out above was already being undermined by a series of significant organizational changes within the BBC during the 1930s and 1940s: the network of local stations was replaced by a more centralized system of London control of the Regional Stations in the 1930s; members of staff were increasingly professionalized; the programme schedule increasingly had more fixed points; the Listener Research Department was set up in 1936; and Reith resigned in 1938.[20]

These shifts are evident in changes that occurred within the realm of children's broadcasting. However, we can also see that a process of 'rationalization' occurred much earlier in the 1920s (cf. Briggs 1961: 260). *Children's Hour* was originally assembled within the local stations. There was no specific department responsible for the Hour and various 'Uncles' and 'Aunts' put together a magazine of different material in their spare time. By December 1923 it was decided that, due to the pressure of work placed upon these members of staff, the *Children's Hour* should be more centrally organized. Each local station was to appoint a woman to arrange a programme for the *Women's Hour* and *Children's Hour*. These local members of staff were responsible not only to their local Station Director but also to a Central Committee in London and to Mrs Ella Fitzgerald, who had been appointed as Central Organizer of Children's Hour programmes, and to Miss E. Elliott, her assistant. Hence although the local stations still

---

20 In France at this time there was also a major structural shift from an assemblage of radio associations to more centralized forms of representation and control (cf. Meadel 1994).

maintained a high degree of autonomy, they were nevertheless more centrally controlled by policy directives from London. This administrative framework allowed local stations to pool their material and to draw upon resources from London. In February 1925 there were further attempts at rationalization. C. E. Hodges (Uncle Peter) was appointed on a part-time basis to run the programme and Fitzgerald was moved exclusively to run *Women's Hour*. In January 1926 Hodges was appointed on a full-time basis and was directly under the control of J. C. Stobart, Director of Education at the BBC. There were directives ordering 'back-chat' to be eliminated and by November 1926 the terms 'Uncle' and 'Aunt' were to follow suit.[21] And later, under cover of the war, McCulloch, Director of Children's Hour, tried to further centralize *Children's Hour* by moving key members of staff from the regions to Bristol (which was the wartime centre of the organization).

This more centralized and professionalized BBC began to lose touch with its audience.[22] New ways of knowing the child audience were beginning to be established. The conception of the domestic nature of the audience began to shift at this time, although its full effects would not be felt until the 1950s after the introduction of television on a popular scale. Central to this shift was the emergence of new knowledges of the audience and the development of new relations with the child population. Instead of understanding this transformation in terms of the internal dynamics of the organizational structure of the BBC, we can see how the exigencies internal to the BBC were constituted in relation to the increasing mapping of social and cultural life generally by social scientific knowledge and specifically by the use of the social survey. In 1947 Adam Smith asked of radio: 'Is it a good effect? Has it enriched family life?' Her response was that personal and

21 Briggs notes that, due to opposition to the changes from children and parents, the ruling was relaxed (Briggs 1961: 261).

22 Scannell and Cardiff state that: 'The regime of control was to replace informality by a studied formality; to replace local variety and differences by a standardised conception of culture and manners; to replace audience participation by a more distanced, authoritative and prescriptive approach to broadcasting; to replace ordinary people and amateur performers in the studios by "authorities", "experts" and "professionals" ' (Scannell and Cardiff 1982: 166). The local stations were replaced by the National and Regional services and those services were mapped out in terms of different conceptions of culture. Scannell and Cardiff state that: 'London, in line with Arnoldian notions of sweetness and light, would provide the best that was available in music, talks, drama and entertainment. The standards and values of metropolitan culture were taken for granted . . . The national culture that the National Programme claimed to embody was of the educated, south-east English variety. If the Regional service rooted in provincial centres, could not match the quality that London could draw upon, its task was to give expression to the everyday life and variety of the areas served by the regional stations—culture "as a way of life" in Raymond Williams' phrase' (1982: 16) Whereas the National Programme could serve to unify the population within a common national culture (in its aesthetic and artisanal sense), the Regional service could continue to pose the task of making broadcasting commensurable with social and cultural life (i.e. culture in its anthropological, but also realist, sense).

parental observation needed to be supplemented by 'generalisations' based on scientific experiment:

> Every parent can give a personal answer, but to generalise is very difficult. There has been no formal enquiry into the subject: no Carlisle experiment, with one group of children docked of wireless and then observed to see if they are more polite, or more musical, or better at homework, than the group with the wireless compulsorily on all day. All is tentative, personal, and subject to the difficulty of disentangling the effect of wireless from the effects of half-a-dozen other modern phenomena, such as the cinema, the combustion engine, the popular press. One can only collect information as widely as possible, and on it try to build some generalisations that, the writer well knows, are open to challenge. (1947: 162)

Eight years prior to this statement, the BBC had enlisted the help of two academics from Bristol University to conduct a survey into the social effects of broadcasting.[23] Hilda Jennings and Winifred Gill undertook a survey specifically into the social effect of broadcasting on individuals and families in a working-class neighbourhood in Bristol. They looked at broadcasting in relation to, among other things: the enrichment of mental background, interest and knowledge of current events, newspaper reading, attitudes to party politics, musical production and appreciation, attendance and membership of religious and other organizations, domestic habits, and school education. The deployment of the social survey allowed radio broadcasting to be conceived within a specific political rationality which linked broadcasting with a whole host of social problems. Broadcasting could provide a mechanism for the moral management of social space. It was conceived as an apparatus for achieving the well-being of the population. In this sense it continued the Reithian ideal of making broadcasting commensurate with the social and cultural life of the population, but the terms of intervention were to be different.

In conceiving of broadcasting in such a way, the degenerative effects of unmanaged social existence were thrown into sharp relief. This was primarily articulated in the form of 'the mob' or 'the crowd'. Although itself an invention with a much longer genealogy, the figure of the mob provided a way of imagining both the nature of social life

---

23 Val Gielgud, in 1930, called for 'some sort of systematic research into the social psychology of regular listening' (quoted in Briggs 1965: 256). McCulloch and Robert Silvey, Head of Listener Research, had engaged in discussion about how to gain information about the child audience using survey techniques in 1947. Davis, in 1957, after discussing how to approach this audience asked 'how do we know what our audience wants' and referred to information gained from surveys conducted by the, now renamed, Audience Research Department (Davis, 1957, WAC R11/51/3).

before the civilizing effects of radio and also starkly presented the dangers of an ungoverned populus. Jennings and Gill stated that:

> Until a comparatively recent period the street and the public-house offered the main scope for recreation outside the home. On Sunday afternoons and fine summer evenings the whole family would stand at the street door or sit on chairs on the pavement. When tension in a street ran high, quarrels easily arose and quickly spread. Witnesses told the survey worker that 'There was a row every night in some streets.' The rougher children 'ran the streets.' Rival street gangs raided each other or even pursued victims into their own homes. The drama of neighbourhood life was watched and discussed at length on the door-steps and at the street-corner, as well as in the public house. (Jennings and Gill 1939: 10)[24]

They also stated that, in comparison, broadcasting has civilized the pleasures of the subordinate classes and brought them within the confines of the home and family:[25]

> It was also generally agreed that comparatively few people now spend a whole evening in a public-house, as they want to get home to the wireless. The children also play less in streets than formerly, partly of course owing to the new public provision of play-centres, but also partly because they like to listen to the wireless programmes. (Jennings and Gill 1939: 21)[26]

The social survey not only made such social changes visible but also made visible the way in which radio broadcasting was imbricated within a wider set of social problems. The social survey enabled the BBC to understand its specific effect upon social and cultural life

---

24 On a similar point, Moores also refers to B. Seebohm Rowntree's survey of York in 1941: 'a large proportion of young working people spent their evenings lounging about in the neighbourhood of their houses or promenading up and down certain streets in the city. The main street was so thronged with them that it was difficult to make one's way through it and a number of policemen were required to keep people moving and to prevent the horseplay between youths and girls from becoming too obstreperous. Youths used to boast how many girls they had "got off with" during the evening . . . Drunken men and women were constantly to be seen in the streets. On Saturday nights special policemen were drafted into the poorer districts of the city in order to deal with fights and brawls' (Rowntree 1941: 468 quoted in Moores 1988: 25).

25 Moores draws upon Donzelot's work in *The Policing of Families* (1979) to argue that radio needs to be conceived in terms of a more general 'withdrawal to the interior' (Moores 1988).

26 Jennings and Gill state that: 'The analysis of the 841 forms filled in by children between the ages of eleven and fourteen showed that 90 per cent sometimes listened to the Children's Hour, while over 80 per cent said that they sometimes stayed at home to listen to the wireless' (Jennings and Gill 1939: 21).

and to understand how it was itself central to the formation of a new public space in relation to the increasing structural changes of social and cultural life.[27]

In the late 1940s the social scientific knowledge of broadcasting's relationship to the social and cultural life of the population began to be matched by an increasing focus on the psychology of the individual listener. Sir Cyril Burt, in 1949, went so far as to question the existence of 'the listener' (Burt 1949). Instead of locating the problem within the 'human mind', as if all mental activity could be defined in terms of a universal and unified conception of 'mind', he referred to the individual mental *differences* within the population in terms of 'the cognitive side of the mind' ('perception, imagination, and thought') and the 'feelings and emotions' of individuals.[28] In categorizing radio listeners in terms of their 'intellectual ability' and in opening up the question of the emotional economy of radio listening he made possible a new way of thinking about and acting upon the child audience. In opening such a discursive space, Burt put into play certain conditions for conceiving the concerns which were to arise with the popularization of television in the 1950s.

Broadcasting was seen to play an ever more important role in the government of liberal democracy. Communities of citizens could be formed through its technical apparatus and new connections could be established between government and governed. As structural changes dissolved and rearranged earlier forms of social and cultural life, broadcasting could participate in the creation of a new public space and new forms of citizenship. The impact of these new techniques of government were not felt widely until the late 1940s and early 1950s. By that time, it was clear that the BBC was failing to address a large proportion of the child population. The new procedures for knowing the audience also threw into sharp relief the failure of its earlier enterprise: the BBC had been primarily addressing 'home service' children.[29] Richard D'A. Marriott, Director of Sound Broadcasting, described Children's Hour in the following way:

27 Jennings and Gill refer to the structural changes in terms of home life, working hours and leisure-time facilities and habits (Jennings and Gill 1939: 9–11).

28 In an article in the *BBC Quarterly* on 'Psychology and the Listener', Professor T.H. Pear talked more specifically about the 'personality' of the listener in terms of individual differences (Pear 1949). He drew upon Jung's analysis of 'introversion' and 'extroversion', which although not in a Jungian sense, became of particular importance in the 1950s and 1960s discourse on children's television viewing.

29 Richard D'A. Marriott, Director of Sound Broadcasting, stated in 1960 that: 'Children's Hour, as at present constituted, is for the children most carefully brought up, in the best homes, and for those of the highest educational potential. It is, one might say, a Home Service rather than a Light Programme audience, although children divide in the same way as adults do' (Marriott, 'Future of Children's Broadcasting', August, 1960, WAC R11/51/3).

They are the programmes of good children, of the attentive and
serious minded, the children of homes where parents are careful
in the influences which are brought to bear upon them, and
this is no doubt a minority of the children and the homes in
this country. (Marriott, February 1960, WAC R11/51/3)

The melancholic realization that *Children's Hour* had failed emerged
with an understanding that the BBC 'should have found a means
of seeking out and talking to children on their own terms'. Marriott
declared: 'but I have a feeling that it may now be too late for this'
(Marriott, February 1960, WAC R11/51/3).[30] He was right. On Good
Friday, 27 March 1964 the last *Children's Hour* was broadcast. Its
share of the radio audience was embarrassingly low.

In a sense, these early discourses and practices concerning children's radio broadcasting form the prehistory of children's television and the child television audience. These practices both support
and become differentiated from the creation of the child television
audience. A particular ethical relation between broadcaster and audience formed the foundational problematic of children's radio: how to
address the audience, how to shape broadcasting as a democratic
medium, and how to overcome the distance between broadcaster and
audience, so that broadcasting could become commensurate with the
everyday cultures of the population. Children's radio broadcasters
were in no doubt that their audience was made up of different kinds
of children, but these children were always conceived and acted upon
inasmuch as they lived their lives and listened to the radio within the
context of the family. Moreover, families themselves were differentiated by class and by their abilities to listen properly (or not). Thus,
there was little sense of the child audience as a distinct and separate
entity. It was neither addressed nor known in its own right. It was not
until after the Second World War, as I discuss in the following chapters, that the child audience began to emerge in its singularity. And
although the ethical concerns remain, the terms and conditions of
their problematization become reshaped and rethought, not because
radio and television are technologically different, but because television as a 'new technology' provides the basis for major rethinking.

---

30 *Children's Hour* was restructured in February 1961. The title was dropped and
programmes were made for different age groups across the Light and Home services.

3
Children's Television: Participation, Commensurability, and Differentiation

ALTHOUGH children's television programmes had been shown before the war in the UK, there was no regular service until after 1946. Initially the driving force behind children's television at the BBC was Mary Adams, Head of Television Talks.[1] By 1947, under her control, the BBC had shown *Muffin the Mule* since the preceding year and one short play. She pushed for a weekly one-hour slot, initially designed to be on Sunday afternoon. She wanted to include plays, 'how to' series (e.g. how to make puppets, kites, and toy theatres), storytelling, 'collectors' corner' (e.g. stamp-collecting, butterfly-collecting, and shell-collecting), programmes on pets, travel tales, 'nature parliament', *Muffin the Mule*, *James Pratt and Molly Blake*, outside broadcasts (e.g. children visiting museums and toy factories), films (e.g. 'Secrets of Nature', 'How the Telephone Works', and 'Instruments of the Orchestra'), current affairs, participation programmes (e.g. general knowledge quizzes and spelling-bees), and 'children's encyclopaedia' programmes. However, the timing on Sunday was particularly sensitive. It would first have to be agreed by the BBC's Central Religious Advisory Committee and gain the consent of other religious authorities. In June 1947 the Director of Religious Broadcasting wrote to the Director of Television Services arguing that the new service for children should not clash with Sunday School and should also be after the religious broadcast at 3 p.m.[2] In July, the Television

---

1 Mary Adams stated in a memo to the Television Programmes Director that: 'At present, children's programmes are my responsibility, and I am very conscious that they have totally inadequate attention. I feel strongly, however, that our child audience is so important that these programmes should have really top priority for the future' (Adams, 8 August 1947, WAC T16/45/1).

2 The child audience was also imagined within the context of rural middle-class routines and habits. For example, Mary Adams imagined the child audience as one that went to Sunday School and went on 'outdoor walks and picnics' on Sunday afternoon (21 January 1949, WAC T16/45/1).

Programme Director, Cecil McGivern, wrote to the Head of Television Service, Maurice Gorham and to his replacement in 1947 Norman Collins, saying that Sunday was not suitable for the children's programmes. He argued that '[c]hildren are fascinated by Television' and that '[t]he correspondence protesting against children being lured away from Sunday School by Television testifies to this' (WAC T16/45/1). Despite these protestations, McGivern announced in November that children's programmes would begin every Sunday from January 1948 between 4 p.m. and 5 p.m. The slot was to be called *For the Children* and Mary Adams was to organize it. In August 1948 there was talk of a daily service.[3] Cecil Madden wanted thirteen staff (organizer, secretary, a clerk to co-ordinate billings and continuity, six producers, and four secretaries) to run one hour on Sunday and half an hour on weekdays. Two hundred and fifty pounds was the minimum per hour of transmission needed. The logistics of organizing the new service was tricky considering there were only two studios for all television output. These were needed for transmission and rehearsal. Most material was broadcast live.

From these early thoughts on the organization of children's television broadcasting we can see how a conception of children's television in the UK drew on an established set of genres developed within children's radio in the 1920s and 1930s. But these forms of programme were themselves conceived in relation to a set of questions and problems about the conditions of production and transmission and the conditions of reception. Moreover, these conditions were taken into account through the ascriptions of particular authorities. In this case the Director of Religious Broadcasting spoke for the audience at home. He spoke of them in relation to particular matters over which he had authority. He was but one of many others who wanted to speak for the domestic child audience. The children's programmes broadcast on Sunday showed a sensitivity to the time and place of reception. Sunday was constructed and ritualized as different from other days. It was a day of Christian worship, of little playing and no seeing friends. It was a day of studied formality and the children's programmes manifested a similar reserve. It was not simply that individual programmes needed to be addressed to a domestic and familial audience, but that an ethos of broadcasting (shaping programmes, programme announcements, and the scheduling of programmes, namely a whole 'language' of broadcasting) was 'intended to be oriented to those conditions' (Scannell 1991: 3).

---

3 Norman Collins, Television Controller, stated in a memo to Nicolls, Director of Home Broadcasting that: 'D.G. [Director General] has already approved in principle that daily children's programmes should be the next development in BBC Television, and with the acquisition of Highbury Studios the whole thing becomes possible' (August, 1948, WAC T16/45/1).

Three sets of problems (concerning participation, commensurability, and differentiation) suggest that, although children were addressed as a television audience, their status as an audience was constantly invoked as a problem. As with children's radio, children's television programmes were constructed within a general ethos of participation. Programme forms and the scheduling of programmes were oriented to their domestic child audiences in such a way as to encourage an intimacy between children's television and the conditions of its reception. In doing so, children's television makers drew upon their repertoires of knowledge as programme makers, but also on other forms of knowledge and authority (i.e. religious, psychological, and educational). There was no single adult authority to which the programme makers referred nor even a single framework for constructing 'fictions' for children. Children's programmes were designed in order to be commensurate with the particularities of that audience. In this chapter I detail the emergence of children's television for the 'very young child'. The child television audience, though, also constituted a problem in terms of the complexity of its internal differences: namely, children's television had to be organized in such a way as to accord with the differences within its audience. Paradoxically, it was only through these problematizations that the child television audience gained any substance, texture, and materiality.

An Ethos of Participation

Children's television broadcasting faced enormous problems right from the start. In all its complexities and difficulties, children's television was conceived as an attempt to produce a range of programmes that would fully represent the diversity of children's everyday lives and experiences, but also to represent to children a range of experiences and lifeworlds, from the UK and overseas, different from their own and in so doing to facilitate their audience's imagination, intelligence, and development. Right from the beginning, the child television audience constituted less a known entity and more a problem: one of how to address this diverse audience and how to organize it. In short, the small makeshift staff of the Department of Children's Programmes at the BBC took it upon themselves not simply to represent a childhood world to children, but to build children into a universal childhood community. Their task was not pursued with arrogance, but with humility. It is clear from memos, policy documents, and various other statements that these broadcasters, if they understood anything of this new and difficult world of television, understood the enormity of the task ahead of them.

Freda Lingstrom, Head of Children's Programmes (Television) from 1951 to 1956, in an article for the *BBC Quarterly* referred to children's television as 'a complete service in miniature, taking in its stride plays, Bible stories, music of every kind, children's classics dramatized and presented as serials, cowboy films, news, ballet, slapstick, how to make things, sport, puppet shows, animated cartoons, not to mention quick glances at arts and sciences'. She continued, 'all find a place and all must be designed to meet the separate needs of children of all ages' (Lingstrom 1953: 101). Similarly, Mary Adams, again in the *BBC Quarterly*, referred to children's television as a 'microcosm of television programme forms: outside broadcasts, films, plays, documentaries, talks, music, ballet, light entertainment' (Adams 1950: 82). Children's television was not conceived as a particular genre of television, but as a collection of genres which were in themselves not specific to particular age categories of audience (i.e. either adult or child). Moreover, children's television was equally conceived as the site of aesthetic experimentation, such that programme forms developed for children's television would be used for adult television. There was a mutual reciprocity in the 1950s as there is now (cf. Holland 1996).

The phrase 'television in miniature' was important because it suggested that children's television was not simply defined in terms of the fact that it contained a variety of genres (equivalent to that of 'adult television') and allotted a smaller amount of air time nor in terms of its audience being 'small in height as well as number' (Lingstrom 1953: 98), but in terms of the *relation between* the mixed schedule of programmes and its audience. As with children's radio before it, children's television attempted to represent its audience in such a way as to become commensurate with the variety of cultures of children's everyday lives. And yet children's television was also conceived in terms of its ability to represent a world of and for childhood, far richer and broader than that experienced by children in their day-to-day experiences.

In this respect, the cultural form of children's television was talked about in the 1940s and 1950s in relation to the perceived capacities of television as a technology. Lingstrom, in her *BBC Quarterly* article, talked about children's television as reflecting 'an external world far wider than can be found in a familiar street. Important events, sport, plays, stories and comedy acts, films, even on occasion transmissions from abroad are to be seen for the mere turning of a knob' (Lingstrom 1953: 100). Lingstrom asked: '[w]ill this powerful, intrusive invention undermine the authority of family life or enrich it; will the speed with which "pictures" can be understood sharpen perceptions or dull them; will television become a despot, encroaching on the liberties of the mind?' (1953: 101). Television as technology did not stand outside of, and separate from, the programme forms it carried.

Children's television was defined by its ability to articulate the spaces and times of the home with those of different and wondrous public worlds. There was an importance attached to children's television's textuality in terms of its ability to constitute a series of diegetic worlds distinct from those of the domestic sphere and yet aligned with it. The capacity of children's television to allow its viewers to travel outside the home was construed through genres such as the adventure play, outside broadcasts, and so on. These programme forms drew on existing genres of social documentary (cf. Corner 1991) and boys adventure fiction (cf. Drotner 1988 and Bristow 1991). In the early years of children's television, these forms of programming were designed not so that children could simply view the world from the privacy of their own homes, but so that they could participate in those wider public worlds. In leading the viewer outside of the home, children's television was conceived not so much in terms of, what Raymond Williams refers to, as 'mobile privatisation' but in terms of a de-privatization of the domestic. Children were invited, as they had been in relation to children's radio, to watch television as a public act. As Mary Adams stated 'Participation is the enemy of passivity. It can make a private pleasure a public act' (Adams 1950: 85). Alongside outside broadcasts and adventure plays, 'How To Do . . .' programmes helped constitute the children's television audience as one constantly making things:

> Children have been shown how to paint scenery and make puppets, and a creditable nursery opera was prepared with properties and puppets made entirely by young viewers. On another occasion children were shown how to design Christmas cards; hundreds of designs were sent in, and a good one chosen and printed for use. Illustrated poems poured in after a programme on the Wordsworth centenary. Nesting boxes, sugar mice, objects seen and made, are legion. One series of programmes sent children into the country, following maps and instruction on the screen, to find Norman arches, country craftsmen, bird song, flints and barge names and all the various sights and sounds of the countryside. (Adams 1950: 85)

The programme forms were geared, as they had been in *Children's Hour* radio, both to construct a normative ethos for the child and to connect the child to an external world in an active form of citizenship and public participation.

Stephen Wagg has argued that the promotion of participation is resonant in contemporary programmes, such as *Blue Peter*, and has argued that such an ethos of participation leads to an understanding of watching television as culturally inferior to other activities (1992).[4] Others, such as Patricia Holland, take a similar view. For example, Holland quotes Monica Sims, Head of Children's Programmes at the BBC (1967–78), as saying 'What would make me happiest would be if they [the children] went away' (Holland 1996: 162). Namely, it is argued that Sims wanted children to 'go away and do something creative themselves' (ibid.). *Why Don't You (Turn Off Your TV and Do Something More Interesting Instead)* is taken as the quintessential example in this respect. It was a programme made in the 1970s that showed children what they could be doing if they weren't watching television (i.e. making things, getting involved in clubs and sports, being with friends from overseas and so on). But it is important to locate such comments by Sims in a broader context than any single television programme. The ethos of participation, which developed in the 1940s and 1950s, was intended to connect children's television viewing to a wider set of quotidian practices. In this sense the ethos of participation was an important means through which broadcasting might align itself with the ordinariness of the everyday lives of all children.

Thus, television itself could become an everyday activity. But in doing so, certain activities were prioritized and made visible as exemplary practices of good citizenship. The 'good' and the 'bad' never simply divided in terms of television or not-television, as Wagg argues, but rather in terms of active/passive. To be an 'active' child participating within the public life of the nation was not to live a life devoid of television. It was precisely to use television in order to be connected to a world of childhood and develop into a 'good citizen'. For example, on 3 September 1952, the Jenkinson Committee *Report on Children's Television* (which I discuss in more detail in Chapter 5) drew up a list of types of programmes which the panel members thought would evoke 'active intelligent responses' from the child viewers at home. The list of programme types included: real world, world of art, music, drama, storytelling, imaginative fantasies, and competitions. Much of the discussion of programmes focused on

---

4 As Wagg rightly shows, the wider deployment of the notion of activity settles on imperialist organizations such as Robert Baden-Powell's Boy Scout movement, as well as liberal progressive organizations such as the Woodcraft Folk. The ethos of participation, though, extended beyond more overtly political citizenship movements to forms of consumerism. In the US, Richard de Cordova has documented the huge growth of Mickey Mouse Clubs in the 1930s (1994). Terry Staples has shown how there were similar cinema clubs in the UK in the 1930s and 1940s. Cinema clubs provided the structure for new forms of public participation. As *The Children's Newspaper* put it in April 1943: 'We may be sure that these Club members will soon be growing into fine little citizens; it will not be they who trouble the police or are run over by motor-cars, or go slouching through the world like ignorant good-for-nothings' (quoted in Staples 1997: 78). Such forms of public participation began to wane in the post-war period and, in their decline, activity and passivity become redefined in terms of the child's cognitive processing rather than public acts.

connecting programmes to children's everyday experiences, facilitating their imagination, intelligence, and development and ensuring that children realized the difference between fantasy worlds and reality. In the discussion of programmes covering the 'real world', the panel wanted to see more programmes 'dealing with the real world, information, news, topical events, etc'. They wanted to see 'more programmes about the everyday life of the child himself, showing him dramatically the kind of problems he is always facing—parental authority, problems of jealousy, etc.—and thus helping him to solve them' (T16/46 3 September 1952: 4) and 'material which will fire his imagination by its creative power and not dull it with a weight of indigestible facts' (ibid. 5). And the panel argued that 'the child's experience should be enlarged by more programmes showing him "How the other half of the world lives"—what goes on in other countries and especially in the Commonwealth; pictures of different sections of our own community—so that they all grow up knowing about each other' (ibid. 4).

A number of contemporary cultural critics have read such comments by children's broadcasters as hollow attempts to conceal the uniformity of their address to the child audience. Bob Ferguson, for example, in his discussion of the British children's magazine programme *Blue Peter* states that children's television constitutes a 'universe of discourse'. He argues that there is an apparent plurality of media messages within children's television, but that this plurality is ultimately reducible to the meanings of the dominant discourse. This universe of discourse, he continues, 'may be characterized as Anglo-centric, often racist, sexist, royalist, pro-capitalist, ostensibly Christian and as generally arguing that the best way to deal with social problems is through benevolence' (Ferguson 1985: 48). Ferguson suggests (this time in another article on *Blue Peter*) that the interests served by these dominant ideologies are concealed through the textual device of 'naturalisation' (Ferguson 1984: 34). He comments, for example, that *Blue Peter* 'has been able to unite a nebulous group of parents and children around televisual discourses which allow for charity, caring, the removal of history and the denial of struggle for change. It is a perverse ideologue's dream' (ibid). Ferguson's account of this 'dream' is bleak: 'There is never any chance for the viewer to discover alternative discourses by watching television' (Ferguson 1985: 48).

This type of criticism, as pursued by Ferguson, reduces the address to the child within a single unitary ideological form (naturalization), ties the meaning of this address to certain underlying interests and constrains children's television within an ideological hold it can never escape. Others make similar, although differently nuanced, observations. For example, Stephen Kline has argued at length that children's television programming has increasingly become shaped by the interests of free-market capitalism and particularly by the transnational interests of toy companies (1993). Shirley Steinberg and Joe Kincheloe have suggested that '[i]n light of the failure of oppositional institutions to challenge corporate hegemony, corporations to a large extent have free reign to produce almost any kinderculture that is profitable' (1997a: 13). I am not suggesting here that contemporary children's television is not importantly shaped by market forces and transnational capital, but to draw on these contemporary theoretical arguments would be anachronistic and would assume a monologic form of address. In these accounts, children's television is seen to deliver child audiences either to the dominant ideology or to the market. To deny the plausibility of such accounts of children's television is not to disavow the way in which children's television broadcasters clearly had a sense of what constituted a childhood community, what constituted imagination and intelligence and what constituted good citizenship. But to foreground the ideological fails to account for how broadcasters attempted to *engage* with children and *address* them as an audience.

In more recent accounts, a more subtle picture of children's television has begun to emerge (Bazalgette and Buckingham 1995; Kinder 1999; Holland 1996). In these accounts, Jacqueline Rose's psychoanalytic analysis of children's literature is drawn upon to argue that children's television reproduces a nostalgic unitary image of childhood innocence. Rose has argued that:

> Children's fiction rests on the idea that there is a child who
> is simply there to be addressed and that speaking to it might
> be simple. It is an idea whose innocent generality covers up
> a multitude of sins. (Rose 1984: 1)

According to Rose, children's fiction is an impossibility. We can never simply speak to the child beyond the text. Children's fiction, she argues, is always written by adults and in relation to adult desire and fantasy. The 'child' is caught up in such fantasy. There is no 'real' child beyond the text. On the contrary, the figure of the 'child' which is addressed by children's fiction serves to hold in place a normative and normalized adult subjectivity (a subjectivity for which the destabilizing forces of language and polymorphous sexuality are held at bay). Rose states that:

> Childhood persists . . . It persists as something which we
> endlessly rework in our attempt to build an image of our own
> history. When we think about childhood, it is above all our
> investment in doing so which counts. The very ambiguity of
> the term 'children's fiction'—fiction the child produces or

fiction given to the child?—is striking for the way in which it leaves the adult completely out of the picture. (Rose 1984: 12)

Despite the sophistication of Rose's analysis, her ideas have been drawn on in such a way that continually marks children's television (even as stigmata) within a singular vision of childhood innocence.

For example, Sean Griffin in his wonderful discussion of the Davy Crockett story in the US, states that '*childhood* is a concept of inno-cence, which has often little relation to the material experience of actual children' (1999: 103). Cary Bazalgette and David Buckingham also draw on Rose to critique a unitary vision of childhood in chil-dren's television: 'The idea that children, like other subordinate social groups are somehow all alike in their tastes, interests and aspirations is powerful and widespread' (1995: 6). Notwithstanding the fact that Rose herself precisely and very carefully disavows the possibility of any simple reference to the 'material reality' of real children, such critics deploy a familiar move which criticizes *textual* constructions on the basis of their inability properly to represent the materiality of the experiences of audiences.[5]

Further evidence for the argument that children's television did not collapse its programmes into a unitary ideology or form of address is provided in discussion concerning children's involvement in the organization and production of their own programmes. The ethos of participation meant not simply that the BBC would produce particu-lar types of programmes for children, but also that children would be encouraged to participate in the production of programmes. In 1948 Cecil Madden, in his early thoughts on a daily television service for children, wanted to offer children 'Plays for children by Grown-up artists', but also 'Plays for children by Children'. In 1949 and 1950, Peter Thompson, television producer, and Richmond Postgate, Head of Schools Broadcasting (both of whom had a central role in organizing children's television at the BBC), talked of getting children to make their own programmes (WAC T16/45/1). In April 1951 Humphrey Lestocq chaired a programme, *Junior Wranglers*, in which panels of four children discussed topics such as 'Should politics be a woman's job?' or 'Make parents adopt a national scale of children's pocket-money, payable on the dot!' The programme was intended to give children a space in which to make their voices heard. In May 1952 the BBC ran a competition for 12 to 15-year-olds to devise a weekly schedule of children's television programmes. Toward the end of 1952 children were similarly invited to make their own programmes for children's television. The *News Chronicle* reported that: 'Children

---

5 Rose, for example, has no time for audience research. She states: 'I am not, of course, talking here of the child's own experience of the book which, despite all the attempts which have been made, I consider more or less impossible to gauge' (Rose 1984: 9).

are going to move into television in a big way' (23 September 1952). A play written by a 13-year-old girl, Irene Lipman, from Willesden, was broadcast in November. In February 1957 children were offered the chance to write, produce, and act in their own TV play. The BBC 'Junior Producers' competition gave the opportunity for twenty finalists to write, produce, and act in three plays. The plays were 10 minutes long and broadcast from the Lime Grove Studios in April 1957. The *Daily Mail* reported that if the plays were popular then a more ambitious contest would be launched in the autumn in which children would be invited to produce longer plays. Even Associated-Rediffusion (one of the regional ITV companies), in 1955, had a fortnightly competition, *Write it Yourself*, in which viewers were invited to write the next episode of an ongoing serial.

Although it is important not to overstate the amount of involvement children had in the production of children's television, such activity forms a significant thematic in the way children's broadcasters understood their relation to their audience and one which still persists to this day.[6] For example, Channel Four's *Wise Up* (Buckingham *et al.* 1999) and also the rationale for the children's channel Nickelodeon clearly demonstrate an attempt to conceptualize children's involvement in the organization of their television. Moreover, evidence of attempts by broadcasters to facilitate children's participation in the making of programmes demonstrates a need to qualify and render more complex theoretical statements concerning children's fiction as simply a product of adult fantasy. Buckingham, for example, argues that:

> children's television is not produced *by* children but *for* them. As such, it should be read as a reflection not so much of children's interests or fantasies or desires but of adults'. The texts which adults produce for children represent adult constructions, both of childhood and (by implication) of adulthood itself. (Buckingham 1995: 47)

Even if we accept, as I do, that children's production has played and continues to play only a minor role in the wider conditions of production of children's television, it nevertheless suggests that our understanding of the making of children's television cannot rest on a theoretical supposition concerning a unitary understanding of adult desire and authority nor on an unproblematically assumed division between adult production and child audience.

Nevertheless any attempts at fully implementing an infrastructure capable of supporting children's involvement in production were always troubled, if not forlorn. In a memo headed 'Plays by Children', Peter

---

6 There are, of course, serious questions concerning the terms and conditions of participation in the production of, and having communicative entitlements within, children's television (cf. Thornborrow 1998).

Thompson argued that such plays were 'not suitable at present I think'. He continued by typifying children's plays in the following manner:

> The wording is brief and to the point, no colour being added. Each scene lasts about half to one minute and action is merely used to get people on and off. Faced with the need to turn an incident into a play the young author has naturally turned it into words. It therefore reads better than it could be presented. (27 June 1949 WAC T16/45/1)

In his notes for this memo, Thompson presented a more sustained argument regarding children's involvement in production. He presented a stark choice:

> Do we want to ofer [sic] children's programmes to children as organisers of items with the producer linking and shaping them *or* do we want to present programmes by adults for children. (ibid.)

Thompson saw the former as 'the ideal'.

> My dream of children's programmes in Television is that Television should be used only as a door to a child community through which by skillful manipulation the child can enter and join their fellows. I believe that children would prefer such a situation in spite of a certain uncoordinated chaos which would be bound to penetrate the production. Under such circumstances a children's committee would plan the programmes and invite adult participation only when they so desire. A studio devoted to these programmes would thus be necessary, so too would one or two rooms for scene painting and the like. A staff of three or four plus secretarial assistance would be an absolute essential; to keep up contact with other children's bodies such as clubs, schools, etc. The practical needs of such a situation would provide great education opportunities while the presentation would provide the sort of entertainment which I feel children both need and want. (ibid.)

Thompson nevertheless recognized the 'many apparently insurmountable obstacles' (involving insufficient money and premises, the weakening of production, the fact that all roles would need to be taken by children and increased viewer participation) which would add to the work load. Thompson did not expand on his definition of these problems. Children's television production in the 1940s and early 1950s was severely limited by the amount of money available for programming and by elaborate technical constraints. Programme budgets meant that most programmes were broadcast from within the studio at

Highbury. Producers and scriptwriters also had to work with strict rehearsal and broadcast spaces and times. A document written in 1954 for children's television scriptwriters and artists stated that:

> Every piece of technical apparatus in use during a programme is almost invariably connected to something. Lights have cables to the switchboard. Cameras have extra heavy cables to the control room. Microphones have cables to the sound engineering section. This means that the floor of the studio more nearly resembles a woven carpet of wire.
>
> Before the programme is transmitted the producer has to work out the moving of every single piece of technical apparatus in such a way that the wires, cables and connections do not become tangled. (1954, 7, WAC T16/45/1)

Any attempt to include children in the production of children's television would have needed to negotiate these kinds of technical difficulties. Thompson was resolute in his opinion that a firm decision was needed to either involve children in production or not. He argued that to mix the two forms of production and associated styles would be 'disasterous'. Given the current circumstances, Thompson concluded 'returning to earth . . . there is no place for material of this sort'. His ideal would remain a dream.

The fact that Thompson took time to elucidate his thoughts in this way emphasizes their significance. But at the same time other forms of organization were being discussed. This time the reference was not only to the child as a source of authority, but to others who were seen to have a stake in children's television. These new dialogues were structured according to normative models of psychological learning and development, but they also paid heed to a growing concern that children's television should be entertaining. Postgate, in a policy document distributed on 20 January 1950, stated the aims of the new regular television service for children:

> Television Children's Hour aims to enrich children's lives and to foster their development by the stimulus and enjoyment of what they see and hear. This aim seems to have several elements:—
>   to entertain and to be liked by the children;
>   to satisfy the parents that the programme is fostering children's development in ways of which they approve;
>   to satisfy instructed professional opinion that programmes are soundly conceived and well executed. This refers both to the entertainment value and aesthetic competence, and to the educational and psychological judgement which the programmes will reflect. So far, Television has to some extent not come under the vigilant gaze of psychologists and educationalists, but when it

begins a daily service of the type proposed we must expect a great deal more comment and criticism to be generated. (Postgate, 20 January 1950, WAC T16/45/1, 2)

Parental approval, professional opinion, children's pleasure and the broadcasters' expertise were now all constituents in the network of making children's television. There was not one subject involved in the creation of children's television, but many, not one authority, but many and not one addressee, but many.

An address to the child audience, although both domestic and public (indicated by that assemblage of child, parent, and expert), was no longer defined in terms of entertainment which is educative in the best sense, but in terms of the alignment of entertainment and psychological and educational judgement. We can see the emergence of a concern about the psychological development of the child and for a professionalization of children's television. For Postgate, as for others, children's television required the expertise not only of broadcasters, but also of the psychologist and educationalist. The authority of children's broadcasters (in terms of their ability to make programmes for particular audiences) was constituted in relation to authorities and institutions outside of broadcasting proper. The possibility of talking about and making programmes for this particular audience required a wider network of expertise and knowledge. Mary Adams called for research into the physiological, psychological and social problems concerning children's television viewing (Adams 1950: 9). Naomi Capon, television producer, stated that decisions concerning children's programming 'must be moulded by the experience we gain in the daily production of programmes, and by our accumulating store of knowledge of what our young viewers need and like to see' (Capon 1952: 31). In August 1950 Norman Collins sent a memo to Robert Silvey, Head of Audience Research, asking for information about the popularity of programmes for 'the very little ones', 'the mid-age group' (7 to 10 years old) and 'the 10 to 14 year olds' (24 August 1950, WAC T16/45/1). Likewise there were also calls for research into the possibility of having separate television programmes for girls and boys on different days of the week (4 September 1950 and 15 January 1951, WAC T16/45/1).

Programmes for the Very Young, Supervised Freedom, and Puppets

Much of the discussion about the use of outside opinion and psychological expertise initially centred on programmes for the very young child. Discussions of programmes for this audience were symptomatic of wider discussions concerning participation, but they carried their own specificity. Nevertheless, some of the features that we would readily associate with pre-school television now were, in the late 1940s and early 1950s, more widely dispersed across television for all children.

In the early days, puppets were used in programmes for young and old child audiences. For example, the magazine programme *Whirligig*—hosted by star personality and ex-fighter pilot Humphrey Lestocq, produced by Michael Westmore (who became Head of Children's Programmes at Associated-Rediffusion in the mid-1950s), and scripted by Peter Ling—was an enormous hit with children of all ages. The programme featured the puppets Mr Turnip and Hank, the cowboy. It was shown fortnightly on Saturday afternoon until June 1954. In 1952 Lestocq was awarded the children's television award for Television Personality of the Year. Annette Mills, the presenter of *Muffin the Mule*, which I shall discuss shortly, came a close second. Moreover, Mr Turnip and his manipulator Joy Laurey were awarded a *Daily Mail* Television Award in 1952. In November 1951, the *Daily Herald* declared: 'It is an incontestable fact that in Britain this is the Puppet Age—and Television is responsible for that' (10 November 1951). However, the overuse of puppets was wearing thin with audiences. The *Daily Mirror*, on 23 March 1954, argued that puppets 'bore older children stiff'. On 1 November 1954 *Whirligig* was replaced by *Jigsaw*. And *Punch* even reported in 1957 that too many items on *Watch with Mother* feature puppets: 'a surfeit of jerking, squeaking, mumbling rag dolls, bunnies, tortoises, hens and so on can be damaging to the most wide-eyed and innocent credulity' (19 April 1957). From this time on, puppets, although initially dispersed across programmes for all ages of children, were increasingly perceived as being best suited for the younger audience. The use of puppets, in part, made it possible for the child to be represented on screen without the ensuing technical difficulties. But their use also had a symbolic role in negotiations between adult and child.

Muffin the Mule was broadcast by the BBC from 1946 and although it had all the hallmarks of a maternalist, infantilizing address to the very young audience, it was nevertheless addressed to and watched by a large age group.[7] Muffin, the star character, performed alongside other puppets, such as Peregrine the Penguin, Oswald the Ostrich, and Louise the Lamb, on top of a piano played by Annette Mills (sister of the actor John Mills). Jan Bussell was the creator of the puppets and the

---

7 Indications of the maternal address can be seen even in the announcement for the programme. For example in 1949 the BBC announcer stated: 'Now if you listen very carefully I think you will hear some most extraordinary noises coming from Annette Mills' piano, and I wonder who's making them. Can you guess? Let's see if you're right' (26 June 1949, WAC T2/104/1). An indication of the audience comes from the *Daily Herald*, which stated that Muffin was an 'overnight sensation causing parents to fight their children for places in the parlour for TV children's hour' (*Daily Herald*, 10 November 1951). The *Daily Express* stated that *Muffin the Mule* had an audience of 'more than a million' (*Daily Express*, 3 May 1949).

husband of Ann Hogarth, who pulled the strings. The programmes were fifteen minutes long and they centred on daily domestic situations such as Muffin having a bath or Peregrine having squeaking shoes. Although difficult to imagine now, *Muffin the Mule* was a great success and stayed on screen until 1957, with a brief spell on ATV (one of the regional ITV companies), after the death of Annette Mills (in January 1955), between 1955 and 1956. It returned again in January 1957 with Jan Bussell presenting the show on guitar, rather than piano. W. E. Williams stated in *The Observer* that 'when a puppet like Muffin the Mule is on view I realise that television is one of the pictorial arts as well as a medium of instantaneous communication' (*The Observer*, 16 February 1949). The *Daily Express* described Muffin as the 'biggest personality in TV' (*Daily Express*, 3 May 1949).

Muffin's success was not limited to the small screen. Muffin and the other puppets appeared on a regular road-show around Britain. The Muffin Syndicate Ltd, jointly owned by Ann Hogarth and Annette Mills, licensed puppets, toys, books, dresses, drinks, soap, puzzles, wallpaper, calendars, china ornaments, and various other character merchandise. The company was reported to have had a three-quarters of a million pound turnover in 1952 (*Evening Standard*, 6 October 1952; *Sunday Dispatch*, 16 November 1952; *Illustrated*, 19 December 1953).[8] There was a *Muffin the Mule* strip cartoon in the *News of the World TV Comic* and in 1952 it was to be distributed globally by PA Reuter Features Ltd (*World's Press News*, 13 June 1952). *Muffin the Mule* had become securely embedded within popular everyday life. Peter Flemming in the *Sunday Times* worried about the 'extent to which television is standardising one particular kind of experience for small children' and that 'all entry into the world of illusion and entertainment' would be 'through the same narrow gate and under the same impeccable guidance'. He was particularly concerned about its effect on our 'earliest memories' and he stated that '[e]ndearing though Muffin the Mule may be, I doubt if he has a right to a place (which he will certainly get) in the first chapter of virtually every autobiography published in this country at the beginning of the twenty-first century' (*Sunday Times*, 30 December 1951).

Muffin the Mule constituted television viewing as a particular space of love and care between mother and child. In an advertisement for Chilprufe woollen children's clothes, in *Woman and Home*, three small children were pictured sitting in front of the television set watching *Muffin the Mule*. The children are happy and contented and the copy beneath the image read, in bold letters, 'Mothers Vision' and

---

8 The *Daily Herald* stated in 1951 that: 'The big stores, the multiple manufacturers are joining in; shops are stocking up with Muffins and the rest for the Christmas stockings. It's a million-pound trade now, and there seems to be no limit' (*Daily Herald*, 10 November 1951).

below it 'seeing the children grow bonnier and sturdier every week, mother blesses her early foresight' (*Woman and Home*, January 1952). Instead of television being presented as the destroyer of childhood, it was aligned, through the imaging of Muffin, with the practices of 'proper mothering' and healthy child development.

The construction of *Muffin the Mule* as safe for children was dependent, in part, upon the presence of the 'mother' within the text itself. Annette Mills is figured in the text as motherly. Through her shrill BBC voice she keeps Muffin and his friends in order and she carefully directs their play. She not only speaks to the characters in the text, but also directly addresses the audience (both mothers and children) at home.[9] Muffin and the other characters who signify early childhood through their various gestures and activities are silent and yet give the impression that they could speak through whispering inaudibly to Annette Mills, who then relays what they have said to the audience.[10] W. E. Williams in *The Observer* stated that 'Miss Mills has no truck with such vulgar devices as ventriloquism, but by repeating to us what Muffin the Mule has inaudibly whispered into her ear she convinces us that thus and thus did really speak'. Mills argued that '[i]n this way we have found that the imaginations of the children are more stimulated and the characters of the creatures are more free to develop. This has been, apparently, a more successful experiment after the spoon-fed entertainment of the cartoon films and comic strips' ('Writing for Puppets on Television', *The Writer*, May 1952). The motherly voice of Annette Mills carefully directs the puppets' play and gives meaning to their activities. Her voice always emanates from the visible space of the screen in which she is present and yet within that space there is a clear division between the space of Annette Mills on the piano stool, the theatrical space on the piano itself and the space of the diegesis, which is audible and implied, but not visibly present on the screen.[11] The camera is always fixed and never ventures outside of the space of Annette Mills and her piano. Although we get a sense of the space of the diegesis outside the screen, inasmuch as we hear sounds off-screen and Annette Mills looks beyond the visible space of the screen, beyond the piano and out of the window, and recounts to

---

9 For example, when Peter the Puppy gets out of the bath and shakes the water off, Annette Mills says, 'They always shake water all over you, don't they!' She was referring both to the actions of a dog and also to the exuberance of a small child.

10 Michael Emmison and Laurence Goldman, in their analysis of *The Sooty Show*, argue that the conversational features of the dialogues between human adults and animal puppets mimic those of conventional adult/child interactions (1997). The programmes I discuss below, in their use of puppets, are no exception. What is interesting about *Muffin the Mule* is that it reproduces such structural relations between adult and child despite the animal puppet/child not having a voice audible to the viewers at home.

11 Annette Mills stated that 'it seemed a pity such a good stage as the top of the piano should always be empty' (*Sunday Dispatch*, 16 November 1952).

the audience what she has seen, this space is always static.[12] In this sense the space off-screen is always represented to the audience in the past (we only have second-hand knowledge of it). It is a world which is always mediated by the mother. Likewise the space on the piano is constituted by the voice and gaze of the motherly narrator. All the activities take place on top of the piano. The puppets' play is carefully located on top of the piano and in sight of Mills. This particular technique of dividing visible and audible spaces constitutes the relations between mother and child (Muffin and characters and Annette Mills) within specific relations of power. The voice of the mother is somewhere between the authority of the voice-over and the diegetic voices of the characters.

Andy Pandy was the first programme series addressed specifically to a pre-school audience and it was initially a short experimental series of four programmes shown on Tuesday and Thursday between 11 July and 20 July 1950. After its initial success the series was shown regularly from 19 September 1950 and scheduled every Tuesday at 3.45 p.m.[13] It was created by Freda Lingstrom and her long-standing friend, Maria Bird, as a programme specifically directed at the pre-school audience. Lingstrom, while Assistant Head of BBC School's Broadcasting, had been responsible for *Listen with Mother* (which only started to be broadcast from 1950) and was asked to make a 'television equivalent on music and movement lines'. *Andy Pandy* contained three characters: Andy, a small male puppet dressed in a clown suit, Teddy, a toy teddy bear and Looby Loo, a female doll. The programme was intended to provide a friend for the very young viewer and '[a] three-year-old actor was out of the question, so a puppet was the obvious answer'.[14] *Andy Pandy* had no linear narrative structure. Instead it presented a series of tableaux with no apparent overarching

---

12 The construction of the off-screen diegetic space was seen as a particular difficulty. Annette Mills stated that: 'For the first few programmes the dialogue was merely a linking up of one song with another or an introduction to a new character. It was Ann Hogarth who first suggested a slight plot, a complete adventure which began and ended in fifteen minutes on my grand piano top. This was not easy at first because only one puppet (except on rare occasions) can be seen with me at a time, and so the script had to be full of descriptions of what was happening off-stage (or outside the window in the garden which is always seen on the television screen)' (*The Writer*, May 1952). In only having one of the puppets on the screen at one time and having them not able to speak to each other, we can see how the childlike characters are constituted as a community only inasmuch as they are voiced and seen by the motherly narrator.

13 There was much concern in 1965 when viewers thought that *Camberwick Green* was to replace *Andy Pandy* and *Bill and Ben*. Doreen Stephens, Head of Family Programmes, reassured the audience stating that they would be shown, although less frequently until 1970 (*Daily Mirror*, 1 October 1965).

14 The production of the programme was very much a local affair. Lingstrom and Bird lived together in Westerham, Kent, and the puppet was made by an old man in the village, supposedly according to the exact proportions of a 3-year-old boy (*Good Housekeeping*, January 1963).

theme. In one programme Andy starts by playing on a swing, accompanied by Maria Bird, the motherly narrator, singing 'Swinging high, swinging low . . .'. He is joined by Teddy. The camera then focuses on Teddy who enacts the movements to the nursery rhyme 'Round and round the garden . . .'. Finally, after a scene with Andy and Teddy playing in their cart and a scene with Looby Loo singing her song, 'Here we go Looby Loo . . .', the two male characters return to their basket and wave goodbye and Maria Bird sings 'Time to go home . . .'. Lingstrom stated that '[t]he tempo is slow and there is no "story": the action moves from one situation to another in a way totally acceptable to the very young child' (Lingstrom, February 1953, 3, WAC T2/7/4). There is an attempt, on the one hand, to represent a stage of early childhood and on the other to imagine an audience as an analogue of such representations. But there is also an attempt to engage the audience at home in such televisual representations.

The programme was designed to bring 3-year-olds 'into a close relationship with what is seen on the screen, and through the medium of a character called "Andy Pandy" to provide a programme which young children may enjoy, taking part in simple movement, games, stories, nursery rhymes and songs, some of which will be traditional and some new' (Bird, 31 August 1950, WAC T2/7/1). The use of nursery rhymes was seen as particularly important as it worked both to establish a relationship between the mother and the development of the child and also to connect the child to a tradition and community of pre-school childhood. The women's magazine *Good Housekeeping*, in an article on *Andy Pandy* stated that:

> Andy Pandy has also helped to revive the nursery rhyme in this country. During the war, with so many mothers and children separated, these old songs and verses were neglected. Miss Bird felt that nursery rhymes could enrich the life of a child to an unbelievable extent. They often provide him with his first experience of melody, and they teach him about numbers, time and space, the seasons and festivals, youth and age. So in each programme Maria Bird gives Andy Pandy a different nursery rhyme to sing, which he repeats several times. The words are always the traditional ones, and so is the music, harmonized very simply so that it can easily be remembered. (*Good Housekeeping*, January 1963)[15]

15 Dr D. B. Bradshaw, Leeds School Medical Officer, in his annual report, argued that television had resulted in a decline in nursery rhymes and jingles. 'Many young viewers', he said 'are missing the valuable experience in speech training which the learning and recitation of nursery rhymes used to provide as a normal part of family life.' He argued that children's speech was 'less mature than it used to be'. The *Yorkshire Evening Post* defended *Watch with Mother* by saying that '[a] child's activity being "endless imitation" we should have thought TV would encourage children to recite rather than otherwise' (*Yorkshire Evening Post*, 27 April 1961).

The invention of this pre-school audience and of programmes suitable for it, was thus construed within the context of a notion of public service working for the public good. Broadcasting was seen to play a role in the everyday life of families and a single programme, and its makers at the BBC took up the responsibility for healing the upset and schisms of war.

Children were invited not only to listen and to 'watch the movements of a simple puppet, naturalistic in form and expression', but also to 'respond to his invitations to join in by clapping, stamping, sitting down, standing up and so forth' (Adams 1950). The programme provided a space in which children could 'build for themselves a heritage of traditional and other stories' and through which preschool children could be constructed as a community for television. The repetition of these different elements and the characterization of Andy Pandy were formed as a specific technique through which children could act out and identify with the forms of pre-school childhood: '[t]here is much repetition and plenty of opportunity for children to become so familiar with the puppets' actions that they regard them as "real"' (Lingstrom, 3 February 1953, WAC T2/7/4). *Andy Pandy* drew upon the language of play in order to make itself, and hence also television, homely: '[t]he puppet comes to the child in the security of its own home, and brings nothing alarming or contradictory to the safe routines of the family' (Adams 1950). In *Andy Pandy*, and also in *The Flowerpot Men*, the fictional world of preschool childhood was presented within the confines of the domestic. Andy, Teddy, and Looby Loo were always presented within the garden or the living room. Likewise in *The Flowerpot Men*, the characters (two male figures made out of flowerpots and a female garden weed) were presented within the garden and in close proximity to the little house which was pictured at the beginning of each programme opening its doors to the diegetic space. In *Andy Pandy* we hear nothing of the outside world. And in *The Flowerpot Men* the only off-screen character we hear about is the gardener, who, never seen or heard, signifies the limits of the imaginary world.[16]

As with *Muffin the Mule* the characters in *Andy Pandy* are voiceless. Maria Bird not only speaks to the characters, she also speaks for them. Andy, Teddy, and Looby Loo play, dance, and do childish things, but they are unable to articulate their own thoughts, desires or troubles. In *Muffin the Mule* the world of children's play was carefully watched over by the 'mother' on screen. However, in *Andy Pandy* the mother is not physically presented. Instead, the mother is signified as outside of, and constitutive of, the diegetic space. Her voice is constituted as

16 Lingstrom stated that the Flowerpot Men and Weed exist in a world secret from adults and only the child watching can know that secret (1953, WAC T2/51).

an authoritative voice and it is able to speak to both the characters within the diegetic space and to the viewers at home. In a scene in which Andy is playing on the swing, Maria Bird addresses the viewer directly saying, 'Andy likes swinging, don't you?' She then asks, 'Have you got a swing in your garden?' and then exclaims, 'I expect some of you have!' The voice establishes a complicity between itself and the viewer and in doing so bypasses the characters. The voice places the image and makes it intelligible to the viewer. However, in being able to cross between the diegetic space and the space of the viewer at home, this authoritative voice establishes an equivalence between the two spaces. And yet this voice is not a disembodied voice. The voice, authoritative because Other, is also embodied as the Mother.

The omniscient and omnipotent, authoritative voice, which constitutes the thoughts and actions of the characters, is formed in relation to the gaze of the camera, always at a fixed medium to medium-close length, which follows the voice. For example, in one scene Andy and Teddy after playing in the pram go off to look for a blanket. The camera, accompanied by the voice, follows them so far and then the voice says: 'Let's go back to the pram and see Looby Loo again.' The camera returns with the voice to Looby Loo and the pram. Just as the voice is embodied as motherly, so too is the gaze of the camera embodied as the Mother's vision. It is at this moment that the diegetic space is constructed as distinct from the screen space. The attention of the mother's voice and gaze focuses on Looby Loo, who 'remains inanimate while Andy and Teddy are there, but who comes to life and plays with the children when they are not looking' (Lingstrom, 3 February 1953, WAC T2/7/4). At this moment we have two diegetic spaces and two forms of complicity between narrator, characters, and viewer. This sequence was formed within a set of hierarchical and secret relationships as follows: between narrator and Andy Pandy and Teddy; narrator and Looby Loo; narrator and child viewer; Andy, Teddy, and Looby Loo; and the child's mediated relationship to the different characters. The relationship between Looby Loo and the child poses a certain anxiety: where are Andy and Teddy (inasmuch as they are not seen or heard) and what position do they occupy (child or adult)? The anxiety that might be produced by Andy and Teddy walking off-screen is compensated by the insularity of the diegetic space itself: they can wander off only because we know they cannot go far. The techniques of the motherly voice and gaze, the imaging of the insularity of the domestic space, the presentation of a pre-school world of play and nursery rhymes and the silencing of the characters were all constituted within a discourse concerned with the production of the *mother as supervisor*. These techniques, although pleasurable to the child audience, were framed within a particular set of relations which constructed television as safe, maternal, and homely.

A concern about giving the child a voice is evident in discussion of *The Flowerpot Men* which was scheduled in the *Watch with Mother* series. Although the characters—Bill, Ben, and Weed—in *The Flowerpot Men* have voices, they speak gobbledegook. This was particularly worrying for some broadcasters and parents who wrote to the BBC. Derek McCulloch stated that:

> I am not so sure about 'The Flowerpot Men'. They are said to have a considerable following, but they indulge in a comic, higgledy-piggledy kind of language which some parents boast is adopted into their children's everyday talk. Grown-ups who embarked upon 'ickle-doggy-wog' babyhood vocabularies, are now faced with the additional complexities of 'flowerpot' talk, may well wish they had stuck to English from the beginning. (*Daily Telegraph*, 25 August 1954)

Similarly, the *Daily Sketch* reported that:

> People are saying that the gibberish Bill and Ben, the flowerpot men, use is rearing Britain's babies in the wrong way . . . It seems the young viewers are imitating the double-talk and so, it is claimed, the children's education is being retarded. Miss Freda Lingstrom, Head of Children's Television Programmes, has called for an investigation into reports that children are conducting long conversations in the new language. (*Daily Sketch*, 2 March 1953)

Lingstrom argued that they had 'decided on a new language—on the grounds that pure English would spoil the "other world" atmosphere of the puppets' (*News Chronicle*, 16 March 1953). She related it to the nonsense language of Lewis Carroll and stated that the 'small child has enough sense to realise that one is fun and the other is reality' (ibid.).

By 1953, partly as a result of the televising of the Coronation, television had become even more firmly embedded in everyday British popular life. In the same year *Rag, Tag and Bobtail* was scheduled within *Watch with Mother*. Unlike *Andy Pandy* or *The Flowerpot Men*, the new programme had a masculine narrator, the characters were given voices and were structured within a narrative. The characters, Rag the hedgehog, Tag the mouse, and Bobtail the rabbit, were placed within the classic fairytale tradition and each story started with 'Once upon a time . . .'. The narration used the third person to frame the voices of the characters and the narrator used direct address to the viewer at home. The narrator impersonated the characters, giving the impression that they had an identity distinct from that of the narrator at the same time as constituting their identity within his voice. The first instalment of the programme, which was shown to parents in the evening beforehand (in order to gain their approval and consent), was described as presenting three 'normal animals in their natural surroundings—they will not wear clothes and will not talk direct' (*The Star*, 31 August 1953). Although the programme escaped from the confines of the domestic, the rural was nevertheless domesticated and tamed. Similarly, in 1955, *The Woodentops* presented an image of rural domesticity and happy family life.[17] Although the narrator is motherly, the characters are given a voice of their own and even the dog has a bark.

The programmes scheduled within *Watch with Mother* were intended each to 'reflect a different aspect of a small child's life' on each weekday. Lingstrom stated that:

> Andy Pandy had satisfied their wish for a friend of their own age; The Flowerpot Men were to cater for their need for fantasy; the little glove puppets, Rag, Tag and Bobtail, were to bring soft, cuddly toys to life; the Woodentops were to illustrate a small child's enjoyment of playing families, and 'Picture Book' was to encourage the creative impulse by giving children things to do. (*Good Housekeeping*, January 1963)

In scheduling the programmes in this way the BBC was able to address and constitute the different needs of the audience at the same time as constituting those differences within a single pre-school child audience. The broadcasting of different programmes within a series provided a means of dividing the pre-school audience from other child, and adult, audiences and, paradoxically, of providing some form of continuity between the different age-groups of viewers. *Watch with Mother* was 'hived-off in the early afternoon' so that the young audience 'need not fear the scorn of impatient elders'. But the 'hiving-off' was also conceived in terms of what Owen Reed called 'the rope-ladder concept', such that children's television was like 'a rope-ladder which children ascend by standing on one rung and instinctively reaching up for the next'.[18] The arrangement of children's programmes both separated children from each other and constituted each division within a hierarchy of the child's development. Such practices did not merely reflect the 'nature' of the child nor did they simply borrow from the discourses of education and developmental psychology. Rather, in producing divisions and continuity, children's television aligned itself in relation to the authorities of education and psychological expertise.

17 The characters included 'Mummy Woodentop and baby, daddy Woodentop, the two twins, Willy and Jenny, Mrs Scrubbit, who comes to help Mummy Woodentop, Sam, who helps Daddy Woodentop and Spottydog' and they all live in 'a little house in the country'.

18 Reed was conscious of the problems with his concept. He stated that 'it is really a very complicated ladder where certain tastes and enthusiasms run far ahead of others, so that a Prudence Kittenite may become a *Sketch Club* fan though not yet ready for *Paul of Tarsus*' (Reed 1961, WAC P660). Reed, however, recognized, as did Lingstrom before him, that the effectiveness of the strategy relied on the responsibilities of the parent.

Watch with Mother was never scheduled within the main bulk of children's programmes between 5 p.m. and 6 p.m. When, in September 1950 the Controller of Television sent a memo to Cecil Madden arguing that *Andy Pandy* should be shown with the rest of children's programmes, Richmond Postgate firmly responded stating that at 5 p.m. three-year-olds should be thinking of bed (13 September 1950, WAC T2/7/1). Initially *Andy Pandy* was shown in the afternoon between 3.45 p.m. and 4 p.m. at the end of the women's programme *For Women* and announcements for the programme were intended to address 'mothers at home'.[19] Maria Bird, in a policy document concerning the objectives of the programme, stated in August 1950 that:

> It appears to be in the interest of the child that the series should be attached to a women's programme and separate from the Children's Hour. The performance should be seen at a time when older children are at school, so that the very young can look without the disturbance of the reactions of older children. If this can be achieved both the pre-school child and his mother may come to feel that this programme is especially theirs. (31 August 1950, WAC T2/7/1)

The programme was designed to fit into the routines of both mothers and small children and changes to its scheduling caused minor revolts widely reported in the press. When in 1963 the BBC planned to show *Watch with Mother* at 10.45 a.m, the *Daily Sketch* declared that 'for most small children 10.45 is a time to "Watch Without Mother". And there's not much joy in that.'[20] However, although the timing of the programme was intended to provide a space 'especially' for mother

19 For example, Sylvia Peters, in an announcement on Tuesday 18 July 1950 after *Shop at Home*, stated: 'And now, may I remind those of you who have been looking at "Shop at Home" that at a quarter to 4 we are putting on the third programme in our short series for very young children—for three-year-olds. Andy Pandy will be shown again at that time. You will know that he is the friendly little puppet who comes to play with the very young children' (WAC T2/7/1).

20 *Watch with Mother* had been scheduled at various times during the 1950s and early 1960s. In October 1957 the BBC moved it from 1.45 p.m. to 2.30 p.m. following complaints that it clashed with *Listen with Mother*. In relation to the changes in 1963, the *Daily Mail*, in a piece entitled 'Tiny tots revolt against a BBC switch', talked about how parents were thinking of starting a petition and it drew upon comments from the Viewers' and Listeners' Association about the 'indifference' of the BBC to 'responsible opinion' (*Daily Mail*, 25 March 1963). A letter in the *Daily Sketch* called the BBC 'a bully' and asked, 'Do they enjoy reducing children to tears?' (*Daily Sketch*, 26 March 1963). The *Daily Sketch* stated that the morning was the 'busiest time for shopping and housework' (*Daily Sketch*, 9 June 1963). The Yorkshire newspaper, the *Telegraph and Argus*, however, referred to 'the little ones whose lives are built on routine' and whose '15-minute treat' came round 'as regularly as bath-time' (*Telegraph and Argus*, 26 January 1963). The *Daily Mail* was pleased to report in September 1963 that the BBC would now show *Watch with Mother* at both 10.45 a.m. and 1.30 p.m. (*Daily Mail*, 13 September 1963). In December 1965, after the morning programme had been dropped two months earlier, the BBC had obviously learnt its lesson and now invited mothers of children under 5 to send postcards saying whether they wanted the programme to be shown in the morning or afternoon (*Daily Mail*, 6 December 1965).

and small child, it is clear that some viewers saw it as a means to do other things. A letter in the *Evening Standard* from Mrs Olive Attwater stated:

> The critics have a lot to say about every programme except *Watch with Mother*. Yet how many mothers, I wonder, are deeply grateful for this simple programme, which gives them at least one moment's relief during the day. (*Evening Standard*, 23 June 1956)

Whether or not mothers actually did watch with their children, what emerges is that the BBC had been successful at creating a 'loving' and 'caring' relationship between mother, child, and television as a specifically discursive space. The techniques of scheduling, programme announcements, the construction of the motherly voice and gaze, the silencing of the child, the imaging of a rural domesticity, and the presentation of specific activities (e.g. nursery rhymes, playing, 'movement', etc.) were formed in relation to specific knowledges which made intelligible the relationship between mother, child, and television.

Andy Pandy can perhaps be seen as the first programme in Britain to be 'pre-tested'. The initial series of four experimental programmes were coupled with audience research into the habits of young viewers and their mothers.[21] The programme makers welcomed viewers' letters and invited further response.[22] Research into the audience was conducted by the Audience Research Department for the four experimental programmes. Mothers were invited to respond to questionnaires.[23] The Audience Research Department wanted to know whether children between 2 years and 5 years old watched television 'fairly regularly', whether programmes for this audience were 'a good idea', whether the children watched alone, with an adult or with older children, whether they were sitting down, standing up or moving about, whether their attention was held throughout, whether they joined in the movements or singing, whether they remembered and used any of the sayings or songs, and what would be the most convenient time for the programme to be shown. Most children of this age

---

21 *Listen with Mother* received similar attention from the Audience Research Department. It is significant that the 'twinkly noises' and so on that McCulloch had been so disparaging about were conceived by both the respondants of the Audience Research Department's questionnaires and the programme makers themselves as a central component within the programme and as accounting, in part, for its popularity.

22 The BBC announced, after *Shop at Home* and *Women of Today*, that some of the suggestions would be 'incorporated' and would help in deciding the future of the programme (see 18 July, 20 July, 1 August and 19 September 1950, WAC T2/7/1).

23 The survey employed two methods: first, 600 questionnaires were sent out to viewers with at least one child under 7 years, of which 290 were completed; and second, questionnaires and the routine weekly logs were completed by the London Viewing Panel (18 August 1950, WAC VR/50/279).

group, it was discovered, watched television regularly.[24] Ninety per cent of the respondents thought that a programme for this age group was a good idea. Two-thirds of the children watched with an adult and others who did not actually sit with their child 'spied unnoticed on their child's reactions'.

The research conducted by the BBC made visible the gap between the original intentions of the producers and the localized conduct of the audience. Whereas the producers had imagined Andy as a friend of the very young child, the research showed that the children at home perceived him as a stranger. While most children, it was stated, believed Andy to be 'real', some children were 'more sophisticated'. The respondents also pointed out that 'great care' needed to be taken 'to prevent Andy doing anything that it would be unwise for a child to imitate' and that when invited to imitate Andy's actions they became 'embarrassed and worried' (due, it was said, to 'children's shyness of strangers'). Similarly, only a relatively small number of children engaged in the games and nursery rhymes. Some stated that it was good training 'in sitting still and concentrating' and that it would allow them to 'focus their interest in television on to suitable subjects and thus make them less apt to demand a share of "grown-up" programmes'. Most children sat to watch the programme and about a third always responded to the songs and movements. The Audience Research Department was able to provide a knowledge of the audience, as distinct from the intentions of the programme makers, such that the ontology of actual children watching *Andy Pandy* is made visible as a difference.

In November 1950 Maria Bird addressed the audience of mothers at home informing them about the type of programme *Andy Pandy* was and inviting further criticisms and comments.[25] The 'talk' referred to the fact that '[s]ome people think there ought not to be a programme for very young children at all', but continued by saying that 'we know that children of this age do look at television, so we have tried to make a suitable programme for them, as different as possible from those for the older children' (14 November 1950, WAC T2/7/1). She also, importantly, stated that:

> I hope very much that you will be able to look at the programmes with the children. I know that in some cases it is not possible, but we do want to know the children's reactions, and you are really the only people who can tell us if we are on the right lines. (ibid.)

The incitement of the responsibilities of mothers in watching with their children fed into a spiral of power and knowledge. The mother

---

24 *Muffin the Mule* was cited as the most popular programme.

25 The research conducted by the Audience Research Department was initiated by the children's television producer, Naomi Capon (19 June 1950, WAC T2/7/1).

acted as a relay not only of the means of supervising the child but also of gathering knowledge of this small audience.

Moreover, earlier in 1950 the programme makers had gathered the expertise of educationalists and psychologists. In the planning stages of *Andy Pandy* there was clearly some hesitancy about the introduction of television programmes for very young children and a concern about their effect on the proper mode of conduct within the home. An internal BBC memo stated in 1950:

> We had a special panel to advise us consisting of representatives of the Ministry of Education, the Institute of Child Development, the Nursery Schools' Association, and some educational child psychologists, and I think they would be pretty sure to squeak if you were to publicise any Television programme for very young children as something that would set Mother free to get about her other business, even though that might in fact be what happened. (6 March 1950, WAC T2/7/1)

The memo indicated a concern about the pre-school audience and the domestic conduct of mothers and it also displayed a range of authorities. The memo clearly presented a concern that mothers should watch with their children and yet it also presents a reluctant acknowledgement that mothers might actually just put their children in front of the screen and do something else. At stake here then was not that programmes were made and audiences researched in the model of normative science, but that expertise and support from other actors were enlisted in the construction of the programme and the audience. The memo, from the Acting Controller of Talks to the Head of Television Talks, about *Listen with Mother*, laid out the 'reasons for bringing Mothers in on this programme'. It stated that:

> Previous suggestions for programmes for Under Fives were strongly discouraged by the S.B.C. [Schools Broadcasting Council] and other advisers and it was only when I came back from Australia with the idea that Under Fives should listen *with* Mothers that they viewed the idea of a special programme with tolerance. (6 March 1950, WAC T2/7/1)

It also stated that there should be co-operation between radio and television broadcasting in relation to this audience and that it would be worthwhile for those involved with the making of television programmes for the very young viewer to draw upon the expertise in broadcasting for schools.

The episodic narrative form, the use of nursery rhyme and song, the presumed interactive relation between programme and child within the home, the speaking relations between narrator and puppet, the invocation of motherly supervision, and the mobilization of research and external expertise all helped to construct programmes for the very young within a discourse of post-war familialism. In this respect the work of the developmental psychologist John Bowlby was of particular importance (cf. Riley 1983; Rose 1989; Hendrick 1990). The writings of Bowlby were significant in that they constructed care for the child in terms of not only physical, but also mental and emotional neglect and that the burden of this care fell upon the mother (Bowlby 1965: 90). Bowlby's work was both popularized in the ideological climate of the post-war period, fitting in with assumptions about women's labour, and also incorporated into social welfare practices directed at mothers and mothering (Riley 1983; Urwin 1985; Wilson 1980; and Walkerdine and Lucey 1989). As a result the concept of 'maternal deprivation' was central to the discourse of mothering. This discursive formation constituted 'love' no longer as 'a moral duty or romantic ideal', but as an element in the production of 'normal and abnormal children'. As Nikolas Rose states:

> Normality was now to be promoted not through coercion after the event—the removal of a pathological child and the disablement of the family—but by inciting the family itself to take on board the business of production of normal subjects. A new relation between subjectivity and the social order was being formed within the matrix of the family. Expertise was to enable the social obligation on the family to regulate the subjectivities of its children to be translated into the personal desire for normal children, and to a set of emotional and intersubjective techniques for securing this goal. (Rose 1989: 156)

It is possible to see the formation of the pre-school television audience within a strategy aimed at rendering families responsible for the production of normal citizens. We can see how programme series, such as *Watch with Mother*, and the practices which surrounded them, were formed as specific elements in a wider web of programmes intended to incite, through a number of devices, certain competencies and dispositions within the viewing population. In this sense, television viewing was construed as a central component in the production of normal families. The consumption of broadcasting, which had been constructed within a set of questions about children's radio and democracy, was now, in relation to television viewing, articulated with a discourse of post-war familialism.

Audiences and Schedules   Although programmes for the very young provided the leading edge for a wider mobilization of motherly supervision, psychological expertise, and broadcasting professionalism, they constituted only one small

segment of the total provision of children's television. Whereas programmes for the very young were framed within, what John Holt has
referred to in another context as, the 'walled garden' of childhood
(1975), programmes for older children were at least more discrete in
concealing the walls and the eyes of protective supervision. Moreover,
there was clearly a tension between satisfying the needs and wants
of particular audiences (and the authorities mobilized around such
audiences) and a general ethos of children's television regarding its
provision of a space of freedom and participation.

Freda Lingstrom had imagined children's television as similar to
the walk between school and home: a time and a space which was
not supervised and which was free from the constraints of adult
authority. She believed that children's television could provide a space
through which children might visit other worlds and peoples. She
envisaged children's television as fitting into their daily routines: '[a]t
an early age children accept the fact that life divides itself into parts'
(Lingstrom 1953: 99).

At five o'clock every day groups, small in height as well as
number, gather round waiting for the now familiar 'stars' to
turn into the words 'Children's Television'. The day is nearing its
end; the younger ones have finished with school, the older ones
are able legitimately to put off the attack on homework which
must follow. A wedge of expectancy has been driven between
the familiar states of having had tea and preparing for bed or for
other employment. A little piece of time has been set apart from
the rest of the day and the child, alert and eager, awaits with an
open mind this small separate part of his daily life. (1953: 98–9)

Television was inserted into this space, not as an intrusion, but as
something which was welcomed by the child: '[t]he child is not forced
to look at the screen, no one says he must. Of his own free will he stands
in happy anticipation ready to receive and observe' (1953: 100).

But within this small time slot and within the general terms of children's television as providing a space of freedom and participation,
children's broadcasters faced a fundamental problem. The child audience was seen to comprise a vast array of differences. An immediate
problem for the children's broadcasters was how to differentiate
between different types of audience. Adams had argued in 1950 that
as a result of the school system, economic change, the influence of
radio and the family, the child audience 'is more homogenous than it
was, and varieties of social experience, although wider than they were
thirty years ago, are more uniform' (Adams 1950: 85). But there was,
nevertheless, a wide discussion (including Adams herself) of how
to tackle the range of differences within the category of the child
audience. There was discussion of having separate programmes for

boys and girls. The Commissioned Report on Children's Television suggested the possibility of explicitly labelling and announcing programmes for boys or girls ('This is a programme for girls. Now boys, off you go, and we'll get on with it' (1952: 24)). But the call for separate programmes for girls and boys was always rejected on the grounds that while girls would watch programmes for boys, boys would never watch programmes made specifically for girls. The intention then was to make 'unisexual' programmes and 'to use the strong narrative book of interest to both' (Spicer, 15 January 1957, WAC T16/45/1).

The main problem, though, was not gender, but age. Adams argued that:

> Practical problems, however, set some limit to this massive objective [of addressing the diverse audience]. The age range, for example. At present, children from two years keep company with teenagers. How shall they be separated, and each provided with adequate satisfaction? (Adams 1950: 86)

Lingstrom added that: 'The under-fives, for whom a special provision is being made, must be discounted: their needs are simple in comparison with those of that vast concourse whose stages of physical growth and mental development are distributed over a span of ten years —a span of "difference" never to be found at any other period of life' (Lingstrom 1953: 97). They had already settled on dividing children's television into two time periods. Thompson had argued that programmes should be divided 'into two defined periods, the first for the younger children and the second for older ones' (30 June 1949, WAC T16/45/1).[26] But Postgate played with the idea that different age-groups might be better served if they made 'certain days of the week specially suitable for particular age-ranges'. Postgate's suggestion, though, cut across the 'idea of a daily Children's Hour of which the essence seems to me that those that will can listen daily and can hope to find something suitable for them each day' (Postgate, 20 January

---

26 Mary Adams in 1949 agreed that it was a good idea to divide children's programmes into 15 minutes for the very young and 45 minutes for the older children (15 December 1949, WAC T16/45/1). However, Spicer argued against this division: 'The Children's Programme should be each afternoon an organic whole, not a string of items each with its age-group or interested minority' (10 May 1951, WAC T16/45/1).

In the early period the BBC employed children to present programmes and to act as announcers. These included Jennifer Gay, Jannette Scott and Elizabeth Cruft. A typical announcement was: 'Hallo everyone. We are doing Thursday's play again this afternoon—"Exercise Hush" which is an adventure thriller for boys—and girls, I think—but definitely not for the younger children. Before that there's the Newsreel and we start the programme with Muffin. Here's Annette with "We Want Muffin" ' (Gay, WAC T2/214). Due to excuses about legal injunctions against the use of child presenters (despite the Home Office stating the contrary), the BBC withdrew them at the beginning of 1952.

1950, 4 and 5, WAC T16/45/1). But whereas the younger audience was black-boxed within a relatively stable network of expertise, the older teenage audience was increasingly subject to instability. In the early 1950s teenagers were still clearly, although problematically, addressed as part of the child audience. The question was what to show them. Adams asked:

> What shall the adolescent be offered? Plays of action or detection? Documentaries like 'London Town', or 'How to be a Doctor'? Travel films? Advice on collecting? Hobbies, such as carpentry or metal work? Coaching for sports and athletics? Dancing lessons? Crafts? Competitions which test his knowledge and abilities? Campanology? (Adams 1950: 87)

She continued by saying that, although there are plenty of subjects to consider, the important question is that of 'scale'. This audience needed to be presented not with models and studio-based programmes but outside broadcasts presenting the 'real thing'. For example:

> In the studio, let them plan and organise a voyage round Britain, round the world. Then charter a vessel and let them go, recording their journey by film, photograph and painting for the others to see on transmission. (1950: 88)

Similarly Lingstrom began to question the place of addressing teenagers within children's television.

> At fifteen, however inarticulate they may be in expressing opinions to adults, they have formed them—indeed, by that time a large proportion will be wage-earners compelled to rely upon their own judgement. It will not be a very mature judgement and it can only be exercised against a set of values gradually built up during childhood. (Lingstrom 1953: 101)

But she nevertheless made no argument that their tastes and needs should be addressed through separate and distinct forms of pro-gramming. By December 1955, however, the discussion gained increasing importance with the impact of commercial television. Lingstrom called for the revival of 'teenage programmes'. As a result of the introduction of commercial television a concern developed that the 'toddlers truce', between 6 p.m. and 7 p.m. might disappear. The 'toddlers truce' had been a space in the day when no programmes were shown in order to aid mothers to get their children to bed. Lingstrom considered what to place in this slot:

> I very much want to revive our teenage programmes and would like to think there might be space for two, one of a magazine character and the other a forum of some kind, each to last half

an hour and occur in alternate weeks. (30 December 1955, WAC T16/45/2)

Although she resisted the idea that children's programmes should be shown between 6 p.m. and 7 p.m., she stated:

> It occurs to me that the period 6 to 7 might well be used for handicraft demonstrations or for a series on careers and trades likely to be of interest to teenagers. (ibid.)

By Saturday 16 February, after the ITV companies had petitioned Charles Hill, the Postmaster General, arguing that 'it was the responsibility of parents, not the State, to put their children to bed at the right time', the toddlers truce was formally ended and the *Six-Five Special* was started (cf. Hill 1991: 90).

The case for splitting up children's television and having separate programmes for children and for teenagers was now being forcefully made. Owen Reed, Head of Children's Programmes (Television) from 1956, presented a discussion document putting both sides of the argument. In the argument for splitting up existing children's programmes he stated that:

> The tastes of older children (i.e. the 12+ age group) are so different from those of younger children that there is nothing to be gained by trying to include them under the title of 'children' at all. Teen-agers are more likely to resent the appellation than to be drawn to it. (Reed, 2, WAC T16/45/2)[27]

He argued that these older children were more interested in watching adult programmes than they were children's programmes. He also stated that:

> These children, whose needs occupy a good half of the Department's effort, are really more interested in adult programmes than in those we provide for them. Their main character as a group is their desire to respond as adults with adults.

Equally there were some programmes, such as *Jane Eyre*, which older children might be more 'emotionally attuned to' and yet which would be 'quite unsuitable for younger children'. It would be, he argued, 'dangerous to attempt to satisfy these contradictory needs in a single programme'.

> As older children are already able and willing to view adult programmes, the illogicality rests in attempting to stretch CTV to include them. They can perfectly well be catered for jointly

---

27 This document is undated but it was produced between 1955 and 1959 and it is likely that it was produced in about 1958.

with adults in the pre-peak, early evening programme planning, and can find the diet they seek in the 'Tonights', 'Whackos' and 'Dixons'. (Reed, 2, WAC T16/45/2)

The 'teenager', as one newspaper put it, was an almost 'elastic' entity.[28] As Petula Clark, President of the newly-formed Teenage Televiewers' Society stated in 1953, it was an audience that had never been properly visible before: 'While I have the greatest admiration for The Children's Programme and—knowing the difficulties under which T.V. producers work—also very much praise for the "adult" programmes, I DO feel that the "in-between" age has been left out in the cold' (Clark quoted in *Heiress*, October 1953). Yet the teenage audience not only constituted a problem for the categorization and organization of children's television, but also in its own right.

In the late 1950s the BBC conducted audience research and set up a Teenage Advisory Committee to look into this question: how successful was the BBC in appealing to young people and in constituting a 'teenage' community? A Report of the Teenage Advisory Committee stated in 1959 that 'the 14 to 19 group is a section of the television audience for which television is less important than for almost any other group' (Teenage Advisory Committee, 1959, 2, WAC R9/13/180). It stated that young people 'are more inclined to go out and do things', that they are starting to make girl- and boy-friends, that they might be in 'some sort of friction with their parents' and that they 'want to be with groups of people of their own age' (ibid.).[29] It seems that television was tainted too much with the familial and the domestic to attract teenagers into the home.[30] The Report also argued that research had indicated that 'there was no such thing as a "teenagers' hour" between 6 p.m. and 7 p.m.': 'We could find little to suggest that, as an audience, they constituted an intermediate third group between children and adults, let alone an extension of the child audience'

---

28 In a report from the Western Union conference, in Rome 1960, on the impact of television on youth, the *Glasgow Herald* stated: ' "Youth", of course, is an elastic state. The 36 delegates from seven countries . . . apparently found themselves unanimous enough on when "youth" ends, but not when it begins, so that the United Kingdom delegation arrived prepared to discuss the 14–20 age group and discovered others concerned about the impact of television on five-year-olds' (25 February 1960).

29 The Crowther Report similarly reported that: 'Less than 8 per cent of the boys and girls who had left modern schools two years before were not still living at home at the time of our Social Survey (when they were, presumably, about 17) but 36 per cent of the boys and 32 per cent of the girls had only spent one or two evenings at home out of the previous seven. A further 28 per cent of the boys and 6 per cent of the girls had been out every evening' (Department of Education 1959: 36).

30 This is wonderfully represented in the British New Wave films *Saturday Night and Sunday Morning* (Karel Reisz 1960) and *The Loneliness of the Long Distance Runner* (Tony Richardson 1962) in which the young male protagonists are clearly alienated from the cosy domesticity and femininity exemplified by watching television (cf. Barr 1986).

(ibid.). Moreover, it would seem, the programme tastes of teenagers (when they stayed at home) were the same as adults. Hence young people did not seem to identify with television nor did they seem to identify with their construction on television as 'teenagers'. Teenagers constituted an audience that did not identify with themselves as an audience. The Advisory Committee stated that the reason for this lay in the fact that it was 'not so much that their specialist interests aren't catered for, but that their *attitude* isn't acknowledged or reflected' (ibid. 7, my italics).

In 1958 Owen Reed stated that he did 'not know whether the existence of the word "children" in our daily title is a source of strength and pride or a damaging weakness in the eyes of the audience we are trying to attract' (2 June 1958, WAC T16/45/2). By 1959 he stated that:

> We must no longer plug 'children', which is a word to which most of our viewers are allergic, and which is a breeder of false attitudes, but think of them simply as unusually selective and appreciative human beings of limited and varying experience. This last point needs stressing. In aiming at this wide bracket we must never forget that many school-goers *are* just children. We must be the more careful about how we approach them, and not treat or greet any part of them in a way that lays them open to the jeers of older brothers and sisters. If we are to hold together the junior and senior halves of our audience we must continue to find an approach which will satisfy both without being offputting to either. That, and *within* each programme to be sure of our target, are the important things. (5 June 1959, WAC T16/45/2)

The dropping of the title Children's Television was also intended to pick up adult viewers and the period was now to be known as 'Late Afternoon'.

The differentiation between and organization into different audiences implied a normative project. Children, teenagers, and adults did not naturally and simply fall into categories and time-slots. As audiences they had to be shaped into audiences. In the early 1950s children's broadcasters had called upon parents to help them 'restrain' children from watching programmes other than those designed for them. Adams argued in the 1950s that:

> Thus, restraint in viewing will be encouraged in the interests of programme quality, as well as in the interests of other pursuits and the demands of homework. It will take some time to make this policy effective; it will need the co-operation of parents, and consistency in planning over a period of time. (Adams 1950: 86)

Similarly, Lingstrom, in 1953, invoked the responsibilities of the parent:

This business of giving a salad to the 15-year-olds which is understandable by the five-year-olds is difficult. It is hard for older children to sit and watch a puppet, for example, put on for the very young. Parents should dissuade their children from looking at items which are too old for them. Children quickly tire of older programmes, and that is not good.

It would be a comfort to know that there is some selection at the other—parental—end. This is important because here in television we do not know what happens to a child when it sees a thing. We could only find that out by invading a man's home.

(Lingstrom quoted in the *Evening Standard*, 9 October 1951)

Lingstrom makes clear in this quote that the limits of broadcasting as a disciplinary apparatus are set within the limits of liberalism. Although the broadcasters could invite the proper responses and responsibilities from parents, they could do nothing but ask. The production of specific programmes for specific types of children at specific and fixed times was accompanied by other techniques such as 'signposting in billing and announcements' such that 'children will be urged to view what suits them best' (Adams 1950: 86).[31] The production of information about the programmes in the *Radio Times*, newspapers, magazines, and importantly on television itself was deployed as a technique for regulating individuals into audiences.

By the late 1950s, the distribution of children's television programming according to age was firmly cemented in place. Children were both separated from adults and divided within themselves. The distribution of bodies was likewise arranged according to a specified logic of development. Programmes both addressed specific age-groups and also provided markers along a line of progression for those climbing up the 'rope-ladder', as Madden called it. The distribution of bodies within this temporal arrangement allowed the construction of specific audiences for television (e.g. the teenage audience and the pre-school audience). Foucault refers to this process in terms of individualization. Such arrangements construct individuals. The technique of scheduling children's programmes as distinct from adult programmes was deployed as a means of dividing the viewing habits of the 'child' population, but also of dividing other populations from it. Likewise the division within children's programmes both divided the viewing habits of the child population and provided a means through which children could progress from the programmes appropriate for one age-group to another. The broadcasters had an understanding of

---

31 Owen Reed, Head of Children's Programmes (Television) from 1956 reaffirmed that position in a policy document to all involved in children's programmes. He stated that the 'age-target of each programme should be carefully considered and made as plain as possible in billing and presentation' (5 June 1959, WAC T16/45/2).

children's development as separate from their particular age and that programmes for older children were necessary in order to provide that 'undiscovered territory' as something to reach for (Reed, 5 June 1959, WAC T16/45/2).

And yet despite the regimentation of children's programmes according to age and development, it was also paradoxically recognized that children did not simply watch programmes designed for them. Reed argued that the 'whole concept of age groups, while necessary for planning programmes, is fallacious'. He stated that:

They are not cut-and-dried entities but interlock and overlap almost infinitely, and it is this very fact which gives the idea of a consolidated children's programme its inner strength and sense of purpose, and evokes that loyalty which is borne out by the audience figures. (ibid.)

It was also clear to the broadcasters that children of all ages watched different programmes for different age-groups: '[n]ot only do different children cross the age-barriers at widely different ages, but they cross them at different ages for different programmes': 'Sooty fans from St. Paul's Girls School rub shoulders with 6 year old boys who write to demand repeats of Nicholas Nickelby' (Reed, ibid. 2). Needless to say concerns about the division of programmes and intended audiences were also voiced by those outside the BBC. The *Daily Mirror* argued that 'blood-thunder stuff does no harm to old children; it gives some frightening ideas to three- and four-year-olds who get sandwiched between a newsreel (which all kids adore) and a puppet show' (23 March 1954).

This configuration of practices was markedly different from those earlier practices concerning *Children's Hour* radio. Whereas the formation in the 1920s, 1930s, and 1940s had conceived of the child audience as a family audience and as isomorphic with *Children's Hour* itself (inasmuch as children were not conceived as listening to programmes for adults), we now see the possibility of children being conceived as an audience in their own right (as distinct from the family audience) and as an audience who might possibly watch programmes other than those designed for them. In this chapter we have seen how children's television was not invented as a means of addressing a pre-existent child audience. On the contrary, although children's television broadcasters could draw on the wealth of nineteenth- and early twentieth-century children's cultural forms and on the radio broadcast forms of the 1920s and 1930s, there were many questions regarding whether children constituted both audience and producer, whether children could be organized as a single audience, and whether certain 'child' audiences could even be addressed as a television audience. Thus, on the one hand, children constituted the object of a series of differentiated forms of address (in the sense that television programmes were being made for children), but on the other hand, they did not in any way constitute a ready-made audience. Nevertheless, despite the questions and problems posed by an address to children, an underlying logic of commensurability organized the different responses. Television broadcasters, as with radio broadcasters before them, sought to construct a televisual world that was intimately connected to the world of children (their interests and enjoyments, their mode of engagement and their temporalities) and organized according to a model of development. By the late 1950s, the question of how to address children was beginning to be more concertedly tied to demands for systematic knowledge of children as a differentiated audience.

4

Geographies of Viewing and the Reconstruction of the Modern Home

THE child television audience is construed as a problem for government, broadcasters, teachers, academics, but also parents. The home and family are significant overlapping sites within which this audience is thought about and acted upon. Child, family, and home are not simply fictions produced by broadcasters. They are not simply the imaginary sites addressed by television institutions. They have their own materiality, discourses, and agencies. Sustained knowledge of the audience, as it were, at home—in all its detail, manners, conducts, and quotidian habits—was initially enunciated not by broadcasters alone, and not by academics in any sustained way, but by journalists, designers, architects, and housewives. These latter commentators divide in terms of expertise, but come together in their focus on the imagining and acting upon the home, family, and television set. It is within this complex of design, social architecture, and viewing conduct that the child television audience is properly understood and importantly governed as a spatialized entity. The figuring of the mother/housewife is central to this story. And so such discourses and practices demand analysis in any investigation of the relation between children and television.

In contemporary academic and public discourse, there is much discussion of the geography of children's and young people's information and communication technology (ICT) use. Research has provided evidence of an increasing geographical segmentation of ICT use. Some researchers talk about the emergence of young people's 'new bedroom cultures' (Livingstone and Bovill 1999). Young people's bedrooms are increasingly equipped with televisions, videos, personal computers, radios, and other music technologies. Other research has provided a normalizing framework within which such trends might become visible and counter-acted. For example, Kimberly Young has pointed to the rise of, what she refers to as, Internet addiction and has argued for the need for parents to bring the ICTs out of the bedroom and back into the living room within the supervisory gaze of the parent (Young 1998). Jon Courtenay Grimwood, writing in the parents' pages of *The Guardian*, reiterates Young's advice:

> Don't take the computer away . . . Make the computer visible. Move the PC out of your child's bedroom. You don't need to stare over the kid's shoulder but he or she does need to know you're there . . . Make the child keep a log of all the time spent online . . . Encourage other [off-line] activities. (*The Guardian* 1 April 1998)

And, in the press, the distribution of ICTs across the household and into children's bedrooms has also proved a cause for concern. In responding to the research of Livingstone and Bovill, the *Express*, a national daily newspaper in the UK, pictured a young person's bedroom in the form of a prison cell (*Express*, 19 March 1999). Three teenage boys were presented as 'inmates of bedroom wing' and video games, computers, and violent videos provided the symbols of their delinquency.

Although the technologies are new, the concerns are not. For example, Conservative MP Kenneth Baker, then Home Secretary, in his address to the National Viewers' and Listeners' Association Annual Convention in March 1991 stated that:

> Watching television is not only popular—it is easy . . . over half the children in Britain aged five or over have a television set in their bedroom. These figures demonstrate vividly the reach and accessibility of television and they point more than ever to the need to achieve standards of taste and decency that would be regarded by all reasonable people as acceptable . . . This is particularly so for young people. We cannot be with our children, nor supervise their viewing at all times. We need to ensure that impressionable young minds are protected and the broadcasters, as well as the viewers, must share some responsibility for that. (Baker 1991: 3–4)

Domestic geography and conduct are differentiated and differently normalized and pathologized. These press reports, expert evidence, and political speeches present the bedroom as a potentially secret part of the home. Like the darks spaces of the home, the city, and society that emerge in the eighteenth century, the bedroom is constituted as a problem. The differentiation of the household in the eighteenth century both allowed the habits of the family to be divided along generational, sexual, and functional lines and permitted a greater detailing of the micro problems of the domestic. These images of the dark and dangerous bedroom are clearly constituted within a historical complex of light/power, public/private and child/parent. They both suggest a space to be made fully visible (and to be supervised thereupon) and a space to be closed-off (in the sense that certain activities in the bedroom are to be proscribed). As with the figure of the masturbating child, the ICT active child cannot be left unsupervised in the bedroom. They must be made visible within the household and their activities overseen.

How, then, was television adopted into the home in the 1950s and how was domestic space, time and conduct accordingly constructed? How were women constituted through forms of expertise regarding the place of television in the home and family? And how did concerns about children's television viewing surface in the context of the motherly supervision of familial conduct? In the 1950s, as today, both ICT development and domestic design underwent massive transformation. Then, as now, television was dispersed in relation to a differential spacing of ICT, and other use, in the home. But whereas now the problem concerns bedroom cultures, then the sitting room was the primary focus of concern, discussion, and governance.

Television Set Design and Gender

Although there is still very little research on the social relations of television set design in screen studies, the research to date makes a clear distinction between those sets which in the early days made no attempt to conceal the internal workings of the technology and those which attempted to hide the various valves and tubes as furniture (cf. Forty 1986; Chambers 1991; Silverstone and Haddon 1996). This distinction can also be found in early writings on set design. For example, Michael Farr in his 1955 survey *Design in British Industry*, distinguished between radio and television sets designed as 'a piece of furniture, suited to a certain standard of interior design' and those designed as 'instruments' (1955: 70–1; Russell 1946). He related this distinction to gramophone design in the late nineteenth and early twentieth centuries. The turn from hand-operated instruments, whose workings remained uncovered, to those resplendently furnished in oak cabinets 'shows the natural tendency in all new and unfamiliar products' (1955: 69). Wireless, but also television, set design drew upon the styles of gramophone cabinets and so the 'progress from the instrument stage (which was essentially amateur and non-commercial), to the "piece of furniture" stage was speedier' (ibid.). In early radio set design Georgian, Queen Anne and Tudor were popular in various 'adaptations and mixtures'. Farr noted that between 1932 and 1939 'the radio set reached the state of wanting its modernity to be expressed in the cabinet'. Jags and angles and cubist sound holes were added. But by 1939 radio sets had become 'straightforward and unpretentious' (1955: 70). For Farr, as for other writers, the history of radio and television set design was one which measured the value of design in terms of either its functional or its aesthetic features. Both have a clearly established, and yet uneasy, relation to modernity.

For writers in popular design and women's magazines the television set was similarly displayed according to such generic stylings. The congregation of 'home entertainment' technologies (as *Ideal Home*, December 1950 referred to radio, television, and gramophone) were presented within a repeated serial history of domestic design. Each new technology was seen to repeat the design cycle from instrument (functional) to furniture (symbolic) and to draw on previous 'entertainment technology' as a resource for design ideas. What is interesting in the representation of these stylings in popular magazines is how such a distinction provided the basis for consumer differentiation and also how it was gendered.

In the late 1940s and early 1950s *Ideal Home* carried a number of articles on television set design.[1] Discussions of different types of television set were largely framed according to their technical features. A genre of writing emerged for introducing television to a general readership. There was much discussion of the lightness of the room and the brightness of the television image, types of aerial, distance from transmitter, AC or DC electrical current, size of cathode ray tube, screen size, baffle area, cost and to a lesser extent cabinet design. Roy Norris, 'radio and television expert' and regular writer for *Ideal Home*, discussed the thorny issue of whether it was necessary to have an 'H aerial'. Norris, in his article 'Decision on Television', talked about the types of aerial in relation to their positioning in the home (i.e. in the sitting room, loft or on the roof) and in relation to their distance from the television transmitter. For example:

> Between 15 and 25 miles a single rod, or dipole, mounted by adjustable bracket to wall or chimney, as high as possible, is likely to be adequate. A second rod, forming the H, acting not as another collector but as a reflector, is needed to increase the signal strength at distances greater than, say, 25 miles, or where the site is screened by trees, large buildings or by hills.

He then went on to discuss how car ignition interference could be reduced 'by efficient suppression circuits built into the receiver'. Typical of all the articles, except one (*Ideal Home*, December 1950) which produced a display of radio and television sets and only captions of

---

1 These included: 'Decision on Television', *Ideal Home*, May 1949; 'Television for the Small Home', *Ideal Home*, February 1950; 'Looking and Listening', *Ideal Home*, November 1950; 'News of the Latest Radio and Television', *Ideal Home*, December 1950; 'Reproduction and Reception', *Ideal Home*, December 1951; 'Television and Radio in Coronation Year', *Ideal Home*, June 1953.

writing attached to the images, was the length of written discussion. Images of television sets, on their own or in sitting rooms, were secondary to the written text. The images served primarily to exemplify the written technical discussion.

There was also a tendency to discuss television set design alongside the design of gramophone and radio sets. In November 1950, an article titled 'Looking and Listening' discussed the latest design in television, radio and gramophone sets. The article started by discussing long-playing gramophone records and then turned its attention to the new Mullard flat screen television set. There was reference to Mullard's supply of the apparatus to other set manufacturers, to the size of the screen, to the fact that the screen was made of plastic and hence able to 'diffuse the light for wide-angle viewing', to the contrast between room lighting and television image and the replacement cost of the cathode-ray tube. It stated that 'the direct-view tubes now give such a bright picture that they can be viewed in strong room lighting —whether artificial or daylight—and there is brilliance to spare' (ibid.). The article closed with a small discussion of radio sets.

In one of the few articles of its kind in women's magazines of the period, Edith Blair, design journalist, presented a range of new record players, radios, televisions, and tape recorders in the mass market weekly *Woman*. The article, which took the same name as its forerunner in *Ideal Home*, 'Looking and Listening' (27 August 1960), presented images of each item and discussed them according to specific themes. The discussion of television was organized according to colour, shape, controls, price, and the right aerial. The colourfulness and sleekness of the sets was accentuated. The volume and brightness controls were constructed as 'easier to operate and smarter to look at'. Aerials were presented in terms of their price and location in the house (i.e. indoor, loft, or roof). A central thematic in the discussion of all items was their mobility. On the right-hand side of the double-page spread was an image of a young heterosexual couple sitting at the end of a punt smiling and embracing each other. To the other end of the boat sat a girl of about eight years playing with a transistor radio. The copy to the left of the image read:

> They can have music wherever they go—no wonder they are thrilled with their new transistor portable radio—they take it on picnics, into the garden, and all round the house without having to bother about aerials or adaptors for plugging in. (ibid.)

The styling, but also the 'context' of use was presented as significant in this display of a consumer product. In addition to the image of outdoor radio use, the article presented images of different room designs within which these new domestic technologies might be located, tables upon which the television set might be placed and a new indoor telescopic aerial (presumably chosen for its aesthetic high-tech features). Such styling and placing of entertainment technologies was typical of the representation of television in women's magazines. In the early 1960s the television sets became thinner, sleeker, and more metallic and also represented in exotic narratives. For example, one advertisement declared 'I'm in a world of dreams-come-true with our new Ultra Bermuda 21'. The image which dominated the advert was of a naval captain walking toward a young woman in a tiara and evening gown. She was standing next to a television set and a bottle of wine and glasses. In the misted background stood a group of Mexican musicians, a row of arches and a full moon.

A number of academics have commented on the history of the domestic reception of media technologies in terms of the gendering of design. For example, the shift from the functional to the aesthetic in radio set design is interpreted in terms of a shift from radio as a masculine hobby to a feminine pastime (cf. Moores 1988; Boddy 1994; Spigel 1992). The construction of radio as decoration is read in terms of both its domestication and its feminization. As Farr said of radio: 'It is as if the cabinet became the radio set's passport to respectability, for it makes an unsightly collection of wires, valves, coils, etc., "presentable" and therefore acceptable in a domestic furnishing scheme' (Farr 1955: 69). The history of the design process of radio and television technology is equally understood in terms of its increasing commodification. Roger Silverstone and Leslie Haddon have rightly argued that the design of information and communication technologies involves the processes of both commodification and familiarization (1996: 45). The former refers to 'the process through which objects and technologies emerge in a public space of exchange values and in a market-place of competing images and functional claims and counterclaims'. The latter 'involves the consumer in appropriation, in taking technologies and objects home or into other private cultural spaces, and in making, or not making, them acceptable and familiar' (ibid.).

The concealment of wires and valves within the radio cabinet is thus read in terms of a wider configuration of radio as an entertainment medium addressed to a predominantly feminine audience. In this sense, the history of the design process of radio sets is seen to encapsulate a wider series of shifts from radio listening as hobby to mass entertainment. However, what is interesting about the domestication of television is that the turn from functional to aesthetic is written not so much in the actual design of the television sets as in the inscriptions which represent television as a domestic medium. There is a clear shift from more 'technical' writings about television set design in magazines such as *Ideal Home* (which had a predominantly middle- and upper-middle-class feminine readership) in the 1940s and 1950s to more 'aesthetic' representations in mass market women's magazines in the late 1950s and 1960s. The domestication of television does not simply settle on the television set itself as in the wider popular distribution and display of its meanings. Moreover, given the readership of *Ideal Home* at the time, it is not possible simply to read the 'technical' accounts of television as masculine. Rather, given the discussion of television in relation to domestic conduct in these magazines, the 'technical' inscriptions of television set design need to be seen in the broader context of a greater seriousness given to the designing and spacing of television within the home in this period. Women readers were addressed in such a way as to take account of both the aesthetic and technical aspects of design. The taking into account of television as technology, unlike radio, was not constructed as a purely masculine endeavour.

These glimpses at the material practices of the home are important for our analysis of the child television audience because they document how women were mobilized around the television set. The attention given in these popular discourses to the design and architecture of objects and space is also significant. It provides the ground for the entrenchment of expert discourses concerning the viewing environment of the child and the lines of its supervision.

Sitting Rooms and Modern Homes

At the end of 1947 only 34,000 television sets were in use in Britain. Only 0.2 per cent of families had sets in their homes. In 1948 the figure had risen to 134,000. In 1955 40 per cent of the population had a television and by 1963 89 per cent now had a television set. The television set was a signifier of modernity and its ownership signified not just status among friends and relatives, but also the presence of the 'modern home' (cf. O'Sullivan 1991). Although the design of the television set changed rapidly from the early bulky wooden and bakelite small-screened model of the 1940s and 1950s to the sleek streamlined metallic design of the late 1950s and 1960s, its insertion into the home during that time signalled a wider set of changes.

The placing of television in the home, but more specifically in the living room, gave rise to a number of discussions concerning the centrality of the hearth in the 'English home'. The displacement of the fireplace by the television set had deep resonances in terms of the connotations of the hearth. For example Davidoff *et al.* show how the 'temple of the hearth' had become an evocative image in literature and house design and they quote *Paved with Gold* (1858) by Augustus Mayhew:

> Then as the dusk of evening sets in, and you can see in the squares
> and crescents the crimson flickering of the flames from the cosy

sea-coal fires in the parlours, lighting up the windows like flashes of sheet lightening, the cold cheerless aspect of the streets without sets you thinking of the exquisite comfort of our English homes. (cited in Davidoff *et al.* 1976: 153)

In advertisements in women's magazines in the 1940s and 1950s, the image of a fireplace with a raging fire comes to represent a quintessential homeliness. For example, one household cleaning company (Reckitt's Blue) ran a series of advertisements entitled 'Home Sweet Home' (*Woman's Own*, 28 June 1946) and 'Homepride . . .' (*Woman's Own*, 14 March 1947). Its images present a table laid for tea, with tea-set, cups, plates and a vase of flowers. The table is set next to the fire and beside the fire are also armchairs. The cleaning fluid company pressed home the message 'This friendly hearth, this shining room remind us that while men make houses women make homes' (*Woman's Own*, 28 June 1946).

Similarly, in January 1945, an advertisement for Oxo beef stock appeared in *Woman*. A family was pictured congregated around the hearth in the sitting room. The father was reading the daily newspaper from the light of a lamp above him. In another armchair opposite him and facing towards the fire was the mother and next to her, sitting on the arm, was the daughter. A clock over the mantelpiece marked the time as 20 minutes to 9 o'clock. A wireless set, probably bakelite, sat on the sideboard. A tray of steaming hot Oxo drinks was placed on a small table. The room was dark and cold except for the light and heat of the fire. Outside of this visible clearing was darkness. We might presume that nobody ventured to the other rooms in the house, which were cold and dark through lack of central heating. The picture was underlined by the copy:

'These simple things . . .' In the quiet of the evening, waiting perhaps for the nine o'clock news. All that is peaceful and restful is centred in the room, around the fireside. Such simple ordinary things—a thrilling book, a special chair, the favourite, homely nightcap—OXO. These are things that make up home. (*Woman*, 6 January 1945)

This advertisement depicted an image of radio as forming and embedded within the routines of familial and domestic life, but it also presented a nostalgic image of the past as a counterpoint to what came to be known as the reconstruction of the modern home (cf. Robertson 1947). It was this type of image of the English home to which Scannell and Cardiff refer in their discussion of BBC radio broadcasting and the formation of a national community. This home was seen to house 'the ordinary English family'. A community of families in 'Acacia Avenue or Laburnum Grove, the tree-lined suburbs of Greater London and the Home counties' (Scannell and Cardiff 1982: 168). Moreover, Scannell argues that it was through the regular, repeated routine of programming, such as news programming, that a national community is lived and imagined (1988a). However, in contrast to an earlier nineteenth-century image of English domesticity, television was to signify an important boundary marker between the traditional and modern home. Television was seen to articulate a different sense of domestic life, a new science of modern living.

An article, 'Fireplaces and Fireplacing', in *Ideal Home* in 1949 presented the binary television/fireplace, but also implicitly modernity/tradition, as a choice for the consumer: 'To-day, when we introduce such benefits of scientific discovery as television into our sitting-rooms, we find ourselves faced with the problem of resolving a new duality of interest: the fireplace and the television set' (*Ideal Home*, October 1949: 37). When read in relation to other articles of the period, this duality is more tempered. The article in fact suggested that the television screen should be placed above the fireplace, but also noted the 'technical difficulties' of this solution to the problem (ibid.). In other articles both television and hearth have a combined centrality. There was discussion of putting television either over or to the side of the fireplace. An article 'Make Room for Television' (*House and Garden*, Spring 1949) suggested that: 'For winter viewing, a good place for television is near the fire where chairs are usually gathered.' However, it also showed an image of a television set built into an existing fireplace: 'An unused fireplace can conceal a television set and, with a removable fabric-covered panel in front, provide a proscenium to the screen.' An article by Edith Blair (*Woman*, 29 August 1953) had an image of a tiled fireplace with surrounding armchairs and a television set placed to the right of the fire on the mantelpiece.

Whereas the mass market women's magazines tended in the early 1950s to present images of the sitting room with a natural fire and no television set, *Ideal Home*, but also the up-market *House and Garden*, displayed rooms with no fireplace. In its place sat the television set. In an article 'Within your Means' (*House and Garden*, December 1950) a living room especially designed to accommodate television was presented. The low pagefold beech chairs pointed not to a fire, but to television. The copy read: 'Television, which only a few years ago was as mysterious as a flying saucer, is now an everyday part of many people's lives.' Similarly, an article 'With a View to Television' (*Ideal Home*, March 1954) suggested: 'Where an open fire is not needed, the area can be used for the fresh focus of many modern rooms—the television set.' It was not until the popularization of central heating systems that television properly usurped the position of the hearth. As homes increasingly gained central heating, the whole of the house could be used. In the past, bedrooms were cold and musty, the sheets only warmed up with a warming-pan before sleep.

Howard Robertson, in his short book *Reconstruction and the Home*, stated that:

> The fact is that houses designed without consideration of heat and light, natural and artificial, can never be proper homes; and that such consideration so properly affects the planning and structure from the outset that decisions thereon have a No. 1 priority. It is necessary to compare a modern open plan, based on the employment of central heating or air conditioning, with the cellular planning of the traditional home which depended on open fires, to realise that the technique of equipment influences design. The whole character of the lay-out is affected; and likewise the way of life within the dwelling. (Robertson 1947: 18)

An advertisement for central heating in *Ideal Home* (February 1949) marked out this same transition from the old, dark, and cold home with an open fire to the modern, light, and warm home with central heating. An image on the top right-hand side of the page portrayed a family doing different activities in different parts of the living room. Grandfather was reading in one corner; father in the other; mother and grandmother sat chatting; and the child played with his toys on the floor. The room was well-lit and everything was clearly visible. Underneath the image the copy read: 'No need to be left out in the cold where there is central heating. The entire room is warm and so are all the other rooms in the house.' On the left-hand side of the page was an image of a family huddled around the fire. The room was dark except for the glow of the fire. Grandfather and father were reading; mother and grandmother sat talking; but the child, not playing, was looking into the fire. The copy read: 'How different when you depend on a fire for warmth. Roasted toes perhaps—but shivers down your spine! And how you dread to leave the fireside to go to bed.'

Instead of the warm glow of the flaming fire in the family's faces, there was now the steely grey flicker of the television's radiation. Television took up the mantle of the home and ousted the cosy hearth from its symbolic centre. Its introduction into the home gave rise to a new set of domestic designs for television viewing.

> Most of the day your set will sit lifeless in the room, so its looks are important. As the cabinet is bulky and creates special problems of accommodation, its position shouldn't be obtrusive. Your room must be re-arranged for its new function. (*House and Garden*, Spring 1949)

Of importance was the lighting of the room, the spatial arrangement of viewers, and the accommodation of other activities while watching television. For example, this article on how to place television within the living room continues by stating that:

> Low chairs are needed, four to twelve feet away. You need not sit in complete darkness when viewing. Many cabinets now on sale are pleasing in design, but if you can't find a set to harmonise with your room, you can build one into an existing piece of furniture, for some makers will sell the chassis without a cabinet. (ibid.)

In *Ideal Home* (September 1949) one article showed an image of a curved Airborne settee upon which a number of people could sit to watch television. The television set could be placed at the apex of the curve so that optimum viewing could be enhanced. Again in *Ideal Home* the seating was arranged in order to maximize viewing: 'by arranging the units at right-angles, each of the five seats gives unobstructed sight of the set and avoids acute viewing angles.' The arrangement of seating helped to 'enclose' the viewers, whether family or neighbours or friends, around the television set 'creating a more intimate group'. Moreover, low coffee tables became popular in order to enable 'refreshment without interruption': 'Low table set before them provides for coffee, sandwiches, drinks and ashtrays within reach of everybody' (March 1954). In *Everywoman* in an article on 'Modern Living: Sitting-Dining Room', the reader was encouraged to arrange the seating around the television and fireplace. The article advised the reader not to 'crowd in too much' or to use 'too bulky furniture'. Moreover, it suggested that television 'has brought us lighter and more adaptable unit lounge chairs' instead of 'the elephantine three-piece suite'. It also argued that television has shown us how to use the whole space of the sitting room including the corners (August 1954).

In the 1950s, readers were increasingly shown how to build furniture into the walls and television was no exception. Some academics have talked about this design and development in terms of the desire to hide television from public view, as if television was something shameful. But the imperative to make furniture light and compact and to design storage space and utilities into the walls of the building was a common feature in architectural discourses. Many of the women's and design magazines were keen to show readers how to make the most of their living space as many of the population lived in, what was commonly referred to as, the 'small home'. Television sets were shown built into cabinets or walls: 'Storage shelves along one wall, or used as a room divider, make an ideal place for housing the TV set, gramophone and records' (*Woman*, 27 August 1960).

Room lighting was a significant issue because the picture quality of the early sets was such that viewers were often advised to sit in a darkened room. But by the late 1940s readers were told that they need not view in a darkened room because of the design of the new television sets.[2] However, there was still an issue of sunlight or artificial light falling directly on the screen.[3] *Ideal Home* (May 1949) suggested the use of soft lighting from lamps, rather than overhead lights. But it also suggested that Sylvania underseat lamps be used.

Given the considerations noted above concerning design for the small home, there was also discussion of how to facilitate different activities within the same living room space. *House and Garden* (Spring 1949) suggested the use of curtains or Venetian blinds to divide up the room:

> In a living-room, when only some occupants wish to view a
> programme two difficulties arise: the viewers need less light
> (especially round the set), while the others may be distracted
> by the performance.

Ideal Home (May 1951) suggested the use of a half-size screen to be used to divide the dining area from the television viewing and living room area. Similarly storage units were suggested in *Everywoman* (August 1956), as well as the use of different types of floor-covering and wallpaper to mark out the different functional spaces of the living-dining room.

Many of these design features were also common in the US in the same period. Spigel refers to their construction as symptomatic of a gendered spatial division of domestic labour such that the home is a site of labour for women and a site of leisure for men and children. The construction of a continuous space between living room, kitchen and dining room and its partial division through the use of a screen or storage units represented both a desire to integrate the 'housewife' into the family circle as well as to keep her functionally separate. As Spigel argues 'the ideals of integration and isolation resulted in highly contradictory representations of domestic life' (Spigel 1992: 91).

In these magazine discussions the emphasis is not simply on a history of entertainment technologies, but on the relation of the television set to domestic technologies concerned with heating, room lighting, and so on. Television is gendered not simply in the design of the television set but importantly in the relations of television to a wider redesign of the domestic. The design of television in the living room was to encourage community as well as maintain existing gendered divisions of labour. There was not one singular design for the ideal modern home, rather it was based on a set of principles concerning the heating, lighting, spacing and entertaining of domestic living. By 1960 *Ideal Home* had presented a series of nine principles for designing the modern living room: unify floor spaces; low, slim furniture; compact

2 *Ideal Home*, May 1949; *Ideal Home*, November 1950.

3 *Ideal Home*, February 1950.

furniture groups; big windows; clear focal point for the room; textures used for contrast and harmony; use of colour to enhance space; limited use of patterns. These principles quickly became encoded through notions of 'space through unity' and 'open planning' (*Ideal Home*, April 1960). Although as Attfield notes (1989), there was some resistance to these principles, in popular representations of the time, space became the principle through which the modern family could use the living room for different activities at the same time. In *Ideal Home* (September 1960) an image of a teenage boy is shown making a model aeroplane on a table, a teenage daughter is shown listening to records, father is reading a book and mother is looking at the daughter. The copy reads: 'In our Room of the Month for open living there is space for all the family to spread, relax and enjoy music and hobbies.' A family living together differently.

These principles emerged in earlier form in architectural and design discourses in the 1920s and 1930s with Le Corbusier and the Bauhaus idea of the home as a 'machine for living in'. In these discourses there was a concern for 'purification through emptiness', to treat the home in the manner of a Taylorized office and to organize domestic space according to principles of efficiency.[4] Television became one of the means through which these principles were articulated. In this sense, television did not simply replace radio as another entertainment technology within the home, but rather it acted as a signifier of a wide-ranging reconstruction of the modern home. To put it starkly, television came to represent a completely different organization and spacing of the domestic to that of radio in the 1920s and 1930s.

In Britain the post-war reconstruction of housing began in earnest with the publication of the Dudley Report in 1944. There were seen to be two main faults in pre-war council housing: lack of variety and lack of sufficient space for modern living. There was a shift away from an earlier design for popular housing: scullery, for washing dishes and clothes; living room/kitchen, for cooking, eating, socializing and generally living; and the parlour/front room, in which the best furniture was kept and which was used only on special occasions (cf. Boys *et al.* 1984). Although the Dudley Report was 'working against the background of the "thirties"' (Ministry of Housing and Local Government 1961: 1), architects and designers in the late 1940s were beginning to reconceptualize contemporary domestic living. Howard Robertson declared that:

> The conception of living is in process of being closely
> scrutinized, and at times drastically revised. Introduction

4 See Benton 1990 and Forty 1986.

of improved mechanical services, obligatory stress on
labour-saving, and an allround reduction in the size of
dwellings have focussed attention on open planning and
'space-making' within a limited compass. More and more
ingenuities go to compensate for less and less super-footage.
(Robertson 1947: 10)

The modern home was opened up to the outside world. It had larger
windows. It was lighter. Bright colours were used in the decor.
Furniture was made to look lighter in weight, thinner and lower to the
ground. Different rooms were no longer distinct and separate from
each other, but were made to merge into one another. However, open
planning, in government architectural reports as well as women's
magazines in this period, articulated not only a gendered division of
labour, but a more fundamental accommodation of both gendered
and generational difference within the contours of the home as a
series of multi-functional spaces. The Ministry of Housing and Local
Government report, *Homes for Today and Tomorrow* (1961), noted in
its opening chapter that two-thirds of households in England and
Wales have a television set, two-thirds a vacuum cleaner, one-third
a car, one-third a washing machine and one-fifth a refrigerator. It
added that children were now staying at school for longer and more
were able to attend further education. It continued: 'All these changes
are beginning to mean an easier, more varied and more enjoyable
home life' (p. 2). The report argued that with increasing domestic
mechanization women, but also other family members as well,
wished to 'live their own lives' within the home:

> Teenagers wanting to listen to records; someone else wanting to
> watch the television; someone going in for do-it-yourself; all
> these and homework too mean that the individual members of
> the family are more and more wanting to be free to move away
> from the fireside to somewhere else in the home—if only (in
> winter at any rate) they can keep warm. (ibid.)

Although the report argued for more space and better heating, the
main focus was 'not about rooms so much as about the activities that
people want to pursue in their homes' (ibid. 4). The report reversed
the normal paradigm which first presents the design of rooms and
then considers how these rooms are used (either as acts of complicity
or resistance). Instead it suggested that spatial arrangements and
rooms were the result, or the outcome, of the spacing of activities.
Instead of providing plans or minimum dimensions for rooms, it
wished to concentrate on the activities that 'occupiers' would want
to pursue. In this sense, certain types of *person*, 'occupiers' rather
than 'non-occupiers', were constructed in relation to certain types of

action. In addition the report constituted these types of person and activities in terms of the development, or life-cycle, of the family (i.e. the space needed for a family with a small child was seen to be different to that with teenage children) and in relation to the spaces of 'privacy' or 'community' (ibid. 8). Domestic spaces needed to facilitate activities such as homework which required a certain amount of privacy with activities such as watching television which might be communal, including all the family. Moreover activities were constituted in relation to certain types of objects (e.g. furniture, cooking or leisure facilities, etc.) which in themselves were seen to have certain spatial and temporal requirements (i.e. the television set takes up a certain amount of space and watching a television programme will take a certain amount of time).

In 1968 the Department of Environment published *Space in the Home*, which sought to detail the recommendation of the earlier report and which mapped the types of private and communal activities of different types of household in relation to their spatial requirements. This report noted the possible range of activities within any particular household and showed how these could be grouped as either 'primary' or 'secondary'.

> The primary activities in the living area generally engage several
> members of the family, and therefore tend to make the living
> room a 'noisy area'. Looking at T.V. is an obvious example of this.
> Many of the occasional activities will be quieter, such as
> homework or sewing. (*Space in the Home*, 3)

The report argued that in the post-war period there has been an increase in consumer expenditure on 'furnishings, decorations and equipment for the home' (ibid. 8) and that a central element of such spending was increasingly used on domestic leisure. Of importance, though, was the way in which the report made visible the spatial requirements of activities (and furniture and facilities) according to the temporal dimensions of the household's daily activities and of the life-cycle of the family. These diagrams represented the 'place' as well as the 'pattern of movement' within the home in such a way that the 'separating out' and 'coming together' of the family, 'points of stress' (i.e. when the house is being most intensively utilized by family but also friends and relatives) and also the 'expansion' and 'contraction' of household needs (e.g. when children get older) were made clearly visible.

These reports, compiled by teams of architects, sociologists, quantity surveyors, and administrators, were extremely influential and would have appeared in 'every architect's and builder's office' (Francis 1984: 83). The thinking behind the reports also appeared in earlier discussion of post-war design which stressed the need to radically change the standards of household design that had existed before the war in the 1920s and 1930s (if not earlier). For example, the Council of Industrial Design journal *Design* stated in 1959:

> Focus on space, a key word, space that gives freedom. Destroy the distinction between rooms. The home is subservient to life in the home. Banish the cold formality of front parlours that attempt to impress callers—then stand unused, to collect dust . . . Push back the wall, bring the kitchen in, dissolve divisions that separate life into compartments . . . Allow freedom to change and space to move. (Cited in Attfield 1985: 219)

The conceptualization of the modern home broke away from the cellular design which we can, to use Foucault, trace back to the eighteenth century:

> The house remains until the eighteenth century an undifferentiated space. There are rooms—one sleeps, eats and receives visitors in them, it doesn't matter which. Then gradually space becomes specified and functional . . . The working class family is to be fixed; by assigning it a living space with a room that serves as a kitchen and dining room, a room for parents which is the place of procreation, and a room for the children, one prescribes a morality for the family . . . the little tactics of the habitat. (Foucault 1980: 148–9)

Domestic space, and the spacing of television, was not conceived (as it is in Foucault, but also as it is in de Certeau's critique and anthropology of tactical resistance) within a Cartesian frame of social order. Space was, of course, geometric in the plans and diagrams of architects, but it was also increasingly construed as action in such a way that freedom (as action) had become the primary focus. Isolation and community became the principles through which gendered and generational division could be reproduced while also maintaining the ideal of family togetherness. Open planning, as Spigel argues, is riven with the contradictions of Victorian domestic social and spatial hierarchies. However, in relation to the spacing of children in the home, we see that they are increasingly spatially separated. Whereas the eighteenth century brings into play a spatial division of sleeping arrangements as a consequence of the emergent discourses of sexuality (cf. Foucault 1979), the twentieth century sees an increasing spatial separation of children's leisure activities in the home. The emergence of bedroom cultures did not lead to children's complete exclusion from the family-centric activities and spaces, rather it provided the possibility of both their inclusion and exclusion. They could do their homework or watch television in the sitting room, but they could equally retire to their bedrooms. My attention to the detail of the space and sociality of the home is so that we might get a sense of the material context within which children's television viewing was placed.

Domestic
Conduct and
Suburban
Mentality

Lynn Spigel has shown how in the US post-war discourses concerning television and the domestic had less to do with increasing privatization and a diminishing of public life and more to do with a set of complex relations such that middle-class families could maintain a distance from the world at the same time as being connected to a wider social fabric (Spigel 1992). For Spigel, as for others such as Haralovich (1988) in the US and Silverstone (1994) in the UK, television, through its sitcoms and soap operas, provided the means through which a suburban imagined community could be constituted.

The knot between domestic modernity and the suburban was tied securely through consumption. The disruption of the boundaries between public and private—a consequence of rendering the suburban home increasingly visible—allowed the home to become a site of consumption and a means of display to other aspirant consumers in the suburban neighbourhood (cf. Silverstone 1994; Spigel 1992). The suburbanization and modernization of the home fuelled consumer demand for new utilities, such as refrigerators and televisions. But the suburban home also offered a set of overlapping spaces and times for the machinations of advertising and one of the central means of addressing this constituency was through television.[5] Moreover, it was the 'housewife' and 'mother' who personified this address (Haralovich 1988; Spigel 1992). The housewife was tied into the home through the (patriarchal) demands of cleanliness, aesthetics, childcare, and family health.

In 1950 Monica Dickens, niece of the Victorian novelist Charles Dickens, wrote an article entitled 'Television—not for me!' for her regular column in *Woman's Own*. This was an article that expressed fears not just about television in general, but about the child television audience; but we will get onto that later. Although the title of the article clearly indicated the author's antipathy to this newly popular technology, its tone was more speculative. It was speculative in that its statements concerned what might be, rather than what is; but more importantly her writing suggested that television, as a social technology, was never merely given. In the opening paragraphs of the piece, Dickens provided an image of Sweden which was presented as clean, well-ordered and without television. The image of rows of suburban

---

5 Vicky Lebeau, in a fascinating re-reading of Wilmott and Young's classic study of class and suburbia in the 1950s, argues that the move to suburbia and its enforced domestication provided the condition for television's popular appeal in the UK (Lebeau 1997).

homes, smoke breathing from their chimneys and each housing families content with their old-fashioned pastimes, was one, Dickens argued, that could also represent an England of the present, as it had in an England of time past. But such a possibility, she continued, was dependent on a fundamental decision: television or not television. If the wrong choice was made, we (the readers, the 'English', the women who maintain the home and family) might tread the same path as the US.

Dickens took the reader on a journey from Sweden to the United States:

> If you go into the most sordid slums of Chicago, seek out a tumbledown tenement building in a filthy alley, climb over the garbage pails to the top flat where poverty, drunkenness and squalor reign, you will find a frig. and a television set. (*Woman's Own*, 27 July 1950)

The story she told of the journey into this exemplary home was a fable. It was a moral tale. The refrigerator and the television set were seen as symptomatic of urban deprivation and depravation. They were seen as signs of excessive ill-afforded spending which were viewed as being mistaken for 'the essentials of life'. She described television as being 'like an imperious queen' which 'claims your undivided attention' and whose effects would be all too apparent:

> If they ever start having TV programmes all day long we might become a nation, not of housewives, but of sluts! I don't say we would, but we might. (ibid.)

The task of the housewife (and also, as we shall see, the mother) was to hold onto the past and to protect the nation. A geography of the future of television was mapped onto the architectural spaces of the home and onto the cultural differentiation of nations. Constructions of time and cultural geography layered each other as the sediments within which television was buried.

Dickens' article signalled a peculiarly English response to the relations between television, domesticity, and the suburban. It is important to remember that her article was written at a time of post-war austerity. The rationing of consumer goods did not end completely until 1953. Television, for Dickens, was a signifier of consumerism and 'Americanness' clearly in opposition to Englishness and suburban domesticity. Her discourse on television was resonant of earlier discourses concerning radio, the suburban and middlebrow culture.

In Britain, television's address to suburban domesticity was tempered by a public service ethos which construed the audience as neither high-brow nor low-bow, but middle-brow. As a consequence of the Reithian struggles over 'culture' in the 1920s and 1930s in relation to radio broadcasting, television has consistently steered a course between 'high culture' and 'mass entertainment'. Or, to put it more accurately, high culture and mass entertainment have been configured, until recently, within an address to a middle-brow sensibility. It addressed, not a mass audience, but a public comprised of individuals in families whose 'home was an enclave, a retreat burrowed deeply away from the pressures of work and urban living, with radio as part of that cosy, domestic warmth' (Scannell and Cardiff 1982: 168). Paddy Scannell has shown how an ethos of public service broadcasting has emerged through attempts to speak as if speaking to someone in the privacy of their own home. For Scannell, such an endeavour 'produces the world, and endlessly reproduces it, as ordinary: as familiar, knowable, recognizable, accessible to all' (Scannell 1988*b*: 3). In addition, it has been argued by Alison Light, in relation to literary culture in the 1920s and 1930s, that such a middlebrow culture can be defined in terms of 'conservative modernism', which is wholeheartedly suburban and 'whose apparent artlessness and insistence on its own ordinariness has made it peculiarly resistant to analysis' (Light 1991: 11).

The Coronation of Queen Elizabeth II in 1953 is often seen as a hallmark of the success of television as a popular medium. Many individuals, beginning to shed the constraints of wartime austerity and to reap the benefits of post-war consumerism, bought a television set for the first time in order to watch the ceremony alongside their friends, neighbours, relatives, and other family members. This event was seen very much as both a public and a domestic occasion. *Woman* carried an article entitled 'At Home on Coronation Day' which stated that 'for the first time in history we are all taking part in one of the most solemn and glorious moments of our lives'. It continued by saying that:

> Television is capturing this moment so that in the heart of all our homes we can join the historic throng in Westminster Abbey and share with them the prayers and rejoicings of this wonderfully exciting day. (*Woman*, 25 April 1953)

The broadcasting of these public ceremonies, as Paddy Scannell has argued, can be seen alongside other broadcast public events, such as the Grand National and the FA Cup Final, and can be analysed more generally in terms of the role of broadcasting in the social organization of time within modern societies (Scannell 1988*a*). These national events are made accessible to everyone with a television set and become interconnected with the spatial and temporal arrangements of domestic life. At the time of the Coronation various women's magazines gave advice about how to arrange the home for this televisual event. The weekly magazine *Woman* and the monthly *Everywoman* advised viewers to sit between 6 and 10 feet from the set, preferably on chairs at eye-level to the screen. If chairs were not available for everyone, then, *Woman* stated, adults, rather than children, should sit on cushions on the floor. The sitting room was to be arranged like a cinema with seats in rows and 'with a row of guests on cushions down the sidelines' (*Woman*, 25 April 1953). Interruptions were to be kept to a minimum and 'inveterate knob twiddlers will have to be curbed by the family once a good picture has been achieved or dramatic moments of the day might be missed' (ibid.). Likewise, meals had to be prepared beforehand and kept as simple as possible so that viewers could remain seated while watching. *Everywoman* gave the following advice to its readers: 'The tactful hostess will, therefore, avoid food which falls to pieces in the hands, scatters on the carpet, or makes loud crunchy noises when eaten!' (*Everywoman*, June 1953).

These articles talked about television as private *and* public, domestic *and* national, familial *and* communal. Television was used to articulate the private life of the family to the public life of the suburban middlebrow nation. Television, in this sense, was constitutive of an imagined national community. But it was also the means through which community was articulated as a lived experience within the context of the household. The address to the housewife/mother in these articles, as in so many others, was such that she was constructed as responsible for the organization of domestic spaces and times through which imagined and lived communities could be formed. In many of these discourses the child television audience is never explicitly discussed. And yet, by the late 1950s and early 1960s, these concerns about the minutiae of the home and family were to become integral to a modern, scientific understanding of the child television audience.

It is important here to stress that television viewing was not conceived, even in its beginnings, as a private experience. Television viewing was not, as Anna McCarthy has shown in the US, only a domestic experience. From its early days television was viewed in public bars, as well as in suburban homes (1995). In these places, the programmes most watched were sports programmes. Also importantly for my analysis here, television was not conceived simply as a familial medium. Or rather television viewing was lived as an experience which cut across family, friends, relatives and neighbours. For example, in a letter titled 'Viewing Today', a woman from Leeds, Yorkshire told the following story of television viewing and neighbourly life:

I am sure the street in which I live in Leeds is one of the happiest in the country. We're all so friendly!
     One woman has a television set and she allows the twenty-four children in the street to watch it.

Naturally, it is not convenient to have the children in everyday and it was rather annoying for her to have to answer about 18 knocks a day from children who asked: 'May we watch television please?'

So now she puts a card marked 'TV' in the window on days when she doesn't mind their coming. (*Woman*, 10 January 1953)

The editor of the letters' page responded by saying:

Many TV owners are as kind as your neighbour. We feel it's up to the parents to guard against their children abusing the privilege. The card in the window is one good way of making sure the children don't call too often. Another 'system' is for the children's names to go on to a rota so that they know in advance when their turn to view will come and they can look forward to the treat. (ibid.)

Other readers, such as Jane Collins from Manchester, argued that it was 'now fun to stay at home':

Up to a few months ago I was hardly ever at home in the evenings, but now I find it's much more fun to stay in. The reason for this sudden change is that my father has recently bought a television set. And it's surprising what a difference it has made to our family. Now, instead of going out for entertainment, we stay in our own front room where our friends and relations are welcome to pop in and join us if there's something they particularly want to see. Today, there seem to be so many interests and diversions taking people away from the home, that family get-togethers have become almost a thing of the past. I think television is the one thing that can bring back those family parties our parents always talk about and seem to have enjoyed so much. (*Woman's Own*, 3 January 1952)

In these family and communal meetings television was not seen to inhibit talk, but rather to provide an occasion for talk and to incite discussion. One letter writer from Rochdale, Lancashire even questioned whether the nostalgic image of family life before television ever really existed: 'I believe many of these so-called "happy family evenings" which anti-TV-ers regretfully recall used to end in bickering and arguments, if the truth were known' (*Woman*, 21 June 1952).

Beverly Nichols, a regular columnist for *Woman's Own*, argued, in a piece headed 'One of the greatest miracles of television is the way in which sincerity triumphs over the machines', that 'the population of this island is rapidly being split into two quite separate divisions—those who view and those who don't'. He refers to the way in which talk about television is met with 'either an enthusiastic response, or a blank stare' (14 May 1953). For him, as for others who watch, television characters and personalities were an intimate part of their lives and provided the basis for talk.

However, only three and a half years earlier Nichols was less positive about television:

> If you had to sit for hour after hour, as I have sat in America, watching a row of gaping faces staring in a sort of daze at a lot of flickering rubbish, never stirring, never talking, never taking their eyes off the screen, you would wonder whether it *was* such a good thing . . . For one thing, it destroys conversation. People with television sets, once they have switched on, become blind and deaf to anything else. (*Woman's Own*, 8 December 1949)

In a letter, headed 'Television? Not for Me!', Mrs Lewin argued that television stultifies conversation and friendship:

> I was recently invited to spend the evening at a friend's house. We usually see each other about once a month. We have tea and then sit back and have a good old chin-wag until about nine o'clock. I set off bright, bubbling with news. We had our usual excellent tea, then four chairs were placed in front of the newly acquired television set and for four solid hours we sat with eyes pinpointed on the screen. I had to fly for the last bus having had no conversation, no fun, none of our usual exchange of ideas. It had been a pleasant evening, but oh! so unintelligent, so unstimulating and devastatingly passive. (*Woman's Own*, 14 February 1952)

Equally, Betty Dale from Leeds argued that:

> Television is certainly a menace to family life. When friends come to see us, instead of a friendly chat or game of cards, we sit in silence in a darkened room. All companionship is lost. And Sunday tea-time, hitherto the pleasantest meal of the week, now has to be taken either impossibly early or late, and is, therefore, seldom enjoyed. (*Woman's Own*, 7 September 1950)

Television is seen to disrupt both talk and the routines of daily family life. Michael Pertwee, an actor from the BBC soap opera *The Grove Family*, argued that: 'The new monster of television, while bringing a percentage of people back again [to the fireside] does little to create a family atmosphere and merely turns any parlour into a miniature cinema, where conversation is frowned upon and relations and friends will sit for hours without exchanging a single word' (*Woman*, 8 January 1955). The analogy with cinema (sitting in a darkened room, not talking) is often used in opposition to a more nostalgic image of the family circle that radio was seen to provide.[6]

These articles and letters which discuss the relation of television to family and friendships are addressed to the mother/housewife in such a way that not only constructs television as 'good' or 'bad', but also constructs it as a dilemma. The decision whether to buy a television set or not is posed as a problem for the mother/housewife in terms of maintaining and facilitating the various family and communal relations within the home. In one letter from a reader in Birmingham, a mother of three is left with the decision of reconciling the different interests and views on television within the household. The father/husband wants to buy a television set. The eldest daughter has for years wanted a radiogram 'but without success'. The son wants a wireless but his interest in it is 'purely mechanical'. He is said to want only 'to twiddle more knobs'. The youngest daughter 'objects to television on the grounds that she considers it ridiculous to sit in semi-darkness "squinting at a far-too-small screen" while there are a thousand jobs waiting to be done'. The mother states that if television is introduced into the home, the daughter has said that she will 'retire to her bedroom'. The decision to buy, so the husband has declared 'in a manner peculiar to his sex', is left with the mother, who is 'perfectly happy with our little wireless set—crackles, buzzes, eccentricities and all!' (*Woman's Own*, 9 March 1950).

In addition to the discourses and practices about television which implicitly embroiled the life of children in the home and environment in which they watched, a small proportion of these early discussions of television also talk explicitly about children. In some of the early discourses there is a concern about children's health. For example, doctors advised parents not to let their children sit too close ('sit about 6 to 10 feet away from the television screen') and to stare at the screen for too long ('glance round the room occasionally, as a change of focus rests the eyes'). They advised children to sit at eye level to the screen and never to view in darkness (due to the effect of the contrast between screen and room on eyesight). They also advised that the set be properly tuned-in ('otherwise the picture may be unsteady and distorted and this strains the eyes') (*Vision*, 1952).[7] Likewise dentists complained about children watching while lying on the floor with head in hands as this was seen to cause 'malocclusion' or jaw displacement. In September 1954 the BBC issued advice to children not

---

6 Again Spigel documents the way in which in the US at the same time television was constructed as a 'home theatre' (Spigel 1992).

7 Among many other such stories, in 1950 George Barnes, Director of Television, BBC, stated that he was worried about children's eyesight and suggested that children's television might be shortened to avoid this danger (27 November 1950, WAC T16/68). Similar discourses were prevalent in the United States (cf. Spigel 1992).

to watch television with their head in their hands, following a warning from a dental association that this was liable to 'make their faces mishapen' (*The Times*, 13 September 1954). These expert discourses soon became the common sense of magazine articles.

Dickens in her far-sighted speculations helped to draw attention to the relation between child and television. She posed the following question:

> And what might our children become? They might become a generation who couldn't read a book, or play games out of doors, or amuse themselves with carpentry or trains or butterflies, or the hundreds of hobbies with which a child can potter so happily. (*Women's Own*, 27 July 1950)

In focusing explicitly on the child, such concerns were not simply about the housewife ordering domestic space, but about the mother governing the family. Thus the significant amount of expert opinion (from doctors, teachers, psychiatrists, and social scientists) regarding general parenting and childcare came to consider children's television viewing and, moreover, came to be considered as having something important to say about this activity. For example, Dickens declared:

> In America, they're getting really scared of television. Doctors are saying that the children's health is suffering because they spend too long indoors. Teachers are saying that their work is suffering, because they neglect their homework and sit up much too late to watch their favourite programmes. Sociologists are saying that although TV may keep people at home, it is changing the pattern of family life, because it destroys conversation and domestic activities and concentration on any work or pastime. (ibid.)

Dickens' article 'brought a storm of protest from readers' and 'roughly, only one in every seven agreed with the views she expressed'. For example, Mrs Boyes from Middlesex was adamant that '50,000 women have benefited from the cookery demonstrations'. And F. J. Camm, Editor of *Practical Television*, strongly disagreed with Dickens stating that '[t]he arguments she adduces in support of these contentions are too specious to warrant special elaboration'. Moreover, he argued that 'on the score of education, radio and television have done more to enlighten the youth of this country than textbooks and homework'. Television was seen as a means to enlightenment, to make 'the world a pleasanter place in which to live' and to make of us 'a healthier and happier race'. Similarly, Mrs Rostrum from Mangotsfield argued that television is no 'glorious toy' but an instrument of enormous possibilities for teaching young and old.

These letters were, in many respects, typical of responses in other magazines also. Although there was much disagreement about the benefits or disadvantages of television, the various statements from readers and journalists circulated around a common set of concerns. At the time there were a number of concerns about children's leisure pursuits. Ruth Martin, a regular columnist for *Woman's Own*, argued in a series of articles that mothers should be careful about what they let their children read in books and comics and see at the cinema. She was concerned not that the films or books would have the effect of turning the children into 'juvenile delinquents', but that they might be frightened by what they read or see: 'No, it is not wise to let a child go to the cinema unless you know exactly what it is he will see; or, on the other hand, unless he is accompanied by someone who is old enough to see that he comes out if the film becomes at all "scary"' (*Woman's Own*, 10 January 1952).[8] The discussion of such leisure pursuits can be placed in contrast to the nostalgic representations of children's more traditional hobbies and pastimes: 'The child who is reaching out in a dozen different directions towards his true interests finds the means of expressing them in familiar things—trains, flowers, the needles and thread in your work-box and such tools as father will let him borrow' (*Everywoman*, June 1952). Writers were keen to discuss television in terms of whether it would take children away from these traditional pastimes. Beverly Nichols in 1953 asked the question 'Is TV responsible for this decline in parlour games?' He suggested that games were 'more fun' than television: 'don't you think that it is better to live than just to watch? I do. Especially at Christmas' (*Woman's Own* 19 November 1953).

Jan Troke , in an article, 'This Changing World—Leisure', for her regular column in *Everywoman*, argued that:

> A generation ago children's play had hardly changed in a hundred years . . . But now, quite suddenly, everything's different. Innovations, one after another, sweep home life along with them at ever-growing speed. (*Everywoman*, September 1950)

She declared that radio, television, cinema, ice rinks, dance halls, and dirt tracks all have a 'deadening mass-effect'. However, she also stated that leisure was not something that could be taught but was something that was learned or 'absorbed unconsciously' at home. For her, drawing on the expertise of psychologists, 'the right use of leisure turns on one thing, and one thing alone: discrimination'. The problem was: '[h]ow to use [television and cinema] to enrich young lives without letting them swamp young personalities'.

---

8 See also *Woman's Own*, 12 April 1951 and *Woman's Own*, 26 February 1953.

Similarly, Dilys Dimbleby, wife of the broadcaster Richard Dimbleby, talked about rationing her children's viewing, not letting them touch the television set ('This is treated as an offence as serious as "playing with fire"') and making sure instead that they got 'fresh air'. She argued that television 'should never be allowed to take the place in the family of the older, simpler pursuits of reading, games or conversation' (*Woman*, 17 January 1952). In *Woman*, the regular column 'Star Gossip' stated that the actor Van Heflin viewed television as a 'threat to children's health':

> TV programmes are day-long in America, and he tells me that indiscriminate viewers let their children sit absorbed by the screen, when they should go out of doors enjoying fresh air and their own inventive games . . . Van talks as a father—his daughters Vara Gay, aged eight, and Kathleen Carol, aged five, looking-times rationed to two tea-sessions a week. And no viewing if punishment is necessary for naughtiness. (*Woman*, 19 April 1951)

Monica Dickens, in a later article entitled 'Every Parent's Dilemma', talked about television as one of the everyday responsibilities of parenting and specifically about the problem of letting children choose for themselves as part of their normal development. Reluctantly accepting the way in which '[f]or good or ill, it [i.e. television] has become part of our national life' and accepting the fact that 'children are learning from it', she argued that '[i]t is up to the parents to decide whether what they learn from it shall be good or bad':

> It is their job to restrict viewing to reasonable hours and to insist that the set is left alone when there is something else to do, their job to prevent their children becoming glued to the screen. (*Woman's Own*, 9 January 1960)

She argued that, however much '[y]ou may hate Westerns and gangster plays as much as I do', 'to try to ban them only makes them more attractive'. Instead, she demanded:

> Teach them good taste. Teach them morals. Teach them to recognize the second-rate, and not to take seriously the cruder entertainment that is offered. (ibid.)

Dickens suggested that parents needed to train their children on how to avoid 'dangers', rather than over-protect them. Television was seen as one of the dangers of modern life (including others such as crossing the road, riding a bicycle, travelling alone in buses and trains, sailing boats, riding ponies and diving off high boards) that children needed to be prepared for, rather than protected from. Over-protection made 'sissies' out of children.

Bedtime and homework were another concern. In 1958 a letter from Mrs Lee in *Everywoman* stated:

> Our three children, aged seven, ten and twelve, have developed such a passion for television that I can't get them either to do their school homework or to go to bed; and then, of course, it's one long struggle to get them up in the morning. (*Everywoman*, August 1958)

She went on to describe the rows she had with her husband because he failed to be helpful. She referred to him as a 'TV fiend'.[9] Mayo Wingate, the magazine's resident psychiatrist, suggested that she have a frank talk with her husband (not with the children present) and '[p]oint out that the children are as much his responsibility as [hers], and that sitting up in this way is bad both for their health and their progress at school' (ibid.)

Apart from one positive article about US family life through the eyes of an English family abroad (*Woman*, 21 January 1950), the 'American child' is held up as the antithesis of the properly behaved child. Monica Dickens, in an article on the future of British children, states that:

> Children in America are spoiled and glorified. They are treated as a separate and superior race entitled to everything. Everyone bends over backwards to see that 'the kids have fun'. (*Woman's Own*, 30 January 1960)

'America' became constructed as 'England's' distopic future. Such discourse about television mobilized and constructed particular social actors and made visible the child, family and home as sites of governance. Appropriate parenting was seen to disentangle television from the crude, the mass and the American. Thus television became construed as a pedagogic device. Proper, disciplined, but caring, parenting became the means through which a peculiarly English suburban culture could be maintained. The space of the home was to become the *mise-en-scène* to a whole drama of expertise and knowledge. A whole drama in which the child television viewer was disclosed as a psychological problem. The innocent signifiers of domestic adornment and familial sociality were to be overdetermined by a game of truth.

---

9 The Editor stated that she got 'many letters from mothers with the same problem!' and that Mrs Lee should point out to her husband that 'the children are as much his responsibility as yours, and that sitting up in this way is bad both for their health and their progress at school' (*Everywoman*, August 1958).

5

Expert Discourses and the Governance of Audiences

SINCE the mid-1980s a growing body of research has emerged which looks at the way television institutions represent and regulate their audiences (Ang 1991; Hartley 1987; Allor 1988; Ettema and Whitney 1994; Paterson 1987). Most notably, John Hartley, in an early polemical essay, has argued that:

> In no case is the audience 'real', or external to its discursive construction. There is no 'actual' audience that lies beyond its production as a category, which is to say that audiences are only ever encountered *per se* as *representations*. (Hartley 1987: 125)

Moreover, Hartley has argued that the figure of the 'child' has played an important role in the governance of television. Television audiences are, he argues, either addressed as if they were childlike or regulated according to the possibility that children might be watching. Television programmes are thus pitched, not to a lowest common denominator, but to an imagined universal childhood. Such a universal notion of childhood allows audiences, Hartley observes, to attach themselves to a form of address which is seen to pre-exist the sociological differences of class, race, and gender (differences which might lead to a greater segregation of audiences and to a diminishing of audience size): 'a fictional version of everyone's supposed childlike tendencies which might be understood as predating such social groupings' (1987: 130). Hartley uses the term 'paedocratization' to refer to this regime of power/knowledge. He even goes so far as to suggest that this might constitute a 'law': 'the bigger the target audience, the more it will be paedocratized' (1987: 127).

Although Hartley's analysis tends to generalize and homogenize the processes involved in the imagining and production of audiences, he interestingly compares the construction of knowledge about audiences to the processes, described by Edward Said, whereby Orientalist discourses construct the East as other, but in doing so also construct the identity of the Western subject (Said 1978). Hartley argues that television audiences 'are so rarely *self*-represented that they are almost always absent, making TV audiences perhaps the largest "community" in the world that is subject to what Edward Said has dubbed the discourse of "orientalism", whereby disorganized communities which have never developed or won adequate means of self-representation, and which exist almost wholly within the imagination and rhetoric of those who speak on their behalf, become "other" of powerful, imperial discourses' (1987: 125).

Hartley's use of this orientalist trope is problematic inasmuch as it construes the audience only through the lens of a pre-constituted powerful subject position. For Hartley, the television institutions have, *a priori*, both power and knowledge over the other. As David Morley has observed, such arguments which importantly prioritize the textuality of audiences, as institutionally inscribed communities, tend to disavow the significance and importance of empirical audience studies and also to presume that the existence of the other is entirely dependent on, and viewed from the perspective of, the subjectivity of the television institutions. For Morley such an institutional insistence can only ever envisage the other as Other (Morley 1997: 130). In this sense, Hartley offers no guide for accounting for how audiences might possibly represent themselves. The press and pressure groups which also speak for audiences are, in Hartley's model, assembled as part of the television institution.[1]

Other writers, such as Ettema and Whitney in their account of the making of audiences, tend to subsume audience relations within a broad organizational apparatus, the television institution. For example, they suggest that '[i]n an institutional conception, actual receivers are constituted—or perhaps, reconstituted—not merely as audiences but as *institutionally effective audiences* that have social meaning and/or economic value within the system' (1994: 5). These institutionally effective audiences might include 'measured audiences' (i.e. those constituted through research companies for advertisers and media channels), 'specialised or segmented audiences' (i.e. those audiences who are seen to have particular interests with regard to types of content) and 'hypothesised audiences' (i.e. those audiences who are in need of protection by regulators). For Ettema and Whitney '[a]ll such audiences exist in relationships with the media—or, more exactly, they exist *as* relationships *within* the media institution' (1994: 6).

I take issue with this type of model, not because it fails to show the congealed relations of power and knowledge endemic to the process

---

1 Hartley divides the television institution into three elements: the television industry (networks, stations, producers, etc.); political/legal institutions (including regulators, government committees, etc.); and critical institutions (academic, journalists, and pressure groups). Hartley is unable to account for the subtle cultural and political interactions between, for example, pressure groups, and television which constitutes the substance of Kathryn Montgomery's wonderful book (1989).

of making audiences, but because it too easily subsumes a number of different agencies within a supra-agentic body, the television institution. In doing so, the model demonstrates a tendency firstly to assume a divide between institution and audience rather than show how such a divide is socially and historically formed and governed, and secondly to assume that knowledge is simply formed within the television institution and not in relation to those constituted as audiences. In this type of model an *a priori* conception of power and agency is assumed such that the agency of the audience is foregone, once it is constituted within the representational practices of the institution. Here I look at the relations between television industry, government, science and audiences, not in order to reduce such relations to a schematic Foucauldian model of power/knowledge or to a form of discursive determination, but in order to understand the contingent relations of agency through which a divide between audience and institution becomes visible to forms of governance.

| Early Academic Research on Children and Television | I start my genealogy not with reference to work developed in television studies, but with reference to work on the social construction of scientific knowledge. Bruno Latour, one of the grand theorists of science studies, tells a tale about the relations between the occident and the orient in order to talk about the relations of agency (of actor-networks) in the social construction of scientific knowledge. Such a tale is useful for thinking about how knowledge and organizational divisions are built up. Latour does not presume that Europeans, in their initial journeys to the East, either have power or knowledge.[2] The early scientists/explorers/colonialists are not interested in the East *per se*. They are interested in mapping its physical geography, economy, culture, and environment in order to return this other place first back to the ship and second back to the colonial centres in Europe. Of importance to the colonial administrative centres of Versailles, London, and Amsterdam, was not that the men on the ships return safely back to their homelands, but that the inscriptions of this other place (the maps, log books, botanical drawings and so on) return in order that more ships could be sent back to the East. The French explorers, aboard their ship *L'Astrolabe*, sailing on their first voyage to Sakhalin, China, were in a *weaker* position than their informants on the island (or was it a peninsula?). On their arrival the sailors do not know the land and its dangers. They are reliant on the information given to them by their 'native' informants. However, ten years later when the English ship *Neptuna* returns to this same place, the explorers are in a |

Early Academic Research on Children and Television

I start my genealogy not with reference to work developed in television studies, but with reference to work on the social construction of scientific knowledge. Bruno Latour, one of the grand theorists of science studies, tells a tale about the relations between the occident and the orient in order to talk about the relations of agency (of actor-networks) in the social construction of scientific knowledge. Such a tale is useful for thinking about how knowledge and organizational divisions are built up. Latour does not presume that Europeans, in their initial journeys to the East, either have power or knowledge.[2] The early scientists/explorers/colonialists are not interested in the East *per se*. They are interested in mapping its physical geography, economy, culture, and environment in order to return this other place first back to the ship and second back to the colonial centres in Europe. Of importance to the colonial administrative centres of Versailles, London, and Amsterdam, was not that the men on the ships return safely back to their homelands, but that the inscriptions of this other place (the maps, log books, botanical drawings and so on) return in order that more ships could be sent back to the East. The French explorers, aboard their ship *L'Astrolabe*, sailing on their first voyage to Sakhalin, China, were in a *weaker* position than their informants on the island (or was it a peninsula?). On their arrival the sailors do not know the land and its dangers. They are reliant on the information given to them by their 'native' informants. However, ten years later when the English ship *Neptuna* returns to this same place, the explorers are in a

2 I am not so much concerned here with the historical veridicality of Latour's account of colonial relations.

stronger position. They have maps, descriptions of the environment, logs books, and so on. They know what to expect. In the first instance, the divide between explorer and 'native' is small. In the second, it has grown. As Latour says: 'what was at first a small divide between the European navigator and the Chinese fishermen will have become larger and deeper since the *Neptuna* crew will have less to learn from the natives' (Latour 1987: 218).

Latour, in his account, overplays the analytical and methodological symmetry between colonizer and colonized, such that we must assume an originary moment (a fantasy of origins) before which there was no divide. Yet his method is important inasmuch as it allows us to consider the processes through which knowledge and alterity are constructed through the mobilization of actors and the accumulation of inscriptions and things that are returned to and help constitute the administrative centres of calculation.

In a similar fashion, the early researchers on children and television did not have a pre-existing knowledge of the child television audience, nor did they have a sense of the child television audience as a discrete object of study. In those early years, in both the US and the UK, the child television audience did not have the status of a 'manoeuvrable "thing" ' (Ang 1991: 23). As we have seen in previous chapters, its becoming an object to be addressed and conquered involved a careful process of mobilization. Children were not *a priori* allocated to one side of the binaries subject/object, institution/audience, knower/known, representer/represented, us/them. On the contrary, the child becomes instrumental in the forging of these divisions and boundaries.

Much of the early research focused on the 'effects' of television on the child (but not as we now often construe the notion of 'effects'), as a means of differentiating television as a medium distinct from other media. In the main, research at this time concerned itself with functional differentiation, displacement effects and differences between television and non-television families. These 'preliminary fact-finding' missions (as Eleanor Maccoby referred to her early research in the field) mapped how television impacted on the daily conduct and manners of the family (Maccoby 1951: 421). Was time in the household now spent watching television, rather than eating, sleeping, doing homework, or consuming other media (such as comics, film or radio)?

These differences (which are seen to construct the specificity of television as a medium and of children's relation to it) are not imposed on audiences. But equally, they are not simply found by the researcher and represented in an unmediated fashion. Rather, they come from the parents and teachers (and to some extent children themselves) who speak to the researchers. These actors tell the researchers how television is different and how the activities and conduct of their children are different. However, the relation between representation and represented is not isomorphic in some naïve naturalistic sense nor is it simply determined by the interests of the researchers or their affiliated institutions (as might be assumed in some audience-construction analysis). If there is a contemporary 'crisis of representation' in media, communications and cultural studies, it cannot be met by a more sophisticated, critical realism (Morley 1997: 132). The problem lies not with the agency of the actors (and whether to place power on the side of the institution or the audience), but with the models of representation used to account for knowledge of audiences and the lack of any account of agency therein. In this early research, as with later research, the voices of the respondents have agency within the process of knowledge construction, but only inasmuch as their voices are *translated* through the voices, categories, and procedures of others. Their voices are significant in the shaping of knowledge, but they are never heard pure.

The early researchers, on return from their expeditions, connected their spoils not to an existing 'knowledge' of the child television audience, but to existing disciplinary procedures, rules of method, established problematics, and expert languages. Carmen Luke, for example, has shown how early research was compelled to reproduce itself within existing intertextual relations. Most obviously citation patterns provide evidence of existing centres of calculation. Luke observes that: 'it becomes evident that the early establishment of the TV–child discourse can be traced in the citation patterns that initially emerged, by reference to authorities who produced the discourse, and by tracing the disciplinary fields of emergence wherein the discourse surfaced' (Luke 1990: 112). Moreover, the process of citation helped to constitute a 'founding tradition' that is, as Luke argues, 'a retrospective discursive construction' (ibid.).

Luke's analysis clearly foregrounds the importance of discursive resources in the construction of a knowledge of the child television audience. In this sense, the audience needs to be made visible in the context of existing discursive elements: '[r]eferencing is always a "return" to a text and a setting of conditions for return by future texts' (ibid.). Events, places and people are translated into things which are mobile, immutable and combinable with existing discursive (and non-discursive) resources (Latour 1987). In order for the child television audience to become visible to wider academic communities and also to other social actors, such as government and industry, the audience must be transmuted into a series of elements (such as diagrams, numbers, and words) such that the audience can be taken from its 'natural habitat' to the laboratories, seminars, journals, reports, and so on of the academic communities. Although inscriptions are important (the notion of the 'text' is the dominant metaphor in post-structural reflexive accounts of audience construction), they are not, as Latour reminds us, the only means through which the 'world' can be made visible in the laboratory: 'the inscription *as the fine edge* and *the final stage* of a whole process of mobilisation' (Latour 1990: 40).

The relative strengths and weaknesses of the researcher and viewer are not necessarily apparent to the individuals involved in actual research. Knowledge does not equate to an authority or sense of power held as a property of an individual (i.e. as a set of attitudes). The viewer has tacit knowledge of her or his television viewing irrespective of the concepts, rules of method, diagrams, styles of writing and referencing used by the researcher. The strengths and weaknesses of viewer and researcher become visible only inasmuch as this knowledge can be combined with forms of organization which bear upon the constitution of the audience. This is to agree with Foucault when he talks about the spiral of power/knowledge. Moreover it is to recognize, against those who interpret Foucault as constructing an equivalence between power and knowledge, that there is always a Kantian tension (even if not an absolute separation) between the constitution of an object and its regulation (Foucault 1977 and 1979).

Early Industry Research

In 1936 the BBC set up the Listener Research Department and in 1939 it conducted a daily Survey of Listening.[3] After Reith's resignation in 1938, Listener Research began to be taken more seriously under the new Director General, F. W. Ogilvie. However, as Asa Briggs states, research was still 'experimental, lively but incomplete, and in places insecurely based' and the 'communication of research conclusions' was still a difficult process: 'policy-making still rested on many other criteria, and most people believed that it should continue to do so' (1965: 279). Until this time the BBC had known its audience through Advisory Committees, programme correspondence, and the personal knowledges and contacts of the programme makers. The Ullswater Committee Report stressed the importance of Advisory Committees as a means of representing the 'views of the general public as well as of experts in each category of broadcast subject' (1936: 16). However, by 1951 the Beveridge Committee Report on Broadcasting stressed the importance of the 'systematic study of audiences' and identified it as one of the responsibilities of the broadcaster (1951: 56 and 59–60). The Beveridge Committee was critical of the BBC's recourse to the conscience of the broadcaster in the governance of programming and

---

3 The lower age limit of the Survey of Listening was 16. In 1951 it included television viewing.

argued that it was imperative for the BBC to know the size of its audiences and the effect of its service:

> Broadcasting authorities cannot serve the public without studying it; they must study deliberately if they have no market quotations as automatic indicators of public feeling. (Beveridge 1951: 56)

Although the 'market' was held up as an index of the BBC's deficit in understanding its audience, the Committee was keen to stress that the BBC should not simply try to 'please as many listeners as possible' (ibid. 59). Audience research was to be used as an instrument to ensure that the BBC fulfilled its public service ethos to reach as wide an audience as possible and not simply to address the select few. More importantly though, audience research was constructed as a means through which the broadcaster could act with modesty and humility. It provided a limit to the potential arrogance of the broadcaster's conscience: 'To whom is the broadcaster responsible? If it is only to his own conscience, the decision might better be described as irresponsible' (ibid.). In this respect market indicators and social scientific research did not so much add to the arrogance of an institution that imagined and represented its audience with no concern for their location, pleasures, size, and conduct. As with the natural sciences, the witnessing of 'truth' (in this case the truth of audiences) was an act of modesty (Haraway 1997; Shapin and Schaffer 1985). Thomas Osborne in his analysis of science, ethics and enlightenment argues that:

> Instead of the 'spirit of system', science embodied a 'systematic spirit'. This meant not a universal rationalization of everything but rather an epistemological *modesty* of approach—observing, calculating, remaining sensitive to the necessary limits of human knowledge—for 'man succeeds best in discovering truths of nature when he first recognizes the limits of his own knowledge'. (Osborne 1998: 43)

From now on the broadcaster needed to include audience knowledge (as constructed by social scientists and their surrogates) in the decision-making process. The broadcaster could not simply presume to act on the audience's behalf without also claiming to know the audience.

Much of the research in which the Listener Research Department (later renamed the Audience Research Department in 1950) was engaged was concerned with providing 'measurements of the extent to which the public has listened to, (or viewed), the programmes which have been broadcast, and the extent to which those broadcasts have pleased them'. Audience measurement and appreciation indices were developed alongside other risk-reducing strategies, including fixed formats and genres and weekly scheduling. Whereas the former coded the size of the audience in relation to particular programmes, the latter measured their investment. They were, as Ien Ang has aptly described them, 'aimed at the codification, routinization and synchronization of the audiences' viewing practices, to make them less capricious and more predictable' (1991: 19). Other forms of knowledge were invented, but discarded. For example, in 1950 it was suggested that 'communication indices' be added to the bread and butter of daily audience research, alongside audience measurement and appreciation indices. The aim was to discover whether or not listeners and viewers actually understood what they were listening to or watching. Tests on military personnel foregrounded the importance of IQ scores in the reception of broadcast communication.[4] Although the cognitive capacities of children were to become significant in the dividing of the child audience, such measures were never adopted in relation to the adult audience.

There is substantial research on audience measurement technologies, especially in the US context, but much of this research assumes a relation between knowledge and control which seems largely unfounded. Many existing approaches assume that knowledge is about control. But audience research tells television executives what programmes fail as well as what succeed. It provides a humility to their decision-making. It disperses and displaces their decision-making across other authorities. There is an alignment of interests, but it would be wrong to assume that 'all parties have a common interest' (Miller 1994: 66). There is no common agreed upon convention or rule through which audiences are understood, even if there is some agreement that audience measurement must be accurate and have a pragmatic value in translating audience figures into current and future revenues. There is no common agreed upon convention or rule because the effect of audience measurement is not to constitute security, but to create a constant sense of one's fallibility in making a decision. Although the intention might be to make audiences predictable and hence to allow the alignment of programmes with audiences, the effect of audience research is not always so. For example, take this much-used quote:

> The phone rings . . . in a . . . Beverly Hills home. The clock on the table registers 5.05 as a man's arm reaches the phone at the instant the second rings starts. Obviously he was anticipating the call, because he is immediately awake and he has a pen and preprinted sheet of paper at hand. After a curt 'Good morning', he begins furiously writing numbers on a sheet. These are Nielson rating numbers for the preceding Friday, Saturday, and Sunday nights

4 Robert Silvey, 13 April 1950, 1, WAC R9/20/4.

being read to him by a research department employee in New York. The man in Beverly Hills is the network's program vice president preparing himself for today's possible repercussions from those rating figures. In somewhat different conditions, perhaps, two other network program heads are also getting numbers at about the same time. (Beville 1985: 186 quoted in Ang 1991: 45)

This is not an image of security and control. Truth is not appealed to as a 'higher order of things' 'necessary for a common ground to emerge' (Miller 1994: 67). Truths about audiences exacerbate an insecurity. Television executives might agree to trust audience ratings but only inasmuch as they would prefer to trust only in their own judgement. Their judgement, though, is always cut with another's authority and knowledge. It is a knowledge that television executives would like to live without, but cannot.

The Social Effects of Broadcasting

Although this type of ratings research took up the bulk of the activities of the BBC Audience Research Department, other research was carried out in-house or commissioned. For example, G. Masterton, from the University of Nottingham, carried out research into the effects of radio listening in 1951. Likewise, A. J. Laird, from the Department of Psychology at the University of Aberdeen, presented a report on the effects of radio broadcasting. Both were very similar, using empirical data from listeners' letters, which were then grouped into different types of effects. Much of the material was similar to earlier research by Jennings and Gill and surveyed the way in which radio listening was bound up within a more complex set of domestic and social activities (1939).

In the 1950s the Audience Research Department continued its investigation into what Silvey called 'the social effects of broadcasting' as distinct from audience measurement, which was referred to as 'broadcasting-centred' research. In 1949, with an annual grant of £10,000, the Department had set up a Projects and Development Section which as Silvey stated would call upon the disciplines of statistics and psychology (Silvey 1974: 137 and 173). Out of this new project emerged the Advisory Committee of Psychologists. With the assistance of Sir Cyril Burt, from University College, London, Silvey drew up a list of prominent psychologists to assist the Department. It included: Sir Cyril Burt, Professor D. W. Harding (Bedford College, London), Professor Rex Knight (University of Aberdeen), Dr R. H. Thouless (a private practictioner), Professor P. E. Vernon (Institute of Education, London), Professor W. J. H. Sprott (University of Nottingham), and its Chairman, Dr Alec Rodger (Secretary of the British Psychological

Society). It also included BBC staff: Robert Silvey, W. A. Belson (a psychologist who later became Head of Survey Research at the London School of Economics), and B. P. Emmett (a statistician). Much of the work of the Advisory Committee of Psychologists was, as its title suggests, advisory. It advised the Audience Research Department primarily on methods of audience measurement and appreciation. It was not until 1953 that it first considered the question of children's television and it was not until 1960 that the daily Survey of Listening and Viewing lowered the adult age range down to 15 and was supplemented by 300 5 to 7-year-olds, 400 8 to 11-year-olds and 300 12 to 14-year-olds. Emmett had argued that interviewing children was in many ways easier than interviewing adults. However, he stated that parental help would be required with the youngest children and that a specially trained group of women interviewers, employing different techniques of sample selection, would also be needed (Silvey 1974: 151–2).

In January 1953, at the request of Freda Lingstrom, the Advisory Committee of Psychologists was invited to discuss 'the fears of children up to the age of seven' generated by watching television and 'in view of public criticism, if Westerns are damaging to children's morals'. The Committee discussed the 'standard fears of children'. The minutes of the meeting stated that:

> The following standard fears of children were suggested by
> members of the panel: (i) malevolent old women (Thouless);
> (ii) dangerous situations and enclosed spaces (Thouless);
> Burt suggested, in particular, 'unfinished' dangerous situations;
> (iii) inanimate objects becoming animate and hostile (Thouless);
> (iv) objects approaching the television camera, and thus
> increasing in apparent size (Thouless); close-ups of the human
> face, particularly teeth (Head of Audience Research). (5 January
> 1953, 7, WAC R9/20/4)

Thouless argued that a child would not be harmed by television viewing 'so long as he is only frightened on the conscious level, but where unconscious fears are aroused, nightmares are a likely result'. Vernon added that a situation is frightening if 'the child identifies himself with the person(s) involved'. And in relation to the Western, Thouless stated that they were 'so fantastic and unusual as to create "distance" between such happenings and the experience of ordinary living' and as a result 'they did not create a code of morals for the child':

> Only where the broadcast situation was similar to the
> surrounding life of the child, was genuine fear likely to be
> aroused or identification with the actions and moral standards
> of the subject likely. (ibid.)

The views expressed were very much informed opinions not based on any specific research and, although the Committee noted the lack of existing research, it made no appeal for research to be carried out in this area.

Even though Silvey stated, in relation to the inclusion of children within the daily Survey of Listening and Viewing, that '[a]fter the war, and even more after the revival of television, the exclusion of children came to be seen as not only illogical but increasingly intolerable' (Silvey 1974: 151), it is noticeable how little psychological concern there was about children's television viewing in the early 1950s. It is perhaps not surprising that the advice of the Advisory Committee of Psychologists was not sought when the Children's Programmes (Television) Department initiated its own survey into the child audience in 1952. The *Commissioned Report on Children's Television* emerged out of the recommendations of the Beveridge Report, which argued that there needed to be more outside expert opinion utilized in the making and planning of programmes. The commissioned report was based on the views of a panel who were required to watch children's television programmes from 18 May to the 30 June 1952. The panel of eight individuals watched in their own homes, wrote individual reports and then met to discuss the issues their viewing had raised and to write the final report.[5] The report was written as a set of fragmentary comments. It was loosely structured around four thematics concerning the activity/passivity of the child viewer, the timing of children's programmes, participation in the community and familial and domestic life. It made no reference to academic expertise nor did it include a bibliography. When comparing the report to the transcripts of the committee meetings, we can see how the voices of individual committee members are articulated in the pages of the report in such a way as to construct a negotiated settlement between those members. The report was a hybrid of different forms of educational, theatrical, parental, and psychological expertise.

This rather fragmentary report is important for our history of the making of the child television audience because it shows us very starkly how blurred the boundaries were between institution/audience and expert/lay person. The report is important because it was not authoritative, since authority had not yet become settled. The report started with the statement: 'We are generally agreed that the aim of the programmes should be to stimulate "active" viewing in the children, rather than to encourage "passive" acceptance of a programme which seems to sweep over them' (1952: 1). But it continued

---

5 The panel was chosen from those who had a knowledge of and contact with children, rather than an expertise in television or the child television audience. Some members even needed to be provided with television sets. I refer to the report as the Jenkinson Report after its chairman.

by stating that television should aim 'not merely to promote "active" viewing but to widen the child's experience and appreciation of all forms of art and culture, and help them to develop into civilised adults' (ibid.). Nevertheless, the report questioned the basis of this opposition between active/passive viewing. It argued that these forms of viewing are not clearly visible to the 'adult observer who is trying to judge the child's attitude' (ibid. 2). First, the report questioned a notion of activity based on the visible conduct of the child (i.e. children's talk, activity, or facial expression) and suggested that active viewing might only be revealed over time through the 'child's unique personal experience' or in the 'inner imaginative life' of the child. Although the panel wanted children's television to facilitate the child's use of their 'intelligence and imagination', the child as a viewer could not simply be represented to a singular authority and knowledge. In the hesitant mix of adult authorities the child is endowed with an agency which could not be easily captured in expert formulation and returned to the reserve of historical authority and knowledge (whether it be aesthetic, educational or scientific). Second, the report problematized active/passive viewing through folding a notion of children's attention to the screen over an earlier notion of participation: 'the fact that their attention is held, if only in a rather glassy way, means they are in some sense participating in the programme' (ibid. 3). This attention was construed as a form of 'mental activity'. In fact, the report was 'doubtful indeed whether such a thing as absolutely "passive" viewing really exists' (ibid.). The issue for them was the 'quality of attention' a programme was able to evoke. Thirdly, the report turned to the notion of 'selectiveness' and here the panel's comments were more categorical. It asserted that new viewers were less selective than regular ones, that less academic children or those with fewer possibilities for doing different things were seen to be less selective; and very young children were seen to demonstrate their lack of selection through ceasing to 'attend to some parts of the programme' (ibid. 4). These subtle, but different, understandings of children's relation to television were also discussed in relation to different genres of programmes.

As yet a psychological knowledge of the child audience had not come to prevail as authoritative. On the one hand the report paid lip-service to psychological categories:

> Programmes about the real world can also help to satisfy the child's growing need to differentiate clearly between the world of reality and of phantasy . . . From an educational angle the drawing of this distinction is also important. Children's awareness of truth, powers of verification, sense of security in their own experience are all closely bound up with their awareness of an inner and outer reality. It therefore seems important on all counts

that adults should give them full support in this growing-point of their developing personalities. (ibid. 5–6)

On the other hand, the report reaffirmed, and prioritized, earlier nineteenth-century aesthetic and moral discourses of the child:

> While recognising that television is the youngest of the arts and still in its experimental stage, we feel that its aims should be wide and its sights set high; not merely to promote 'active' viewing but to widen the children's experience and appreciation of all forms of art and culture, and help them develop into civilised adults. It should introduce the child to good home conditions, good designs and decoration, beauty in every-day life. This is already being done to a certain extent, but we feel that it could be done even more effectively. (ibid. 1)

It is possible to see, from the report itself and from the minutes of the meetings, how there were quite distinct authorities which were negotiated and contested within the dynamics of the group. For example, Miriam Langdon, a developmental psychologist, although profuse and authoritative in her own writing, was circumspect and almost absent from much of the discussion. When she did speak, her comments were often ignored or circumvented. In a discussion about children being frightened by television programmes, Langdon said, 'You get a strange emotional expression set up, and it is awfully difficult to make any general statement about how they react to these things. I think a lot depends on the adult's make-up—as was seen in the air raids.' Langdon's professional expertise was politely dismissed by Mary Fields (a well-established figure in children's arts, theatre, and film), who replied, 'This may be something for the psychologist—I don't know' and she continued, 'but I should think it was the more abnormal children who are more easily frightened. But there is no doubt that some groups enjoy that sort of thing to no end.' This marginalization of the expertise of the psychologist was clearly expressed in the conclusion of the report, which stated that there was a need for the BBC Children's Programmes (Television) Department to form contacts not with psychologists and educationalists, who were not even mentioned, but with those involved in children's radio, theatre, music, art, film, and libraries (ibid. 22).

Although audience measurement was quickly embedded within broadcasting institutions as a resource for knowing audiences, research into the social effects of broadcasting (both the *ad hoc* and the expert) was more transient. This was not because the broadcasters did not recognize the expertise of those social scientists researching the effects of television on children or because, for example, the *Commissioned Report on Children's Television* was undervalued. In the case of the findings of social scientists, the results were inscribed, through printed articles, diagrams, and graphs, within an intertextual domain specific to the social sciences. Notwithstanding the fact that such research was read by individual broadcasters, the inscriptions of the social scientists were not easily intelligible within the institutional context of broadcasting. It was not sufficient for the truth to be represented, it had to be translated (i.e. made intelligible) and to address the institutional concerns of broadcasters.

In the case of short-lived commissioned reports in these early years, it is noticeable how although the expertise inaugurated by the broadcasters was intelligible to them and easily translated into institutional decisions (i.e. if children are scared of witches and close-ups of teeth then don't show them when children might be watching) it too was ultimately transient. The members of the advisory panels and committees did not display a knowledge of the child television audience through inscription devices that would have lasting authority and that could be distributed outside of its particular context of production. The *Commissioned Report* was read by Lingstrom and others in the Department of Children's Programmes, but it did not figure elsewhere in the BBC or externally at the time. Thus, whereas the early social scientists external to broadcasting had inscription devices which were immutable and mobile, but not translatable within the institutional context of broadcasting, those experts working closely with the broadcasting institutions were able to translate their knowledge into immediate (but localized) policy, but their findings were not inscribed in such a way as could be disseminated outside of a very localized context. In contrast, audience measurement had been constituted in such a way as to make it central to the governance of programming, but also in such a way that individual results (the rating of a week's schedule of programmes) were short-lived. The shelf-life of the data was such that repeated measurement was required.

The Nuffield Report

Psychological knowledge of the child television audience was uneven in its deployment within different sites of discursive production. However, over the next few years this was to change. In July 1953 the Advisory Committee of Psychologists proposed to initiate a detailed survey of the effect of television on children. In 1954 the Nuffield Foundation was approached to fund the survey and in 1958 Hilde Himmelweit and her fellow social psychologists from the London School of Economics published *Television and the Child: An Empirical Study into the Effect of Television on the Young*. There had been research into the child audience in the United States in the early 1950s and research into the use of television by adolescents in Britain, but this was the first major piece of research into children's television viewing not only within Britain but across the globe.[6] It was closely followed by major studies in the United States, Japan, and Australia (Schramm *et al.* 1961; Furu 1962). As a form of social enquiry the research was not in itself interesting. It continued the protocols of the social survey into the realm of children's television viewing, but it did not offer any novel ways of researching this specific audience. Nonetheless, if audience measurement was able to quantify the size and demographics of the audience in relation to particular programmes and times of broadcast, the social survey was able to add texture to those distributions of intelligence, sex, age, education, and social class. It made possible a social scientific judgement of the moral topographies of home and nation. It provided a sophisticated language of viewing and made the clusters of familial conduct and the viewing habits of the nation visible to government.

Taken as a particular social document, the Nuffield Report provided an exemplary account of a new set of intermeshing knowledges of the child audience, recoding the responsibilities of the broadcaster and bringing to the fore the responsibilities of the parent. The research looked at children's reactions to conflict, crime, and violence on television, effects on their values and outlook, effects on knowledge and school performance, effects on leisure and interests, and other effects on eyesight and night rest, and the family. Tucked away in a small corner of the table of contents was an item which held the key to understanding the introduction of a psychological knowledge of the child audience. The complex of discourses which surrounded the figure of the *television addict* provided a way of making intelligible the discursive formation of the child television audience and the way this discourse was caught up in a web of disciplinary techniques.

For Himmelweit children's television viewing was not linked to any notion of passivity: 'there is no evidence whatsoever that makes television passive; viewers are as active, independent, and imaginative as controls' (Himmelweit *et al.* 1958). Instead of the opposition between active and passive viewers, an opposition which is readily banded around in contemporary discourse, Himmelweit's analysis rested upon an opposition between discriminate viewing and addiction. The concern about discriminate viewing was (as I have shown earlier) voiced in women's magazines, but it was also prevalent in educational discourses. For example, both the Crowther Report and the Newsom Report referred to the need for teachers to teach children how to be discriminate and critical consumers of the mass media (Ministry of

---

6 For example, in the United States Eleanor Maccoby had carried out small-scale surveys into school children's viewing (1951, 1954) and in Britain M. Gordon had published a *Report on a Survey by the Coventry University Tutorial Class on the Adolescent and Television* (1951).

Education 1959; Department of Education and Science 1963). Again the imperative was predicated upon a need to regulate the relationship between freedom and choice in an age where it was perceived that the old authorities of 'home town, county, church and father's political party' had given way to the influence of 'public opinion' (Ministry of Education 1959: 43). The problem was that children and teenagers were not 'thinking for themselves' and the task of the teacher, and others, was to form within these individuals the capacity to make critical judgements: to help children govern themselves. Although the specific mechanisms deployed within the educational apparatus are beyond the boundaries of this book, inasmuch as they function within a quite separate governmental formation, it is nevertheless clear that educational practices provide one of the conditions of existence of the discursive formation of the child television audience, inasmuch as educational authorities legitimate a particular forming of the child viewer within the home.

Nevertheless, the 'television addict' was formed as a particular pathology within the wider axis of discriminate/indiscriminate viewing. The Nuffield Report initially identified the television addict as a 'heavy viewer', a product of a specific set of statistical techniques.[7] In this way the Report aligned the discourse of the child audience with a longer history of statistics as a particular technique of government. The deployment of statistics as a form of science of government dated back to the middle of the eighteenth century and importantly to Galton's invention of the 'normal curve' as a statistical technique for measuring normality in the late nineteenth century (cf. Nikolas Rose 1985). This technique, in the Nuffield Report, rendered the child viewing population calculable and governable. This particular form of government produced the television addict alongside other social problems within a specific moral topography of psychological instability, family disharmony, delinquency, and crime.

The addict was classified in terms of the biological factors of age, sex, and intelligence, and the sociological factors of education and class. Of these, intelligence and class were centrally important. The survey stated that among 10 to 11-year-olds 36 per cent of heavy viewers had IQs of below 100. Among 13 to 14-year-olds the number was 50 per cent. And while class was not seen to play an important role in the older age group, it was seen as significant in the younger age group.[8]

7 The group designated as addicts were 'the one-third of each age group who spent the longest time viewing'. This was, according to Himmelweit, a purely arbitrary designation (Himmelweit *et al.* 1958: 385).

8 In the older age group 36 per cent of middle-class and 31 per cent of working-class children were identified as addicts. In the younger age group the figure was 25 per cent of middle-class children and 37 per cent of working-class children (Himmelweit *et al.* 1958: 386).

The differential importance of class in the figures was seen as being due to the way in which 'the closer control exercised by middle-class parents diminishes when children reach early adolescence' (Himmelweit *et al.* 1958: 386). These different factors of analysis took on their strategic importance when they were connected to the specification of the television addict as a type of personality. Himmelweit defined the television addict in the following way:

> an addict type emerged who is not exclusive to television; his
> emotional insecurity and maladjustment seem to impel him
> towards excessive consumption of any available mass medium.
> If television is available to such a child, he will view excessively;
> if not, he will go very often to the cinema, listen a great deal to
> the radio, or become a heavy reader of comics (but not books).
> Such children were characterised by lack of security, by being ill
> at ease with other children. Their teachers often described them
> as shy and retiring. (1958: 29)

The addict was constituted in relation to a set of discourses concerning the emotional economy of the family. These discourses, as Nikolas Rose argues, were formed in the 1920s and 1930s with the emergence of 'new psychology' and were, in turn, constituted within a longer genealogy of the invention of psychology as a particular governmental technology. The 'socially adjusted' child was 'the natural outcome of the child's development and the normal outcome of family life'. The 'normal family', as Rose puts it, 'could now be specified in psychological terms' (Rose 1989: 155). Likewise, Rose states:

> But if the family produced conflicts in wishes or emotions,
> denied them expression, associated them with unpleasant
> feelings, or reacted in terms of their own fears, hopes, desires,
> or disappointments to the child's feelings, what would be
> produced would be *maladjustment*. And maladjustment, from
> bed-wetting to delinquency, had become a sign of something
> wrong in the emotional economy of the family. (ibid.)

In the Nuffield Report children's television viewing was clearly added to this list of pathologies. Whereas children's radio listening was framed in terms of cultural training and good moral influences, children's domestic television viewing was conceived much more as an element within the dynamics of intra-familial emotions, wishes and expressions. The television addict 'turns to viewing because of the kind of person he is, and viewing in turn reduces his feeling of isolation and insecurity by giving him imaginary companionship and satisfying his need for vicarious excitement' (Himmelweit *et al.* 1958: 395). The types of programmes an addict liked were seen to be the same as those within his/her age group 'except that he enjoyed plays especially family serials, adventure, and mystery—plays which permit identification with the type of active person he would like to be, or with the happy family of which he would like to be a member' (1958: 390 and 395).[9] The child was seen to develop an emotional investment in television in response to the lack of emotional support and security provided within the 'real life' of the family. In place of the image of television as providing children with a 'window on the world' and an extension of citizenship that was presented across a number of institutional sites, this discourse presented an image of the child viewer as an 'introvert' who turns to television to escape from 'reality' and the duties of public life. Such an image, as we can see from an article in *The New Statesman and Nation* by Richard Strout in 1949, had been in circulation prior to the publication of the Nuffield Report. Strout pictured television as bringing the world into the home. He presented an image of television viewing as pacifying and breaking down communality. Strout stated that:

> The effect of this illusion is spectacular, and upon children it acts like a drug. I have seen a gang of noisy unmanageable boys huddle before a set for hours, hardly speaking. Is this a good or a natural thing? (28 May 1949)

Although Himmelweit does not talk of television as a drug, Strout's comments have the same import: namely discussion of television makes visible the withdrawal of children from public life. Whereas other discourses of the popular were concerned about the production of new forms of youth *community*, the discourse of the child television audience pathologized the child's *retreat* from public life. Unlike the discursive formation of the child radio audience in the 1920s, which presented the overcrowding and rowdiness of working-class families as a problem, this discourse focused on the problem of the withdrawal to, what we might call, the interior space of the mind (cf. Moores 1988).

The introduction of the expertise and language of the psychologist reframed the relationship between the public space of broadcasting and the democratic life of the population and constituted the relationship in terms of the social problems of delinquency, familial disharmony, crime and social decline. The post-war period continued the process of rendering social and cultural life more visible, and in the late 1940s and 1950s, that process was intensified in relation to domestic and familial conduct. The proliferation of images of light, spacious, and yet small, homes was now reconstrued within a discourse of the psychology of children's television viewing and the (dis)harmony of the family. The aesthetics of domestic space and the

---

9 Similar findings were made in the United States (cf. Schramm *et al.* 1961).

medical discourse of viewing posture and position were rearticulated within an architecture of the psychology of children's viewing. The addict not only shied away from other children and public life, but also watched within a womb of darkness. Richard Strout, in his article 'Every Cellar a Cinema', declared of his own family that:

> The children dash in every evening for permission to see
> 'Howdy-Doody' at a neighbour's before dinner. Squatting there
> in the darkness will be a dozen watching a television marionette
> show. Other shows follow. The children are dragged away by brute
> strength. A recent *New Yorker* cartoon puts the point: 'Remember
> the good old days,' a wife says to her husband with a gesture at the
> crowd round the television set, 'when we didn't know where they
> were?' (28 May 1949)

There is an obvious play here between the darkness of the viewing space and the increased visibility of children for the parent. Himmelweit argued that more addicts than others watched (and would like to watch) in the dark, duplicating at home the setting of the cinema in which familiar surroundings were obscured. The isolated child, the insecure child, the delinquent child, the maladjusted child and the 'dull' child were seen to congregate silently around the television set in darkness.

However, it was not that television produced delinquent children (for example, through the effects of violent television images), or any other of these 'pathologies'; rather, a psychological interpretation of children's viewing made possible a whole infrastructure of problems and concerns through which familial and domestic conduct could be managed. This was a more insidious manoeuvre. As Himmelweit stated '[t]he solution of the problem is not primarily to restrict children's viewing, but to attack the various underlying causes'. Television viewing acted as a 'barometer', to use Himmelweit's term, of the insecurity of the child:

> A reduction in the amount a child addict views is likely to be a
> sign that his personal relations have improved: an increase may
> well reflect tension and anxiety. Viewing, it would appear,
> might well serve as a barometer to indicate the extent to which
> the child's life is satisfactory, provided it is considered in relation
> to the child's age, intellectual calibre, and background.
> (Himmelweit *et al.* 1958: 396)

Whereas the concern with the causal connection between television content and children's attitudes and behaviour was strategic in the government of television content, the discourse which I have outlined above was able to shape familial and domestic conduct as a particular area of intervention. This manoeuvre connected concerns about television viewing to a wider set of social problems and forms of intervention.

The Nuffield Report had a major impact upon the broadcasting institutions and the press at the time. It was reported in the late 1950s alongside various other reports and pieces of research concerning children and television.[10] An analysis of these discussions allows me to display more clearly how the discourse of the child television audience was formed in relation to two strategic objectives of making middle-class parents conscious of their responsibilities and of making broadcasters assume responsibility for the irresponsibilities of working-class parents. The Nuffield Report was keen to stress that it found no evidence to support the view that supervision of children's viewing was greater in middle-class than in working-class homes (Himmelweit *et al.* 1958: 44). However, despite protestations, 'class' was clearly central to the formulation of its knowledge of children's television viewing. The report stated that:

> Parent viewers have a vested interest in presenting television as something of a benefactor, and as a result, especially in working-class families, it tends to be regarded in an uncritical manner. (1958: 379)

The report then included an example of a working-class family in which television provided a common point of interest and conversation and in the same paragraph provided another example of a mother who kept 'her baby quiet by holding it up to look at television' (1958: 380). However, only two pages later it talked about how middle-class parents 'pay more attention than working-class parents to [the] potential uses of television'. These uses included young boys making things by hand with their fathers and girls sharing interest with their mothers in sewing (1958: 381–2). The report then went on to state that '[n]o rules for avoiding conflict can be a substitute for unstrained relationships, for perceptive parental handling of the child, and for a home atmosphere which is conducive to the development of many alternative interests to viewing' and it provided an example from a middle-class mother of four children (aged 6–18) whose 'family has rules for viewing, flexibly adhered to, and the children have many other interests' (1958: 383). The positioning of working-class and middle-class families within this discursive formation was picked up in the press, institutional reports and government committees

10 Of these the most significant and widely reported in Britain were: Mark Abrahms' research on the child television audience for the BBC Audience Research Department (WAC R9/10/2, 1955); the ITA Report on *Parents, Children and Television*, 1958; the ITA/BBC O'Connor Committee Report, 1960; the Knight Committee Report on television and the family, 1960; and the Pilkington Report on broadcasting, 1962. There was also a report conducted for the Council for Children's Welfare, 1958 (cf. Blishen 1958; Birk 1957).

primarily in relation to the problem of when and in what space children watched television, whose responsibility it was to regulate the situation and how it could be regulated.

The recognition that children constituted a distinct audience in their own right and did not simply watch programmes designed for them was clearly established in this period. Broadcasters attempted to separate the child audience from the adult audience through various techniques, including the 'toddlers truce' which supposedly intermeshed with the routines of normal family life (e.g. washing the children and putting them to bed) and the distinct separation between children's programmes and adult programmes. However, the Nuffield Report repeatedly stated that the problem was not how much time children spent watching television but the 'nature of the programmes' they watched (1958: 44). Thus, as *The Times Educational Supplement* put it, the report would not flatten the carping minority of critics, but would be like a 'drink with a kick in it' and would 'jolt the thoughtful adult into new anxieties just when he is feeling secure' (12 December 1958). The paper also referred to the way in which children 'trespass determinedly and extensively into the programmes that are meant for adults' and the inability of the broadcasters to 'parcel out the day between the young and their elders'. As *The New Statesman* commented in the same month:

> One particularly useful corrective is the report's insistence on the impact on children of 'adult' TV programmes, up to 9 p.m. or later; in future, no one discussing this subject will be able to do so in terms of 'children's television' alone. (Driburg, 20 December 1958)

Himmelweit had shown how a large number of children stayed up watching television until 9 p.m. and that significantly large numbers stayed up later.[11]

From the late 1930s, when television was first regularly broadcast in the UK, the BBC had issued warnings about certain programmes. A television announcement would be made concerning the suitability of the programme vis-à-vis children's viewing. It had also been suggested that 'a carefully-written synopsis of the programmes should be printed in the Radio Times' (Adams, WAC 20 April 1949, T16/166). Another consideration was the use of a continuous warning symbol in the corner of the screen. Although these mechanisms of certification were regarded as insufficient, there was seen to be, nevertheless, a pressing need to regulate domestic viewing.

---

11 *The New Statesman* had reported on a survey in 1958 on school children in Widnes which had discovered that 65 per cent of children aged seven and eight were watching television between 9 p.m. and 10 p.m. (Blishen 1958).

Problems concerning children watching unsuitable programmes were, as I have already argued, framed within a discourse of the emotional economy of the family. A consequence of constructing children as watching programmes other than those designed for them was that the audience for programmes after children's television was now seen to include children, adolescents and adults. Likewise the inclusion of children into the imagining of the temporal arrangements of television viewing, other than between 5 p.m. and 6 p.m. and after school during school term-time, was connected to the particular spatial arrangements of television viewing in the home. Himmelweit had stressed that television viewing was 'after all a family affair', that it took place 'in the only room available in a home containing children of very different ages' and that 'effectively they [young children] cannot be sent out of the room' (Himmelweit *et al.* 1958: 53). It was not that the imagining of broadcasting as a 'family affair' was a novel idea, but that such an imagining in the 1950s was embedded within a wider deployment of techniques directed at the government of domestic and familial conduct.

The space/time relations of family viewing constituted the main concern of the joint Independent Television Authority and BBC O'Connor Committee Report which stated that:

> The television-set is generally kept in a single living-room used by all the family. No-one in the room can avoid giving it at least some of his or her attention. The television audience ought, therefore, to be considered as having no analogy with any other. Not even radio offers a satisfactory parallel. It is possible to turn the mind away from mere sounds issuing from a box, but much harder to ignore the pictures moving in the corner of the room. At least up to 9 p.m., then, the television audience is largely a family audience, concentrating their attention upon the screen. (1960: 3)

Although the BBC, through its programme policy, could deploy dividing practices in order to separate and individualize the child audience, the construction of television viewing as a familial activity led to calls for greater regulation of both the broadcasters and parents. These calls were also tied to a wider set of concerns arising from the introduction of commercial television in 1955, after the Television Act of 1954, and a concern about attacks on the moral framework of society from the Western and other 'American' programming.

The O'Connor Committee Report called for the introduction of three different temporal–spatial arrangements: programmes suitable for children, programmes not unsuitable for children and programmes unsuitable for children. These categories in turn refer to children's programmes, family viewing time and adult programmes. In this sense, television programming had become regulated in relation to the figure of the child viewer. The Independent Television Companies Association (ITCA) was resistant to such a conceptualization and argued that an adult had a 'right to expect that entertainment at the peak viewing hours of the evening will be designed for him rather than for children, whose needs have already been catered for in schools and children's programmes earlier in the day': '[i]s Television for children or adults?' (ibid. Appendix C, 2). They argued that the logic of the argument for a family viewing time between 6 p.m. and 9 p.m. could extend 'in the interests of children over the whole viewing period, and would preclude any attempts at more sophisticated programmes and stultify much creative talent' due to the fact that large numbers of children viewed until 10 p.m. and even until 11 p.m. (ibid. Appendix C, 3). As a result they declared that '[p]arents must surely accept the main responsibility for what their children are allowed to see during the hours intended for adult entertainment, and the responsibility cannot be transferred' (ibid. Appendix C, 3). In 1960 the Pilkington Report on Broadcasting (published in 1962) received a number of submissions from individuals and organizations concerned with television violence and children and as a result of the evidence reaffirmed many of the recommendations of the O'Connor Committee. There were also a number of calls for the setting up of an advisory council to supervise the relationship between the television broadcasters and children.[12]

Framing these discussions was a sense that children needed to be able to watch television in a secure and stable familial environment which would facilitate their mental and emotional development. Family viewing time was invented as a means of providing such an environment. However, such regulatory measures were not introduced to 'dilute' or 'emasculate' television programming:

> Indeed, the protection and security offered by the family to its younger members should provide the right circumstances in which children can be introduced to many problems of adult life. What matters, as the Committee sets out later, is that these problems should be properly introduced. (op. cit. 3)

---

12 The O'Connor Committee called for a joint ITA/BBC advisory council which would contain 'people who have a special knowledge of the mental and emotional development of children as well as the medium of television' (BBC/ITA Joint Committee on 'Television and the Child': 13). The Pilkington Committee considered the idea of a viewers' council, but rejected the idea and even relieved the ITA of its statutory obligation to appoint a Children's Advisory Committee (cf. Sendall 1983: 164). Demands for such a council had been made consistently throughout the mid- to late-1950s from the Council for Children's Welfare and other organizations. For example, Alma Birk in 1958 in *The New Statesman* argued that it 'should include doctors, social psychologists, teachers and parents, and its function should include the preparation (and supervision) of a production code, the right to propose changes in programmes and the publication of an annual report both on children's programmes and on their impact' (Birk 1958).

In this sense family viewing time was imagined as providing the context for 'normal' viewing as well as excluding programme material, such as horror, science fiction and even *Jane Eyre*, which might be harmful to children at risk.[13] As I have argued above in relation to the Nuffield Report, this discourse was not simply predicated on a notion of the defencelessness of the young child, but rather on a notion that certain parents were seen to be too irresponsible to supervise properly their children's television viewing. The O'Connor Report stated that:

> The Committee does not consider that broadcasters can discharge their responsibility simply by leaving to parents the question of what their children see. Parents are not always present when children are viewing, nor can they always tell from published information the nature of the programmes about to be televised. There are other parents too irresponsible to care what their children see. The broadcaster must accordingly recognise that he has the responsibility for providing programmes not unsuitable for children at those times when it is known that large numbers of children are viewing. (ibid.: 10)

Whereas some parents were deemed responsible for supervising their children's discriminative viewing, other parents were not. *The Economist*, in an article on the O'Connor Committee Report, made it clear who those parents were:

> there is a grain of common sense in the BBC and ITV contention that parents have a responsibility to send children up to bed when anything unsuitable comes on; but there has always been a clear class distinction in Britain between the parents who drive young people to bed reasonably early and those who do not. Until middle class standards are commoner in this matter of child welfare, the BBC and ITV can at least voluntarily remind their programme makers that, when in doubt about how far to go during family listening time, they should adopt the maxim of Victorian Grundyism 'Not before the children.' (30 July 1960)

Although broadcasters could rely upon the responsible supervision of children's viewing in middle-class homes, programme makers and planners, regulators, and others concerned with children's television viewing could not rid themselves of a vision of the pathologies of working-class families. The working-class home was deemed to be an environment which was potentially harmful to the development of the child.

---

13 Himmelweit stated that '[t]elevision in so far as it is more of a family activity than radio listening is likely to arouse less fear, but television's visual impact in darkened rooms could well make up for this' (Himmelweit *et al.* 1958: 19; see also BBC/ITA Joint Committee on 'Television and the Child', Appendix B, 7).

It is not that a psychology of the child television audience is an 'anti-social' science 'focusing on the properties of individuals abstracted from social relations, reducing social issues to inter-personal ones, servicing an unequal society', but that it is profoundly social. It is not simply that 'childhood', and 'children' even, are socially produced categories or that the truth of the child television audience is constituted socially ('the outcome of a complex process of con-struction and persuasion undertaken within a social arena'), but rather, as Nikolas Rose comments, that 'the birth of psychology as a distinct discipline, its vocation and destiny, is inextricably bound to the emergence of the "social" as a territory of our thought and our reality' (Rose 1990: 103). Rose, drawing upon the work of Jacques Donzelot (1979), argues that the 'social' is 'an historical achievement, a shifting and uncertain terrain that began to consolidate in western societies in the nineteenth century'. For Rose, as for Donzelot, the 'social' is a discursively constructed domain which refers to institu-tional and practical arrangements, including the emergence of social security, social welfare, social workers, and social services (cf. Hirst 1981). He observes that:

> The social is a matrix of deliberation and action, the object of certain types of knowledge, the location of certain types of predicaments, the realm traced out by certain types of apparatus and the target of certain types of programmes and ambition. Psychology as a discipline—a heterogeneous assemblage of problems, methods, approaches and objects—was born in this social domain in the nineteenth century and its subsequent vicissitudes are inseparable from it. And psychology, as a way of knowing, speaking, calculating, has played a constitutive part in the formation of the social. (Rose 1990: 103–4)

In the 1950s psychological discourse began to become established at a popular level as a resource for thinking about and acting upon fam-ilial practices and domestic arrangements. It did so by making the child (more specifically the child's mind) central to the governance of the home. Psychology provided not simply a discourse, but an author-ity for bringing together a number of actors, focused on a common problem: the mental health of the child (cf. Rose 1989; Walkerdine and Lucey 1989). Psychology did not merely offer opinion, but truth, a veritable science of the child and a means of correctly governing the domestic. This is not to suggest that 'psychology' designates a unitary phenomenon, but that, in broad terms, the mental well-being of the child viewer becomes the object of social scientific concern as distinct from issues concerning the moral, cultural, or physical well-being of the child.

6
Children's Television Grows Up: The Good, the Bad, and the Ugly

THE fourth set of problems significant in the making of the child television audience regards the coming to maturity of the organization of children's television. This set of problems sits alongside and draws upon the problem spaces I have discussed earlier, concerning the address to the child television audience as a distinct, but differentiated whole, the formation of conditions of domestic supervision and geographies of familial viewing and the congealing of relations of expertise and governance. In the late 1950s and early 1960s, children's television and the child television audience were increasingly understood within a logic of commercialism and also posed as a matter of public and political concern. The children's broadcasters at the BBC sought to shape themselves in relation to the rigours of competition, but also to present themselves (to the press, government, and the public) as defenders of tradition and the welfare of the child. In this new context of both defence and competition, the television Western became a prime site of debate and mobilization.

The Effect of Competition

In 1954 the Television Act broke the monopoly of the BBC and paved the way for the first broadcasting of commercial television in the following year. The Act of Parliament allowed independent companies to gain a franchise to broadcast within designated regions across the UK. The independent television companies were regulated by the Independent Television Authority. In the early days, the BBC only faced limited competition as independent television (ITV) only broadcast around London and the South-East. Nevertheless, the popularity, and populism, of commercial programming caused some concern at the BBC and drove it to place an important focus on children's television as 'entertainment'.

Owen Reed, Head of Children's Programmes (Television) at the BBC from 1956, argued in 1961 that the BBC Children's Programmes

Department faced competition from ITV children's programmes and also from the evening programmes of both channels. He stated that the only way of resolving the dilemma was to 'make good programmes popular—in other words, to achieve entertainment in depth' (*The Times*, 20 November 1961). The attempt to articulate 'quality programming' with 'popular entertainment' was evident in a number of organizational changes in this period. There were shifts in the aesthetics of programming (more emphasis on film entertainment than on live television, more Western and adventure programmes), in the scheduling of programmes (more serializations) and in the 'professionalism' of the broadcasters. In many respects those working on children's television at the BBC recognized that things needed to change and that the old broadcast model based on radio broadcasting was not sufficient to sustain 'good popular programmes'. Needless to say, instead of a clean sweep of the old programmes, we find an attempt to construe classic BBC children's drama as popular programming and to construct it as equivalent to the type of adventure serializations being shown on commercial television. For example, earlier in 1958 Reed had argued that *Little Lord Fauntleroy* had greater similarities than differences with *Robin Hood*, *The Lone Ranger*, and *Ivanhoe* (all three filmed serials were broadcast on the ITV system). He claimed that all the programmes had strong dynamic stories and a central predicament that attracted the child audience. They also had an appeal to 'space': the wide open plains in *The Lone Ranger* and baronial architectures in *Little Lord Fauntleroy*. Equally, each type of narrative is serialized. In constructing an equivalence between the types of programmes shown on commercial television and the types broadcast on BBC, Reed readily conceded ground to the argument that the BBC needed to make popular programmes (in terms of ratings), but that the difference between the different services was marked by the BBC's ability to offer 'quality'. The exigency to make BBC children's programmes popular and entertaining was tied to a need to modernize the children's broadcaster in line with a post-war modern world. Reed stated in 1959: 'I don't want to denigrate the old uncle, but he wasn't quite up to the modern child.' He continued by saying that these modern children are 'tough individuals, with a hunger for realism not to be satisfied by gnomes and little elves' (*Sunday Times*, 13 December 1959).

In a series of policy documents and discussions, which were eventually presented to a BBC General Advisory Council meeting on children's radio and television programming, Reed set a clear agenda for the future of children's television. The context for these debates was the success of ITV in attracting the majority of the child television audience to its children's programmes. Reed forcefully declared in August 1957 that the existing Department of Children's Programmes was 'amorphous and unwieldy'. He argued that the development of children's television since the war had been 'piecemeal'. Children's television as it had developed under Lingstrom was both emphatically and diplomatically identified as a central problem. Reed characterized Lingstrom's aim and achievement as being in the 'same tradition as Sound Radio Children's Hour'. Lingstrom's leadership of children's television 'was directed to offering children of all ages from three to sixteen a balanced and wholesome diet'. But he also recognized that Lingstrom wanted children's television to be 'appetising' and her menu included (against her 'more high-minded critics') a number of Westerns and 'good-time' programmes such as *Crackerjack* (August 1957, 4, WAC T16/45/2). Reed's policy of change, thus, was not simply posed in relation to an opposition between entertainment and more high-brow programmes (with all the connotations that those terms carried). In June 1958, he also pointed out that any change meant a change in staffing.

In contrast to Lingstrom's vision of children's television, Reed typified the ITV provision accordingly:

> What is there in ITV's Children's Programmes that holds this fascination? The main reasons are two. First, the reliance on a daily quota of American 'Westerns'; secondly, and in conjunction with this, the constant reiteration of habit-forming titles on a weekly plan. (August 1957, 5)

The central terms of the contrast between Lingstrom's and the ITV's provision of children's programmes concerned not the Western *per se*, but the 'reliance' on them and a weekly schedule designed according to programme ratings and programme genres which could deliver high ratings. The pattern of ITV children's programming included thirty minutes of 'straightforward entertainment' and twenty-five minutes of film. Reed noted that there were about eight films per week including *Roy Rogers, Hopalong Cassidy, Rin-Tin-Tin, Scarlet Pimpernel, Brave Eagle, Lassie*, and 'the most popular' *Robin Hood* (September 1957, 1, WAC T16/45/2 5). The Western made up the bulk of the ITV filmed material, apart from the adventure serial *Robin Hood*. But all programmes were construed as 'American': 'These film programmes are either made in America for the American audience (not always for a *children's* audience) or made in this country by American executives with stories, action and dialogue actions slanted for an American audience' (ibid.). More specifically, Reed argued, the Western was problematic because it interested both adults and children, contained adult material (such as sex, brutality, and fights), was often historically anachronistic, incited too much 'tension and excitement' (which was seen to be bad for children's health) and was predominantly aimed at older children.

Reed offered three alternative solutions to the problem of restoring the BBC's child audience: 'persevere with the present pattern', increase the amount of film-material (which would result in a lowering of standards and might not increase the size of the audience) or 'adopt the pattern of ITA' (while trying to learn the lesson of some of its disadvantages as noted in the list above). In relation to the final solution, Reed proposed that the BBC make its own film programmes. But this would limit the overall range of children's programmes, take some time to establish and 'be very expensive indeed' (September 1957, 8). In making these changes it could begin to properly address, what Reed referred to as, the 'real child audience' of 8 to 12 years old (Reed, June 1958, WAC T16/45/2).

Just as the BBC Children's Television Department was undergoing significant changes in its organizational thinking, so too were those involved in children's television production in the commercial sector. The children's television departments in the ITV system were housed with talented individuals from film (notably Mary Fields), theatre, the arts and from ex-BBC staff (including Michael Westmore). It would be a mistake to think of these individuals as having only a superficial interest in children's programming and in the welfare of the child. For example, Michael Westmore, Head of Children's Programmes at the ITV company Associated-Rediffusion, talked with detail and care about the schedule of programmes for 'Tea-V Time' accordingly: Monday included a hobbies and sports programme titled *Venture* and a 30 minute play for boys aged between 9 and 15; Tuesday contained *Elizabethan Fanfare* which included shadow puppet films, 'stories told with flowers', interviews with children in the news and a 'gentler drama' for girls of 9 to 15; Wednesday had *Telebox* for all the family; Thursday contained a competition show called *Flickwiz* for older children plus a Western; and Friday contained *Bubble and Squeak* for 5 to 9-year-olds (*The Times*, 29 November 1955). Westmore claimed that he hoped to encourage children to have their own viewing days and to watch discriminately: 'What . . . is the good of fighting passivity and stimulating all kinds of activities if you do not leave the audience time for hobbies to which they have been introduced?' (ibid.). Similarly, Associated Television's *Junior Club*, shown on Saturday, was intended to 'create an informal, friendly club atmosphere, and great pains are made to feel that they belong' (ibid.). The club, in 1955, had a membership of 5,000. It is also worth noting at this point that the ITA was statutorily obliged to appoint a Children's Advisory Committee. The Committee was comprised mainly of educationalists with one minister of St John's Church of Scotland and one psychologist. The BBC was under no such obligation and had no such committee.

On 22 November 1960 a group of children's television producers was called to a meeting to discuss children's television for a BBC report to be sent to the Pilkington Committee which was conducting a government enquiry into broadcasting. The main lines of discussion were focused on the effect of competition on BBC children's television and the corresponding need for a new professional ethos. After much discussion of changes in the scheduling of children's programmes, Reed observed that:

> I think we would admit that we have hardened. We have hardened in presentation. There is less of the cosy, deliberate children's own approach. There is a big stiffening in the total amount of drama and story-telling and action, and a greater disposition on our side to take risks in search of that. (Meeting on Children's Television, 22 November 1960, WAC T16/45/3)

Dorothea Brooking, children's novelist and scriptwriter, argued that it was not competition from the ITV companies that had led to changes but 'learning a little bit about the business'. Others in the meeting referred to change in terms of becoming less 'amateurish' and more 'professional'. It was also mentioned that the BBC Children's Department was 'growing-up' and becoming more 'adult'. Thus, although there was some dispute as to the cause (competition or increased competency over time) of the greater professionalism, there was agreement as to the nature of the change. Moreover, the language used to describe the change clearly reproduced relations of gender and generation. Notwithstanding the ethical commitment of the broadcasters, children's television broadcasting was increasingly conceived as a business. As a form of business, the language used to describe the programmes likewise changed. There was much discussion of the rhythm of programming. It was argued that commercial pressure lead to a new rhythm of television. There was now greater continuity between programmes. One television producer, David Goddard, was resistant to such changes. He emotively stated that:

> The fact is that on Sunday you finish your play or Sunday Special and up comes the news straight away with some terrible pictures and news of some girl being taken off into the bushes and that sort of thing. (ibid. 19)

The scheduling of programmes was clearly conceived as having moral implications. Goddard was in favour of 'proper, peaceful entertainment as opposed to commercial entertainment, which is thump, thump, thump every time.' Nevertheless, this did not imply a return to an earlier 'cosy' attitude, but a way of thinking about a modern professional children's television broadcasting. The change in the rhythm of programming was also discussed in terms of the increase in serializations and the decline in the number of single plays: 'Plays had to go in the awful thing of competition, because serials were the thing' (ibid. 30). There was a greater emphasis on filmed entertainment rather than live material. It was understood that the rhetoric of the programmes needed to be 'punchier'. A difference was mapped out between programmes such as *Whirligig, Jigsaw, Teleclub*, and the programmes aired now. Star quality was increasingly seen as important. The panel, for example, discussed the star qualities of Michael Bentine and Eamonn Andrews (both high profile children's television presenters at the time).

An important change in the language used to describe children's television programming was that the quality of a programme was now defined in terms of the programme's ability to capture an audience: 'whether a programme is good or bad is decided not only on whether it is intrinsically a good or bad programme for children, but whether it is a useful programme for keeping children with you' (ibid. 17). Reed used the phrase 'the art of being compulsive' to describe this shift. However, compulsiveness did not mean programming should be dictated by the exclusive criterion of entertainment. On the contrary, although the department had more money than in the past and although the department was larger than in the past, pragmatic programme choices had to be made. Thus in order to have two 'quality' plays rather than three 'average' plays, it was argued that a cheap Western could be used to 'fill the gap'. Individual children's programmes were seen as elements within a broader strategy of maintaining an audience. The panel talked about the audience in terms of its division according to age and about the suitability of the title 'Children's Television' for all age groups addressed. They also talked about how children were now more educated in the ways of watching television and how they switched from channel to channel according to the best programme. Reed noted that: '[Children] are more selective than adults. They hunt for their favourite title. That is why we must have a popular title in the bill every day' (ibid. 27). Although children's selective viewing (and listening) had been one of the primary goals of public service children's broadcasting, there was no discussion of how this very same technique of viewing was now thought to undermine that system: namely, that greater selectivity might lead to an increase in 'entertainment' programmes and less diversity. As one producer stated, 'The whole thing is titles. We now sell titles' (ibid. 29).

The earlier ethos of children's television (of participation and of providing a deeply embedded closeness between programmes and the everyday lives of their audience) was now foregone. Once made visible as a distinct audience (one that watched programmes other than those designed for it), a new strategy was to be pursued. Audience research was seen as important in this respect. Research could provide evidence of how children watch television and this could inform programme makers and planners in their overall strategic aim of holding an audience. And it was because of this shift in the strategic aim of children's television, that the BBC now began to take more seriously the notion that entertainment, rhythm, and scheduling were important for achieving a mass audience. Audience measurement, in this respect, would become of central importance. It would become the only way that children's broadcasters would know if their strategy was working. Nevertheless, the appeal to a mass children's audience did not mean simply becoming more commercialized or 'American'. Central to this negotiation was the way in which BBC broadcasters constructed themselves as responsible and able to provide a balanced schedule of programmes. In this sense, the mixed schedule, which had been central to an earlier ethos of participation, was now constructed not only in relation to its child audience, but also in relation to a wider range of actors who were critical of the increased commercialism and Americanization of television.

A constant thread in this discussion was whether children's television had become more 'grown-up'. As a means of thinking about and assessing the change brought about by competition, comparison was made to *Children's Hour* radio. It was argued that Lingstrom's vision of children's television was comparable to that of *Children's Hour* radio and that, as children's radio had not faced competition, it 'would now broadly represent where our programmes would have got to had it been left alone' (ibid. 24). Thus, 'an analysis of Children's Hour, Sound, its basic character and age range, is very relevant' (ibid.). Brooking posed the question 'do people think that Sound Children's Hour is less adult, on the whole, than television?' (ibid. 23). She continued, 'As far as I can see, judging by the title of their serials and the things they do, they are not less adult'. Another panellist, Shaun Sutton, replied, 'They are very juvenile' (ibid. 24). Reed pushed the question again and extended its reach:

> Do we think it more juvenile from what little we know of it? . . .
> Do we think David Davis's [Head of BBC Children's Hour radio]
> programme is more mature than ours, or less mature? Is it more
> civilised or less, more middle-class or less? (ibid.)

To which Brooking replied, 'Looking over the weeks, it is very well balanced' (ibid.). The Department of Children's Programmes' sense of itself as comparable to children's radio, and hence its sense of maintaining institutional continuity and tradition, meant that the BBC department could still claim an authority from its earlier history and not be seen as reacting solely to competition.

Reed, in summing up the discussion, stated that children's television 'would have hardened and matured in certain ways, but it would certainly give more emphasis to the needs of younger children and it would certainly be less Americanised' (ibid. 31), but also that 'as a result of competition, children's programmes have been given far more priority in the service as a whole than they would otherwise have enjoyed' (ibid. 31–2). What is striking about the use of the metaphor of children's television 'growing-up' is that, in this room full of people involved in making children's programmes, in a discussion which explicitly refers to the problems of the title of children's television, there was no reflection on its use as a way of accounting for change in the organization, no reflection on the oxymoronic ascription of children's television as 'more adult'.

The Western, the Pressure Group and the Regulator

In the press at the time, a wider public discourse framed these debates, one which favoured old 'English' institutions, such as the BBC, and feared the new Americanized culture, such as that aired by ITV. This public discourse focused, to a great extent, on the genre of the Western. This genre in particular condensed a set of problems concerning commercialism, Americanization, but also increasingly television violence.

Let me trace a brief genealogy of this discourse. In the early 1950s concerns were expressed about the use of close-ups, teeth, ghosts, and witches. In a speech to the Society of Film Teachers, which was widely reported by the press, Freda Lingstrom stated that if she were to include witches and dragons in children's programmes, 'they must on no account have teeth, for children are terrified by teeth' (*The Times*, 9 October 1953). It was particularly close-ups of teeth which were seen to be most frightening.[1] Likewise, Ursula Eason, television producer,

---

1 The speech was delivered on 4 October 1953 (cf. *Birmingham Mail*, 5 October 1953; *Manchester Guardian*, 5 October 1953). The concern about teeth is raised in the *Commissioned Report on Children's Television*. In a section on programmes which were thought to be frightening, the Report stated: 'The directors and producers of television programmes are to be warmly commended for the care they have taken in reducing frightening situations to a minimum. We feel they have taken the sting out of those things which most obviously produce fear—things which appear to be common denominators in children of varying ages and environments—for example, sudden loud noises, close-ups of intense feeling portrayed on adult faces, emotions which seem out of control, eerie music, wailing of wind in the dark, close-up shots of animal's teeth etc.' The Report went on to state that: 'without the help of psychologists, or perhaps even with it, we believe it would be impossible to make every programme fear-proof for every child. Children's fears are often quite unpredictable and are highly correlated with temperament, individual experience, the adults in the child's environment, etc.' (Jenkinson Report, 1952, WAC T16/46). The Report also mentions children being frightened by the sight of animals or other children being hurt. However, it neither catalogues the lists of contemporary concerns nor considers 'frightening' programmes with the current intensity of investment.

stated that '[g]hosts, witches, and figures with ghoulish faces are strictly censored for children' (*Daily Mail*, 11 December 1954).[2]

Although it could in no way be constituted as a child's potential fear, there was also a concern about the acceptance of gifts of programmes from the USSR. In reaction to a programme entitled *Children of the U.S.S.R.*, the *Daily Mail* alarmingly declared that 'the film was a massive propaganda job for Russia' (*Daily Mail*, 9 October 1954).[3] And while on the whole 'Britain's new TV family', as the *Daily Mirror* called it, was welcomed by the press, some did voice their criticisms of *The Appleyards* (the first British television soap opera family). Councillor F. V. Scopes, of Derbyshire Education Committee, was particularly worried about 'young people' being 'shown betting on horse racing' and teenagers smoking (*Derbyshire Advertiser*, 28 November 1952).[4] The *Daily Herald* reported that 'American-style jiving between girls in sweaters and boys without jackets has been banned from TV's *Teleclub*'. It stated that 'Viewers have complained of the tendency to "Americanise" the programme' (22 March 1954). But the BBC was caught between two camps. On 1 June 1954 the *News Chronicle* stated, with regard to *Teleclub*: 'It just doesn't click.' The majority of press reports on children's television in this period were not especially critical of either the programmes or the broadcasters, but the reporting of the Western tells a different story.

The influx of Westerns into the UK in the 1950s was partly a result of the reorganization of television in the US. The Western had become, in the 1950s, the dominant television genre in the US. Its serialized, action-adventure, filmed, entertainment form was ushered in as a risk-reducing strategy, whereby audiences would be able to view, with certainty, regular quality programming (cf. Comstock 1991). The genre, though, went into decline in the 1960s and by 1975 no Westerns were scheduled on US television. The Western, in the US as in the UK, typified a set of aesthetic and organizational struggles. Boddy has shown how, in the US, the live 'anthology' drama was being

2 Eason went on to become Assistant Head of Children's Programmes at the BBC from 1955 to 1970. The *Manchester Guardian*, which reported Eason's speech at the Institute of Education, stated that '[t]he list of proscriptions [carried out by the BBC Children's Programmes Department] merely covers obvious things such as close-ups of the grotesque and, of course, ghosts' (*Manchester Guardian*, 11 December 1954).

3 The *Daily Mail*'s concern about the programme was matched by its concern about the representation of the United States. '"Children of the U.S.S.R." was followed by a new American Western film series. Thud went the hooves and bang went the rifle. "He didn't have a chance," said the range rider examining the first body' (*Daily Mail*, 9 October 1954).

4 This was at odds with most of the reporting, which stated that, even though it was shown within children's programmes, *The Appleyards* would appeal to 'thousands of women with TV sets who devotedly follow Mrs. Dale and the Archers on radio'. The Appleyard family were described as 'ordinary, workaday folk' (*Daily Mirror*, 2 October 1952).

replaced by the filmed series and how the centre of production had shifted from New York to Hollywood (1990). Moreover, the writer was increasingly becoming secondary to the producer as the creative heart of television production (cf. Comstock 1991; Newcomb and Alley 1983). Boddy has argued that:

> By the early 1960s commercial television in the United States had achieved unprecedented levels of set ownership (91 per cent of all US households in 1963), audience viewing (over five hours a day), and advertising revenues within the commercial and regulatory structures which would remain generally stable for the subsequent two decades. The period also marks the confident march of American program exporters in pursuit of a burgeoning international TV programming market. (1991: 1)

Given the limited resources available to both BBC and ITV children's television producers, the UK was eagerly seen as a major English-language market for US programmes.

The reaction to the Western in the UK press, even in the early 1950s, was dramatic. The reporting was slow to build up, but build up it did, mobilizing a range of criticisms and condensing a number of television genres into the single problematic figure of the Western. The *Birmingham Post* reported that George L. Reakes, Chairman of Wallasey Juvenile Court, had criticized the showing of *Murder on the Yukon*. Reakes asserted that it was 'not fit even for adults'. This criticism was presented within a speech about a 'wave of brutal crime' in which he attacked the 'dangerous and senseless sentimentalism which inspires opposition to restoration of corporal punishment' (*Birmingham Post*, 5 November 1952). The *Wallasey News* added that the programme provided 'a demonstration for murder, theft with violence, fighting and battery on a full scale' and that 'such television stories could do nothing but harm to children and prepare the groundwork for more juvenile delinquency' (*Wallasey News*, 8 November 1952).

The press though was not uniformly hostile to the Western. The *Evening Standard* enthusiastically quoted Freda Lingstrom, after her recent appointment as Head of Children's Programmes at the BBC:

> So long as we have nothing frightening, nothing cruel and nothing 'vulgar', nothing is barred. I am fully in sympathy with the children's desire for a good healthy Western or having clowns—or whatever it is. (*Evening Standard*, 9 October 1951)

In 1953 the *Liverpool Echo*, in an interview with Lingstrom, stated that 'Western films cause no alarm in children' and that, because the genre is so 'remote' from the children's lives, they 'count Westerns good entertainment and aren't a bit worried by flying arrows and bullets' (*Liverpool Echo*, 28 September 1953). There were, though, parents who were worried about Westerns. Lingstrom was reported in the *Manchester Guardian* as saying that, while the children made no complaints, there was a 'large group of parents who had a strong reaction to "Western" shows'. She went on to say how these parents always referred to Westerns as 'gangster films' (*Manchester Guardian*, 5 October 1953).[5] At this time, although some individual press reports were dramatic, there was no widespread concern about the Western or television violence. Even when Mr M. Gordon, psychology tutor at the Extra-Mural Department of Birmingham University, who had published research into adolescent viewing (Gordon 1951), addressed the Coventry Rotary Club in 1953 concerning the way in which television could effect the moral development of children, the *Coventry Standard* simply reported that a 'large section of responsible psychiatrists said that violence on television provided a harmless outlet for the normal and natural aggressiveness of all children' (*Coventry Standard*, 28 August 1953).

The concerns expressed at this time were ones raised initially by individuals and only rarely taken up at a party political level or within orchestrated campaigns. For example, David Llewellyn, Conservative MP for Cardiff, was one of the first MPs to discuss children's television when he attacked *Billy Bunter of Greyfriars School* and *Desert Adventure* and called children's television a 'national scandal'. This outburst, though, was a specific attack on the BBC and contained within an argument for the introduction of commercial television (*The Western Mail*, 3 September 1953). In January 1954 it was reported that Llewellyn had drawn the attention of Sir Ian Jacob, the Director General, to a girl who had gone 'into hysterics on seeing the film [*Wallaby Jim of the Islands*], which depicted a man being hit on the head with a bottle, a man being whipped for theft, and fights with guns and knives'. As a result the BBC announced that 'a closer check is being kept on western and other adventure films shown on Children's TV' (*The Times*, 15 January 1954). Llewellyn had argued that he wanted to 'break down the B.B.C. monopoly, especially of children's TV' and that '[f]reedom of the air would give parents a wider choice' (*The Western Mail*, 3 September 1953). But Llewellyn was very much in a minority. Even the *Yorkshire Evening News*, in its coverage of the

---

5 The 'misrecognition' of Westerns as 'gangster films' owed much to the concerns in the 1920s and 1930s about American crime thriller films. The use of the term allowed a condensation of images of crime, Americanization, and unruly youth to be deployed in relation to the concern about the Western (cf. Pearson 1983). Lingstrom was also reported as saying that '[d]uring the controversy over the Craig and Bentley case, I was directly accused by some people who said that Bentley was looking at the children's television programme when Craig came to call for him to go on that terrible mission' (*Manchester Guardian*, 5 October 1953). Of more concern to Lingstrom and the press was the problem of children watching too much television, which Lingstrom associated with children's television viewing in the United States (*Birmingham Mail*, 5 October 1953).

story, focused on the governance of children's television viewing and not on political arguments against the BBC. The *Yorkshire Evening News* commented on 'how children's eyes can be kept away from unsuitable TV programmes' and on the problem of children 'peeping over the shoulders of their elders at the television set'. The paper also wondered whether 'the best way to solve it would be to reduce the amount of TV for the younger people, and let the children fend for themselves' (*Yorkshire Evening News*, 15 January 1954).

In the late 1950s and early 1960s a number of lobby groups began to take an interest in children's television and to articulate their concerns through the press. Notably in 1957 the Council for Children's Welfare conducted a survey of parental attitudes to children's viewing. The chairman of the Council for Children's Welfare was Dr Phyllis Dobbs and one of its vice-presidents was Sir Frederick Messer MP. The group had played an important role in a campaign against 'horror comics' in the 1950s (Barker 1984a). Their survey of parental attitudes was widely reported in the press. The *Daily Mirror* laid out the arguments of the Council for Children's Welfare side by side with a response by Sir Robert Fraser, Director General of the Independent Television Authority (*Daily Mail*, 27 November 1957). Edward Blishen, a London schoolmaster at the time, speaking for the Council for Children's Welfare, stated that parents thought that there were too many Westerns, too much American influence, too much violence 'for its own sake' and too much 'moronic' comedy. The Western carried the connotations of Americanization, violence and low-taste. Sir Robert Fraser defended the ITV service on the grounds that it 'had never been in the slightest doubt about the responsibilities towards its child viewers' and that it aimed to provide a 'balanced' service. Thus, although the attack was made against particular programme forms (and types of content), the defence was in terms of the ethical responsibility of the children's broadcaster.

In 1960 the *Evening Chronicle* argued that parents could no longer trust the BBC to 'supervise the youngsters viewing at that hour' (*Evening Chronicle*, 24 February 1960) and in 1961 there was widespread concern about a children's programme called *Paradise Walk* which, according to Owen Reed, then Head of Children's Programmes, was about 'the twin evils of hooliganism and race-hatred' (Reed, 1961, WAC P660).[6] Reed ill-advisedly stated in the same article that 'had we been doing *Oliver Twist*, which is far more violent and harrowing, this would have passed without comment' (ibid.). No sooner had he made his comment than in March 1961 Reginald Bevins, Postmaster General, joined MPs' protests in the House of Commons

---

6 See the articles and letters in: *Yorkshire Post*, 26 January 1961; *Lancashire Evening Post*, 30 January 1961; *Birmingham Mail*, 14 January, 31 January, 3 February, and 6 February 1961; and the *Beckenham Advertiser*, 9 March 1961.

against the violent killing of Nancy in the BBC Children's Programmes Department's production of *Oliver Twist*: he thought it 'brutal and quite inexcusable'. Victor Yates, Labour MP, called upon the Postmaster General to use his powers to require the BBC and ITA to refrain from showing scenes of brutality and violence when children were viewing. Dame Irene Ward, Conservative MP, asked the minister 'who advised as to what time children went to bed?' Mr Yates also raised the issue of 'four cases of boys who had been found dead from hanging after watching television programmes about crime, including hanging scenes' (*The Daily Telegraph*, 28 March 1962). Despite these protests, Owen Reed insisted that children did not share their parents' view: 'the Department had received many letters from children saying how much they enjoyed it!' (*Luton News*, 7 June 1962). Reed had argued that children's television should not shy away from violence, but that it should be presented within a moral framework:

> Of course, there are things that can damage, and against which we keep constant vigil: bad habits in a hero, sudden reversal, for shock dramatic effect, of a 'good' character into a 'bad', anything that really strikes deeply at a child's trust and sense of security, experiments inviting dangerous imitation, or bad taste. Shall I add violence?. . . It is violation rather than violence which is the enemy. (Reed, 1961, WAC P660)

Again, the defence against criticism of violence, Americanization, and commercialism was conducted through a discourse of responsibility, trust, and security. The case for interpreting the BBC's mixed schedule of programme as a form of violation was thus harder to make.

This debate, about the dramatization of violence within a Manichean world of good and bad characters, found its exemplary form in the Western. Reed had argued that 'Westerns are basically a good thing for children because they present a tremendous panoramic sweep and basic healthiness with a knight errant there for a good purpose' (*Southport Visitor*, 27 February 1960). His views echoed Sir Robert Fraser's defence of the Western and of commercial television in 1957:

> What is the moral fabric out of which television films for children are constructed? If someone would point out to me in what way they do not in general embody the salient moral values of Western civilisation, I should be obliged. (*The Times*, 7 December 1957)

And the joint BBC/ITA O'Connor Committee Report (1960), itself caught in the tension between constructing the Western (and television violence) in terms of a psychological discourse of effects and seeing it as a contemporary form of moral drama, complained that 'too often the good and bad characters in Western and modern crime series are indistinguishable in the methods they employ to achieve their different ends' (O'Connor 1960: 6). The concerns about Americanization, commercialism, and violence were in the late 1950s and early 1960s now being voiced by specific campaigning organizations and lobby groups. The Council for Children's Welfare in its submission to the Pilkington Committee (a government committee looking into the organization of broadcasting and concerns about taste and triviality) specifically focused on the Western and the crime series. They argued that, even though these programmes might deploy a moral framework, they would automatically lead to an 'accumulation of violence' (Pilkington 1962: 1202). Later, in the mid-1960s, the National Viewers' and Listeners' Association (NVLA), which had been formed, in part, as a consequence of this emerging configuration of interests and concerns, drew specific attention to a spate of hangings and other scenes of violence which had been increasingly catalogued in the local and national press.[7] In an essay entitled 'A Power in the Land', the founder of the NVLA, Mary Whitehouse, referred to the 're-enactment' of a hanging in a Western by a 12-year-old boy from Dudley in 1964 and to the dangers of children playing cowboys (Whitehouse 1967).[8] Whitehouse argued that the problem of the Western and television violence could not be reduced to a discussion of the moral framework of the programmes, but needed to be thought about in terms of the way in which violence was presented as normal: '[i]f violence is shown as normal on the television screen it will help to create a violent society' (ibid.). Counter views, such as those voiced by Dennis Potter, were rare. In the *Daily Herald* he stated that: 'If they frighten children, it is surely a "fear" which must not be judged by adult standards. Children need these symbols as much as they need a box of bricks' (24 November 1962).

The BBC attempted to distance itself from the views of pressure groups such as the NVLA, at the same time as differentiating itself from the commercial children's television service. It did so by continually constructing itself in terms of an ethos of care and supervision. The BBC Children's Television Department was able to position itself

7 See Tracey and Morrison 1979; Weeks 1981; and Newburn 1992.

8 Whitehouse referred to an article by Rosemary Ross Skinner in the *Weekend Telegraph* which discussed the 'disruptive effect [of television] on some children'. Skinner stated that: 'Where there are a lot of small children television appears to be a godsend to a mother—her little ones are presumably warm, quiet and safe. The fact that they are being exposed to a dangerous and insidious influence is not immediately apparent' (*Weekend Telegraph*, 15 July 1965, quoted in Whitehouse 1967: 71). She then went on to say that even though responsible parents might raise 'good, intelligent, independent children', they cannot account for children whose parents are not responsible. These children play, for example, with airguns as if they were cowboys: ' "Shoot you dead," he says. "Cor, wouldn't dare! I'd tell your dad." "So what? Bang, bang, you're dead." Well, not dead, just blind. And don't think this is far-fetched; it happened near here last week' (ibid.). The strength of such stories lay in their being anecdotal and commonsensical and yet drawing upon scientific authority.

as a 'responsible parent' by means of the possibility that the 'real' parent might be absent. The O'Connor Committee, for example, stressed that the main responsibilities of the broadcasters were firstly in relation to the unknown potentialities of the new medium and secondly to the 'privileged position' accorded the BBC by Parliament to act 'consistently in the public good' (O'Connor 1960: 10). It continued: 'This responsibility cannot be fulfilled if drivel, brutality and debased moral standards are significant features of the programmes provided in the peak period of family viewing' (ibid.). It is noticeable that although these responsibilities were pertinent to children's television broadcasters, they were explicitly addressed to those responsible for family programmes. The responsibility toward the child audience now clearly involved those not specifically making children's programmes.

In the Pilkington Committee Report, the ITV sector was castigated and the BBC praised for its service. The Report focused on questions of 'triviality' and 'balance', but also on representations of violence, particularly in Westerns and crime series. A survey of programme content presented by the Council for Children's Welfare provided a significant piece of evidence used by the Committee. The ITA had argued that the main responsibility of the broadcaster was to 'mirror' the tastes and values of society and that crime and violence were, and had been, a staple diet of drama. In a speech of Sir Robert Fraser submitted to the Committee, the violence of contemporary serialized drama was compared to the violence of Shakespearean and classical Greek drama. The Pilkington Committee were dismissive of such claims. Although they recognized, as had others at the time, that broadcasting could not be organized either according to notions of what the audience wanted or according to notions of what the audience needed, they were keen to assert that broadcasting, because of its power of influence, required a positive responsibility. These deliberations in turn tapped into a wider set of debates concerning the Americanization of 'English' culture. Richard Hoggart, a leading member of the Pilkington Committee and a literary critic, had typified this cultural assault in terms of the increasing influence of 'shiny barbarism' (Hoggart 1957). Quality was construed in opposition to American culture and triviality, but also in opposition to the flattening of individuality. The levelling of individuality was presented as an issue concerning the formulaic standardization of commercial television production, but also one concerning the reduction of personality and character to the level of the 'unit'. Labour MP Christopher Mayhew vilified commercial television accordingly:

It must play down to the lowest common factor in us all, treating us as units in a mass, without personality, without individuality. This is why so many commercial programmes are so utterly

without character of any kind. Long experience shows that the
perfect formula for a commercial broadcast is variety plus sex
plus crime. (Mayhew 1953: 7 quoted in Corner 1995: 164)

The television Western was caught within these tensions. An aesthetics of moral drama and noble character was played out in relation
to the Western (as a shifting signifier) but also in relation to those
claiming responsibility for the child television audience.

The BBC Children's Television Department differentiated itself on
the grounds not that it was against entertainment or the Western, but
that its basis for broadcasting to the child was predicated on a notion
of care. The BBC could claim to address the concerns of anxious parents inasmuch as it was publicly recognized as a guardian of taste and
protector of the young, but it could also begin to try to win back its
young audience from the ITV sector. Older notions of 'mixed broadcasting' were articulated with newer notions of the welfare of the child.
The commercial sector was thus typified as purely concerned with
entertainment. As a strategic move the BBC could schedule Westerns
and other popular programmes as well as maintain a moral high-
ground. Far from being popular because its conventions bore 'a close
relationship to the dominant ideology of the time' (Fiske 1987: 112),
the Western was the focus of a deeply embedded field of problems and
social relations. The Western provided the object of concern and the
mode of narration for a social drama in which the BBC could claim
moral authority as well as reorganize itself to meet the challenge of
new market conditions.

7
Postscript: Production, Markets, and Expertise

By the early 1960s, the child television audience had become a substantial and material entity. It could be invoked as a matter of concern by parents and the press alike; it could be addressed and differentiated by broadcasters; it could be researched and understood by academics; and it could become an important figure in regulatory and governmental thinking. Moreover, the distribution of responsibility, and the terms and conditions of its thinking and enactment, had been carefully demarcated between parents, broadcasters, and government. None of this, however, is to say that the child television audience was not problematic, that it stopped being the site of innovation and change, a site of new questions and solutions, but that the relations and languages of care and responsibility had become congealed in such a way that any innovation necessarily rested and leaned upon the child television audience's status as already being a recognizable object of concern.

In the 1970s and 1980s there are a number of significant shifts in children's television and the child television audience: cognitive and developmental psychology constitutes the child television viewer as a cognitive subject whose learning is facilitated through the appropriate play-centred environment; children's television becomes much more 'child-centred'; and children's television occupies more time on the schedules, most notably on the Saturday, then Sunday, then weekday morning slots. Yet despite being significant, these changes do not mark a break with the network of discourses and agencies discussed in this book so far: open planning provides the space of facilitated cognitive development; the imperative not to 'talk down' and patronize the child is yet again the mechanism through which programme makers get close to their audience; and the daily life of the child outside of school is easily filled with children's television. In contrast, the current situation is of a different order. The economic, although not the determinant, is the matrix through which these earlier problem spaces are now made intelligible and through which the child television audience is thought about and acted upon as a site of innovation.

The very nature of the child television audience is shifting, in very broad terms, from psychology to economics. Its material basis is shifting; the network of actors who conduct its conduct are changing; and the language to define the problems and issues have been radically transformed. As with the shift from the 1920s and 1930s to the 1950s and 1960s, the change to the present does not mark a complete transformation. Earlier cultural and technical forms are drawn upon, but as resources within a new strategic game. To conclude my analysis I want to consider the present. My reasons are that an analysis of the difference between present and past helps bring out the uniqueness of the initial formation of the child television audience and that my account of the 'origins' of the child television audience helps us to make intelligible the present.

In a pan-European survey of television provision for children conducted in 1996 Jay Blumler and Daniel Biltereyst state that:

> European public broadcasters have endeavoured to serve children as all-round developing personalities and future citizens for many years . . . In stark contrast, children's programmes in the more market-oriented system of US commercial television have been dominated by entertainment (mainly animated) and geared to the interests of advertisers and toy manufacturers. (1998: 5)

The authors ask whether the traditional values of public broadcasting still apply to the provision of children's television in Europe or whether a more market-oriented approach has come to dominate. Although this formulation of the problem appears to restate an old problematic concerning the fragility of public service broadcasting in the face of the hegemonic might of a US market system, the arguments are underpinned by widely recognized strategic shifts in the television environment concerning globalization, trade liberalization, increased national and international competition, new communication technologies and a diminution in the role of the state in the provision of services (cf. Sinclair, Jacka, and Cunningham 1996). Three major elements of change from the tradition have been recognized concerning the making of children's television and child audiences in the late 1980s and 1990s: the transformation of children's television production, the increasing differentiation, segmentation and hybridization of child audiences and the proliferation and dispersion of expertise regarding the child television audience. These changes mark both continuities and discontinuities with regard to the practices of children's broadcasting described in the earlier chapters of this book.

**Restructuring
Children's
Television
Production and
Professional
Training**

Recent discussion of the digitalization of television and the changing media environment often revisits, in some form or another, an earlier set of debates which surfaced in the 1980s with the setting up of a fourth channel in the UK and the generation of new organizational languages and forms of governance for television. An important element of these earlier debates was not simply the notion of Channel Four as a 'publisher-broadcaster', but wider economic, social and political issues concerning 'post-Fordism' and 'flexible specialisation' (Piore and Sabel 1984; Hall and Jacques 1989; Murray 1989; Hirst and Zeitlin 1991; Kumar 1995). In terms of television broadcasting, the breaking up of the 'cosy duopoly' of the BBC and the ITV sector was seen to usher in greater flexibility and choice in production and consumption. There is more than a hint of such arguments in the broader contemporary debates concerning 'convergence' and the impact of 'new technologies'. A form of technological determinism is linked to an economic liberalism. Together they provide, for example, the underlying logic of Bruce Tuchman's (General Manager of Global Networks at Nickelodeon) discussion of the new markets of the Commonwealth of Independent States (CIS) and the Balkan republics after the collapse of the Soviet bloc: 'On a long-term basis, the CIS and Baltic republics are going to be huge multi-channel markets, and we want to get in now when a lot of other people may be getting cold feet' (quoted in *KidsTV*, 28 September 1998). His argument, underpinned by a critique of paternalism and anti-populism, rests on an unswerving faith in the child-centred success of Nickelodeon in mobilizing its viewers: 'Nick always wins on screens—we always connect with viewers and develop a fanatical loyalty' (ibid.).

The new digital technologies are seen to accelerate the process of increasing flexibilization and choice. As Kevin Robins has argued, the basis of such arguments could be found as much in the camp of neo-liberals, as in the radical Left. The shift to greater flexibility through vertical disintegration, which had been advanced in the White Paper on Broadcasting (1988) and the subsequent Broadcasting Act of 1990 (with its statutory requirement that BBC and ITV broadcasters make up 25 per cent of their television programme schedule from independent production companies), found echoes in those who argued that flexible specialization promised 'a new political pluralism and cultural diversity, maybe a kind of socialism after Fordism' (Robins 1992: 192):

> From this perspective, the proliferation of independent producers during the course of the 1980s was a good example of a more general shift from the era of 'Fordism'—characterized by the

dominance of large, vertically integrated corporations—to a coming 'post-Fordist' era of broadcasting characterized by the vertical disintegration of large corporations and the emergence of a complex division of labour between a myriad of small and specialized firms. (ibid.)

Robins is critical of claims for flexible specialization.[1] Beyond the heyday of the workshop sector period of Channel Four, '[a]s the demand for independent production grew, supply grew faster, bringing about intensified competition within the sector' (1992: 194). The alternative source of programmes and the increased competition led to broadcasters reforming their organizational structures in order to gain higher levels of efficiency. In the BBC, this took the form of 'Producer Choice' and the new organizational divisions of commercial exploitation, transmission, commissioning, and programme production. Similarly, in the terrestrial commercial sector, ITV endowed the Network Centre with more power over commissioning and scheduling of programmes. Instead of heralding a new era of cultural diversity, 'the independent producers have come to be seen by many within the industry—including some producers themselves—as agents of rationalization' (Davis quoted in Robins 1992: 194).

It is not simply, then, that structural changes occurred, but that new organizational languages have been developed, new problems made visible, and new mechanisms for tackling such problems invented. These are issues concerning governance. The organizational language that gains credibility with the establishment of Channel Four, and is ushered in across the different sectors, has implications for the relations of governance within, and across, the television sectors. Vertical disintegration, functional differentiation (vis-à-vis commissioning and production, but also public service and market-oriented functions), and increasing autonomization of such functions introduce new problems of governance. Moreover, (perhaps as a consequence of such problems of governance) the objective of achieving cultural diversity as a corollary of production plurality has clearly faltered.[2]

How do we make sense of these changes with respect to children's television in the UK? The externalization of production (outside the traditional broadcasting centres), far from introducing greater

---

1 See also Keane (1991) and Graham (1999).

2 For example, Graham identifies four factors leading to the creation of private media monopolies: media products are expensive to produce (high fixed costs), but cheap to reproduce (low marginal costs); unit costs are low if a large audience is reached (i.e. economies of scale) and if the product is used in a variety of formats (i.e. economies of scope); in addition, there is a natural scarcity of talent (which replaces spectrum scarcity as a condition of monopoly); and finally there is a tendency to bottleneck in gateways (Graham 1999).

diversity, has made possible a continued integration and concentration of resources and has not led to an increase in aesthetic risk-taking. Some critics would even argue that there has been a serious reduction in aesthetic innovation. For example, Blumler (1992), Blumler and Biltereyst (1998), and Davies and Corbett (1997) all state that although the provision of children's programming has increased, the range of programmes has reduced and that the quality of programmes has 'dumbed down'.[3] Buckingham *et al.* are more sceptical and attempt to qualify some of the claims of the earlier research. Nevertheless, they still agree in broad terms with its findings and state that 'very little of this increase [in provision of children's programming] has been achieved through the provision of *new* programming—particularly home-produced programming' (Buckingham *et al.* 1999: 66, my italics).

The commissioner–producer relationship, far from providing greater autonomy for the producers, shifts the creative balance to the commissioner. Producers are locked into the control mechanisms of the commissioners through the form of legal, and other more informal, contracts. Small independent production companies lack the economic muscle to negotiate contracts on their own terms. Thus, for example, even healthy companies such as Ragdoll Productions (producer of *Tots TV* and *Teletubbies*) negotiated a deal such that distribution and merchandising rights for *Teletubbies* are held by the BBC for countries outside the UK, except in the US. In the US, Ragdoll sold the rights to the programme to Itsy Bitsy Entertainment for just £500,000. The programme is expected to bring in £15 million in royalties on sales of £150 million in the US market. By-and-large, many small independent production companies remain without significant assets and a long-term workforce and hence remain dependent on the control of the broadcasters (cf. Sparks 1994). Equally, existing centres of excellence for children's television production, found predominantly within the old broadcasting structures (e.g. the BBC and Carlton), are susceptible to reductions in size and face competition from other departments (both children's and non-children's production centres). Such organizational fragility is typical of, what has been termed, the new ethos of contractualism (Burchell 1993; du Gay 1996; Davis, Sullivan, and Yeatman 1997). Social relations increasingly take the form of contracts and risk is increasingly transferred downwards.[4]

3 Blumler (1992) refers to the potential changes, rather than the actual changes in quality and diversity. The claim that children's television was dumbing down was made by the Broadcasting Standards Commission in its press releases, but Davies and Corbett are more circumspect and hesitant about such claims in their report.

4 Mark Oliver has discussed this issue in relation to the ITV Network in the 1980s (Oliver 1990).

Furthermore, those few commercial organizations large enough to exploit the relation of independence are led to pursue expansionist corporate policies that encourage the merger and buy-outs of small to medium-size production companies and to maintain their own satellite of smaller service companies (companies specialized in, for example, programme packaging, post-production, or other facilities) which float in the waters at their periphery. Equally, co-production and co-finance deals allow the large corporations to share their risks as they facilitate their own expansion. For example, Nickelodeon UK signed a £15–20 million co-production deal with Granada Media to develop sixteen animation projects with at least five going into full production in the next three years. The programmes will be shown on Nickelodeon UK, but Granada will hold the international rights (*Kids TV*, 23 November 1998). However, it should also be noted that such deals are not always advantageous. For example, the BBC's involvement with a French production company in the making of *The Prince of Atlantis* was not all plain sailing, when the company went bankrupt mid-production (*Kids TV*, 28 September 1998).

Robins has argued that the concentration of capital in a relatively small number of firms is not the only issue at stake, but that '[f]lexible specialization was also about a new geography of broadcasting' (1992: 197). He refers to a report published in 1989 which found that of 459 independent production companies surveyed, 73 per cent were based in London and the South-East and that these were generally larger than the companies in the regions. In 1998 a survey of those working in children's television in the UK found a similar geographical distribution: 57 per cent lived in London, a further 25 per cent in the South of England, 13 per cent in the Midlands and the North of England, 3 per cent in Scotland and 2 per cent in Wales (Hillman and Oswell 1998). The demographic make-up of those involved in children's television broadcasting, moreover, has not changed so as to represent a greater cultural diversity.[5] Although there was an equal distribution of male and female respondents (53 per cent male, 47 per cent female) and an even distribution of respondents from across the age range of the working population, a majority of those working in children's television in the UK are white, English and from grammar or public (i.e. fee-paying) schools (Oswell 2000). Unlike the cultural intermediaries that Bourdieu describes in his work on the social construction of taste, these professionals do not comprise a 'new petite bourgeoisie' (Bourdieu 1984). Instead there seems to be a correlation between a more entrenched cultural aristocracy and the provision of children's television. Many working in children's television have

5 Buckingham *et al.* state that structural changes have 'begun to open up the industry to hitherto under-represented groups' (Buckingham *et al.* 1999: 73). Hillman and Oswell's findings suggest that, although this might be happening, it is not a significant factor yet.

specifically chosen to work in a 'creative industry' over and above any specific desire to make programmes for children. The old ethos of children's broadcasting has clearly seen its day. Moreover, despite claims regarding the professionalism of children's television broadcasters, there is no formal training and there is high job mobility. [6] Children's television producers have no sustained formal or informal means of training or systematic means of apprenticeship that would explicitly equip them for the very specific problems and issues raised when dealing with a child television audience.

Niches Audiences and Global Markets

Despite recent attempts by the new Director General of the BBC, Greg Dyke (2000–) to return the BBC to its core values of creativity and programming, and to restructure the BBC, there is little evidence that there is a recognition of the need for specialist training for those involved in children's television given the current flexibility in the labour market. Instead of functional divisions between commissioning and production, Dyke has returned to an older notion of 'sociability and solidarity' (*The Guardian*, 3 April 2000). He has also declared the BBC's commitment to children's television by announcing two new digital children's television channels (one pre-school, the other for older children). These fall short, though, of fully addressing the problem, which is not simply about the number of dedicated channels or the amount of air-time, but the reproduction of children's television programming as a 'quality' service inasmuch as the centres of children's television production are also centres of knowledge and expertise vis-à-vis children's television.

The BBC strategy of increasing its children's television output through establishing a portfolio of dedicated channels is not untypical of the UK market nor of other national markets. In the UK there are already ten children's channels and five terrestrial broadcasters providing children's television. In addition to the proposed BBC children's television channels, Disney is establishing three new children's channels (3 September 2001, *Broadcast*). Despite fears voiced by children's television campaigners, such as British Action for Children's Television (BACTV) in the UK and Action for Children's Television (ACT) in the US, that 'deregulation' would lead to the death of children's television, there has clearly been a proliferation of dedicated channels and an increase in provision generally.

---

6 In this sense, although I use the term 'professional', it is highly problematic with respect to this group of workers. Although not purely a notional application, it neither simply identifies an 'interpretative community' (Buckingham *et al.* 1999: 73) nor a form of status and expertise in normative terms (cf. Abbott 1988; Elliott 1979; Macdonald 1995; Perkins 1989).

The new children's television market is divided in terms of *generalist* provision (i.e. catering for all age ranges of children) normally on terrestrial services in the UK and *segmented niche* channels targeted to particular audience constituencies (i.e. pre-school, middle-childhood, youth, and family). Whereas in conditions of spectrum scarcity, time is scheduled according to particular aged-based constituencies of audience, in conditions of plenty the branding of separate channels becomes the means through which audiences are differentiated.

In the late 1980s campaigners had assumed that certain specialized children's television markets (e.g. pre-school children's television) would suffer because of the limited size of their national audiences. In the twenty-first century, the thinking is that markets are increasingly global. Specialization goes hand-in-hand with globalization. Hoskins, McFayen, and Finn state that '[n]iche channels directed at narrow audience segments would become more viable, but aggregating demand across space (international markets) and time' (1997: 133). Moreover they argue that:

> Implementation [of segmentation strategies] requires selection
> of the target audience segment and positioning of the offering
> to attract members of the target segment . . . Grounds for . . .
> similarities [in consumer responses] can be identified across
> different national markets and provide the opportunity for
> standardization based on serving cross-national segments.
> (1997: 119)

Programmes can be shown on specialist segmented children's television channels in a number of national contexts. Moreover, these programmes are either produced, or rights for distribution held, by a relatively small number of dedicated children's television channels (or their parent companies): primarily Nickelodeon, Fox Kids, and Disney. It is this market that the BBC is increasingly interested in.

The trend toward niche audiences/global markets in children's television is a complex phenomenon. A number of strategies are visible which play on the cross-over value of children's television in addressing multiple constituencies of audience. First, Marsha Kinder has put forward the concept of 'transgenerational address' as a way of explaining how a single text (whether film or television programme) is able to address generationally different audiences. She argues that films such as *Home Alone* address both adults and children. She argues that 'this convergence of generations moves in both directions—not only are adult spectators "paedocratised" but also young spectators are encouraged to adopt adult tastes, creating subject positions for a dual audience of infantilised adults and precocious children' (1995: 77).

Second, we see forms of children's television programme that very explicitly target one age-group of children, but which are then taken up by a range of other audience constituencies. In some ways, pre-school children's television has always addressed both parental and child audiences as a means of facilitating inter-generational talk and the child's cognitive development and so on. Unlike the strategy deployed in *Home Alone,* this form of multiple address does not necessarily lead to a convergence of adult and child positions. *Tele-tubbies* was a prime example of one form of this lack of convergence. *Teletubbies* was ostensibly addressed to a young pre-school audience, but clearly found favour with both teenagers and adults and quickly became a focus of national discussion and interest, not just in the UK, but globally.

Third, we can document a strategy typically used by Disney in marketing its movies as 'classics'. The marketing of films from *Pinocchio* to *Pocohontas* places them in a timeless realm of the classic such that they can be shown and reshown endlessly in a way that plays on the dominant cultural connotations of childhood as timeless and a-historical (cf. Mattelart and Dorfman 1975; Forgacs 1992). Buckingham, for example, argues that:

> one could argue that the core of Disney resides in a certain notion of *childhood*—a notion which can, of course, be sold to both children and adults. It is this dual address which would seem to be crucial to Disney's appeal: Disney both constructs and speaks to elements of children's lived experience, while providing adults with opportunities for nostalgic fantasies about their own past. (1997: 286)

The re-selling of the BBC's *Watch with Mother* on video in the 1980s was another example of a transgenerational address. Parents bought the old black and white videos to be watched as classic children's television. Television companies have long been aware that existing archives of old children's television programmes can to be drawn on to gather mixed child and adult audiences through forms of trans-generational address.

And fourth, the children's television audience is one that is con-stantly reproduced anew. As one generation of children grow up, a new generation can be shown the same programmes. Jane Lighting, Managing Director of Minotaur International, has suggested that:

> Broadcasters assume that because a few programmes can be such a big merchandising hit they don't need to invest as much. And they see kids' programmes have a longer shelf life than other genres, so can earn money back in that way. (quoted in *Broadcast,* 24 September 1999)

Bob the Builder (an animated television series for pre-school children, shown in sixty-six countries and fourteen languages) can be shown to today's 3 to 4-year-olds and tomorrow's and so on. Peter Orton, Chief Executive of HIT, producer of *Bob the Builder*, has argued that 'old shows can be shown again and again. It keeps costs low' (*The Guardian*, 5 February 2000). As Emory Woodard, in a report on children's television for the Annenberg Public Policy Center, University of Pennsylvania, explains: '[t]he explosion of programs is not the result of a burgeoning production community. Though many new shows are airing, one still sees a large percentage of shows from the 1950s, 1960s, 1970s and 1980s' (1999: 3).

One of the problems that arises from this highly differentiated complex of markets is that the strategy of niche audience/global market favours forms of programming that address a global audience, albeit differentiated by age. This is a problem concerning the types of programme that will get made. As Celia Leaberry, analyst for Dresdner Kleinwort Benson, has argued of HIT and Brit Allcroft:

> Their programmes do not carry any cultural baggage when they are dubbed. With drama it can be more of a problem. Thomas the Tank Engine is sold to 120 countries, broadcast in 11 languages and is one of the most popular licensed characters in Japan.
> (quoted in *The Guardian*, 5 February 2000)

Typically concern has been expressed about animation and programmes imported from the US. Blumler and Biltereyst have noted that, although 'careful to avoid exaggeration . . . one sees certain North American patterns glimmering through many European public channels' approaches to children: in the intensification of scheduling strategies to build loyalty and habit among young viewers; in reduced diversity and higher proportions of animation; and in a growing dependency on US imports (Americanization literally!)' (1998: 33). The problem though is not animation or US imports *per se*, but the reduction in traditional forms of children's television, such as drama, news, documentaries, and culturally specific programmes, and the devaluation of traditional notions of programme diversity within a mixed schedule. Animation is seen to have, what Hoskins has termed, a low 'cultural discount': 'A particular television programme, film, or video rooted in one culture, and thus attractive in the home market where viewers share a common knowledge and way of life, will have a diminished appeal elsewhere, as viewers find it difficult to identify with the style, values, beliefs, history, myths, institutions, physical environment, and behavioural patterns' (Hoskins *et al.* 1997: 32). Thus children's television programmes which carry signs of national cultural specificity are less likely to be made in conditions where broadcasters employ a segmentary, rather than generalist strategy and where producers hope to recoup their investment across different national markets. In addition, given the importance of marketing tie-ins as a source of revenue, and given the dominance of certain global toy brands (such as Mattel and Hasboro), producers are less likely to produce programmes which are not able to sell programme-related products across national contexts.

However, the emergence of these new conditions for children's television production and distribution has not yet led to a transnational unitary global children's television market. At present, there are a number of nationally and regionally differentiated, or discriminated, markets, rather than a single global market. The pricing of children's television programmes is differentiated according to the relative value of these markets. For example, the BBC or ITV pay $20,000–100,000 per fifty minutes of US programming, whereas in Zimbabwe the price is $200–250 (Hoskins *et al.* 1997: 69).[7] There is no universal price for programmes. Price discrimination occurs as a result of the seller's ability to separate markets (such as through licence agreements), their relative market power in setting a price and price elasticity of demand (i.e. the differential elasticity of demand within different markets).

Thus programme rights can be negotiated and differentiated in order to gain the highest revenues. The global distribution capacity of the Internet clearly adds yet further changes. Nevertheless, as is still the case with television programmes generally, given the size of the US domestic market and given its relative dominance vis-à-vis cultural discount (namely the acceptance of US programmes globally in contrast to the reluctance of US consumers to accept non-US programmes), the US has maintained a competitive advantage over non-US countries. Although specifically in relation to children's television (because of the low cultural discount of animation) US dominance is open to contestation, in practice due to the global spread of US-centred children's television channels, such as Disney, Fox Kids, and Nickelodeon, these channels carry much weight in terms of distributing their home-grown programmes globally across their channels or in owning the rights to programmes, produced by independent production companies, shown on their channels. Thus although content has a prime value ('content is king') in global markets, the control of the means of distribution and programme rights is still a central axiom of power. Drawing on a different critical language, Nicholas Garnham stated some years ago regarding the film industry that: 'If we want to examine "the real relations" of the movie business rather than "its phenomenal form" it is upon distribution that it is necessary to focus' (1990: 183). His statement is still applicable to the television industry today.

---

7 These figures are indicative of the relative price differences, rather than actual prices for children's television programmes per fifty minutes.

The Proliferation of Expertise

In these new conditions of production and distribution, research has taken on a primary importance. Just as audience measurement technologies in the 1950s and 1960s helped constitute one of the defining features of post-war television, so the new niche markets and specialized television channels are reliant on reliable data about their audiences. As Barnes and Thomson argue:

> the logic of the specialization process—that smaller, more homogeneous audiences offer advertisers more value per person than larger, more heterogeneous audiences—requires acceptable audience data to operate. Without that data, the audience has no reality for advertisers and, consequently, no value (or, at least, greatly reduced value relative to a 'known' audience). And, if the audience has no value, the medium will not attract advertiser support. Thus audience measurement technologies play a vital role in sustaining the media whose audiences they measure. (1994: 91–2)

Audience measurement technologies are supplemented increasingly by sustained market research into programmes and audience reactions. Ellen Wartella, for example, quotes Linda Kahn, then vice president of production at Nickelodeon:

> We don't buy the series unless we go out and test it with kids . . . We talk about them on a lot of levels, just on the shows themselves, on the characters, on what happened, on what they think might happen in other episodes, on things they might like to see happen . . . And being in touch with the constituency is the key in anything we do. (quoted in Wartella 1994: 49)

Market research has become a major factor in programme development, but is also important in testing broader public reaction to programmes which might be seen as potentially problematic.

In addition to market research, Wartella argues that a different kind of research is used in programme development and to evaluate children's reactions to programme content. She refers to 'formative research' as that which is conducted 'before and during the production of a television series' and 'summative research' as that which 'is conducted to ascertain the effects of the program on child audiences and whether or not the educational goals were met' (1994: 50). In particular, she refers to the Children's Television Workshop, the producers of *Sesame Street*, and to the kind of research which is explicitly aimed at evaluating the educational content and impact of certain forms of programming. She states that 'while both educational and commercial children's television increasingly use consultants, advisers, and research to create programs, the research is directed at different goals and different sets of needs' (1994: 51). Wartella, in making this distinction, tends to simplify the goals of commercial research in terms of its ability 'to assess what children will watch, what they enjoy, what will sell to them' (ibid.). But the distinction between the educational and commercial value of research is far from clear-cut. One of the strategies that has been used to accredit a programme with educational value—irrespective of whether the programme 'really is' educational or commercial—is the use of academic consultants. Thus for programmes ranging from *Sesame Street* to *He-Man and the Masters of the Universe*, academic consultants have been adopted as advisers and named in the programme credits. Heather Hendershot, in her discussion of *Fat Albert*, argues that:

> There is no question that *Fat Albert* was legitimized as an educational cartoon, at least in part, by the educators involved in the show's production. The scripts were reviewed by a panel of sociologists, educators, and psychologists, all Ph.D.'s credited in each episode . . . The intellectual clout of the people who worked on *Fat Albert* helped establish the show as quality entertainment in spite of its status as a TV cartoon. (1998: 196)

Although Hendershot tends to overplay the use of Ph.D. consultants, she identifies an important strategy deployed by children's television programme makers in order to accredit their programmes with educational value. Academic consultants were hired by Filmation, the production company which made *Fat Albert*, to advise on *He-Man* and were used to fend off criticisms regarding its merchandising tie-ins and its representations of gender. The important issue here is that academic expertise is always subsumed within the economic concerns of the company: either reports are not released into the public domain or paid-for advice is not taken or just that expertise is taken selectively.

The distinction between commercial and educational programming has become increasingly problematic in the US, since the 1990 Children's Television Act and the Federal Communications Commission (FCC) regulation concerning, what has been termed, the 'Three-Hour Rule'. The Children's Television Act required every station to broadcast material that 'furthers the positive development of the child in any respect, including the child's cognitive/intellectual or emotional/social needs' (FCC 1991: 2114), to limit advertising on children's programmes to twelve minutes per hour on weekdays and ten and a half minutes per hour at weekends and to provide funding for educational programming through the National Endowment for Children's Educational Television (NECET). The three-hour rule, which became effective from September 1997, obliges broadcasters to air, between 7 a.m. and 10 p.m., a minimum of three hours of educational or informational television which is designed to meet the above needs of children under the age of 16. Moreover, broadcasters are required to label such programming both on-screen and in television listings. The Children's Television Act and the FCC regulations were clearly designed to improve the quality of children's television in the US. One of the effects of these changes, though, has been to increase the amount of outside experts involved in the making and accreditation of children's television. Amy Jordan, in a report for the Annenberg Public Policy Center, University of Pennsylvania, states that '[w]hether to ensure that the programs are meeting the spirit of the regulations or whether to obtain a seal of approval, programmers and producers are now regularly involving outside educational experts, or consultants, in their process' (1999: 12). One network executive quoted in the report explained that:

> There was enough ambiguousness in the law, there was enough to cause the creative community to say, 'We may need the help of somebody who knows more about child development and education than we do.' And I think it was a very legitimate need, and it resulted in a greater outreach to that community. (quoted in Jordan 1999: 12)

Thus, although since the 1950s academic experts had been consulted in the development of pre-school programmes and more widely in ascertaining the social and psychological impact of television, from the 1980s academic experts have been drawn on more concertedly in the development of a range of programmes and more widely across the production process. In this sense, the use of academic expertise does not represent a departure from earlier practices so much as an intensive proliferation. Moreover, academic expertise is now strategically positioned both to strengthen regulatory arguments regarding the need for more 'educational' programmes and also, by commercial companies, as a resource to counter such arguments.

The new economic language of children's television and the child television audience is the leading edge of a deeper socio-technical reorganization. The language articulates the restructuring of relations of production, the segmentation and address to child audiences and the commercialization of relations of expertise and knowledge. At the beginning of the twenty-first century, children's television is burgeoning. But where once the imperative was to make programmes within a mixed schedule commensurate with the population of children watching at home, the objective now has radically changed. No longer is it possible to make a close correlation between children's television and its child audience. Not only are children clearly documented as watching family and adult programmes (even identifying such programmes as their favourites), but children's programmes themselves are designed to address a much wider constituency than just children. Moreover, where once children's broadcasting was perceived as a chosen vocation, as a way of living out one's being for the child (as an ethos), now it has become a job, such that the particular skills and knowledges required to address a very particular audience are now contracted out to various experts outside of broadcasting proper and with little control over its outcome.

Bibliography

Files Consulted at the BBC Written Archives

When referring, in the text of the book, to material from the BBC Written Archives at Caversham (WAC), I use their file index notation (e.g. T16/45/1). I have not referred to specific sub-sections of files.

R11/27—Children's Hour—General Correspondence 1923–1938
R11/51—Children's Hour—Policy 1939–1963
R11/57—Children's Hour—Radio Circle 1926–1933
R11/58—Children's Hour—Radio Circle 1926–1933

R9—Audience Research
VR—Viewer Research

T2—Television Children's Programmes
T16/45—Television Policy—Children's Programmes 1946–1966
T16/46—Television Policy—Children's Programmes: Commissioned Report on Children's Television 1951–1952
T16/68—Television Policy—Eyes and Eyestrain 1949–1953
T16/166—Television Policy—Programme Policy—Unsuitability for Children 1938–1966
T16/303—Nuffield Foundation Enquiry 1953–1959
T16/689—Himmelweit 1959–1960

P654, P657, P660—Press Cuttings—Television Programmes 1950–1962
P37—Press Cuttings—General Policy 1955–1958

Periodicals and Newspapers

BBC Handbook
BBC Quarterly
BBC Yearbook
Beckenham Advertiser
Birmingham Mail
The Birmingham Post
Coventry Standard
Daily Express
Daily Herald
Daily Mail
Daily Mirror
Daily Sketch
The Daily Star
The Daily Telegraph
Derbyshire Advertiser
The Economist
Evening Chronicle

Evening Standard
Everywoman
Good Housekeeping
The Guardian
Home and Garden
The Independent
Ideal Home
Lancashire Evening Post
Liverpool Echo
Luton News
Manchester Guardian
National Viewers' and Listeners' Association Newsletter
News Chronicle
New Statesman and Nation
The Observer
The Sketch

—— and WOOLLACOTT, JANET (1987), *Bond and Beyond: The Political Career of a Popular Hero* (Basingstoke: Macmillan).

BENTON, CHARLOTTE (1990), 'Le Corbusier: Furniture and the Interior', *Journal of Design History*, 3(2–3).

BILLIG, MICHAEL (1997), 'From Codes to Utterances: Cultural Studies, Discourse and Psychology', in Ferguson, Marjorie, and Golding, Peter (eds.), *Cultural Studies in Question* (London: Sage).

BIRK, ALMA (1957), 'Captive Children', *New Statesman*, 14 December.

BLAIR HILTY, ELEANOR (1997), 'From *Sesame Street* to *Barney and Friends*: Television as Teacher', in Steinberg, Shirly R., and Kincheloe, Joe L. (eds.), *Kinder Culture: The Corporate Construction of Childhood* (Oxford: Westview Press).

BLISHEN, EDWARD (1958), 'The Mechanical Nanny', *New Statesman*, 4 October.

BLUMLER, JAY (1992), *The Future of Children's Television in Britain: An Enquiry for the Broadcasting Standards Council* (London: Broadcasting Standards Council).

—— and BILTEREYST, DANIEL (1998), *The Integrity and Erosion of Public Television for Children: A Pan-European Study* (London: Broadcasting Standards Commission).

BODDY, WILLIAM (1985), ' "The Shining Centre of the Home": Ontologies of Television in the "Golden Age" ', in Drummond, Phillip, and Paterson, Richard (eds.), *Television in Transition* (London: British Film Institute).

—— (1991), 'TV in Trouble: The Politics of Prime-Time Violence in 1960s American Television', paper presented to the *International Television Studies Conference* (London: British Film Institute).

—— (1994), 'Archaeologies of Electronic Vision and the Gendered Spectator', *Screen* 35(2).

BOURDIEU, PIERRE (1984), *Distinction: A Social Critique of the Judgement of Taste* (Cambridge, Massachusetts: Harvard University Press).

BOWLBY, JOHN (1965), *Child Care and the Growth of Love* (Harmondsworth: Penguin).

BOYS, JOS, *et al.* (1984), 'House Design and Women's Roles', in Matrix (ed.), *Making Space: Women and the Man-Made Environment* (London: Pluto Press).

BRIGGS, ASA (1961), *The Birth of Broadcasting: The History of Broadcasting in the United Kingdom*, vol. 1 (Oxford: Oxford University Press).

—— (1965), *The Golden Age of Wireless: The History of Broadcasting in the United Kingdom*, vol. 2 (Oxford: Oxford University Press).

—— (1979), *Governing the BBC* (London: BBC).

—— (1985), *The BBC: The First Fifty Years* (Oxford: Oxford University Press).

BRIGGS, SUSAN (1981), *Those Radio Times* (London: Weidenfeld and Nicolson).

BRISTOW, JOSEPH (1991), *Empire Boys: Adventures in a Man's World* (London: Harper Collins).

BRUNSDEN, CHARLOTTE (1981), '*Crossroads*: Notes on Soap Opera', *Screen* 22(4).

BRYANT, SARA CONE (1910), *How to Tell Stories to Children* (London: George G. Harrap and Co.).

BUCKINGHAM, DAVID (1993a), *Children Talking Television: The Making of Television Literacy* (London: Falmer Press).

—— (1993b), 'Introduction: Young People and the Media', in Buckingham, David (ed.), *Reading Audiences: Young People and the Media* (Manchester: Manchester University Press).

—— (1995), 'On the Impossibility of Children's Television: The Case of Timmy Mallett', in Bazalgette, Cary, and Buckingham, David (eds.), *In Front of the Children: Screen Entertainment and Young Audiences* (London: British Film Institute).

—— (1997), 'Dissin' Disney: Critical Perspectives on Children's Media Culture', *Media,Culture and Society*, 19.

—— HANNAH DAVIES, KEN JONES, and PETER KELLEY (1999), *Children's Television in Britain: History, Discourse and Policy* (London: British Film Institute).

BURCHELL, GRAHAM (1993), 'Liberal Government and Techniques of the Self', *Economy and Society*, 22(3).

BURNETT, JOHN (1986), *A Social History of Housing, 1815–1985* (London: Routledge).

BURT, CYRIL (1949), 'The Psychology of Listeners', *BBC Quarterly*, 4(2).

CANTOR, MURIEL (1987), *The Hollywood TV Producer* (New Brunswick, NJ: Transaction).

—— (1994), 'The Role of the Audience in the Production of Culture: A Personal Research Retrospective', in Ettema, James S., and Whitney, D. Charles (eds.), *Audiencemaking: How the Media Create the Audience* (London: Sage).

CAPON, NAOMI (1952), 'The Child and the Dragon', *BBC Quarterly*, 6.

CHAMBERS, DEBORAH (1991), 'Domestic Communication Technology: The Television Cabinet's Design Message', paper presented to the *International Television Studies Conference* (London: British Film Institute).

COLLINS, RICHARD, and MURRONI, CHRISTINA (1996), *New Media, New Policies: Media and Communications Strategies for the Future* (Cambridge: Polity Press).

COMSTOCK, GEORGE (1991), *Television in America*, 2nd edn. (London: Sage).

CORNER, JOHN (1991), 'The Interview as Social Encounter', in Scannell, Paddy (ed.), *Broadcast Talk* (London: Sage).

—— (ed.) (1991), *Popular Television in Britain: Studies in Cultural History* (London: British Film Institute).

—— (1995), *Television Form and Public Address* (London: Edward Arnold).

CORRIGAN, PHILIP (1983), 'Film Entertainment as Ideology and Pleasure: A Preliminary Approach to a History of Audiences', in Curran, James, and Porter, Vincent (eds.), *British Cinema History* (London: British Film Institute).

CROOME, HONOR (1949), 'The Family Listens', *BBC Quarterly*, 4.

CUNNINGHAM, STUART, and JACKA, ELIZABETH (1996), *Australian Television and International Mediascapes* (Cambridge: Cambridge University Press).

CURRIE, DAVID, and SINER, MARTIN (1999), 'The BBC: Balancing Public and Commercial Purpose', in Graham, *et al. Public Purpose in Broadcasting: Funding the BBC* (Luton: University of Luton Press).

DE CORDOVA, RICHARD (1994), 'The Mickey in Macey's Window: Childhood, Consumerism and Disney Animation', in Smoodin, Eric (ed.), *Disney Discourse* (London: British Film Institute).

DAVIDOFF, L., L'ESPERANCE, J., and NEWBY, H. (1976), 'Landscape with Figures: Home and Community in English Society', in Mitchell, Juliet, and Oakley, Ann (eds.), *The Rights and Wrongs of Women* (Harmondsworth: Penguin).

DAVIES, MAIRE MESSENGER, and CORBETT, BETH (1997), *The Provision of Children's Television in Britain: 1992–1996: An Enquiry for the Broadcasting Standards Commission* (London: Broadcasting Standards Commission).

DAVIS, GLYN, BARBARA SULLIVAN, and ANNA YEATMAN (1997), *A New Contractualism?* (Melbourne: Macmillan Press).

DONALD, JAMES (1992), *Sentimental Education* (London: Verso).

DONZELOT, JACQUES (1979), *The Policing of Families* (London: Hutchinson).

DRIBURG, TOM (1958), 'Father of the Man', *New Statesman*, 20 December.

DROTNER, KIRSTEN (1988), *English Children and their Magazines, 1751–1945* (Yale: Yale University Press).

DU GAY, PAUL (1996), 'Organizing Identity: Entrepreneurial Governance and Public Management', in Hall, Stuart, and du Gay, Paul (eds.), *Questions of Cultural Identity* (London: Sage).

DUGGAN, E. P. (1955), 'Children at the Television Set', *Times Educational Supplement*, 11 November.

ELLIOTT, PHILIP (1979), *The Sociology of the Professions* (London: Routledge and Kegan Paul).

EMMISON, MICHAEL, and GOLDMAN, LAURENCE (1997), '*The Sooty Show* Laid Bear: Children, Puppets and Make-Believe', *Childhood* 4(3).

ETTEMA, JAMES S., and WHITNEY, D. CHARLES (eds.) (1994), *Audiencemaking: How the Media Create the Audience* (London: Sage).

FARR, MICHAEL (1955), *Design in British Industry: A Mid-Century Survey* (Cambridge: Cambridge University Press).

FERGUSON, BOB (1984), 'Black Blue Peter', in Masterman, Len (ed.), *Television Mythologies: Stars, Shows and Signs* (London: Comedia).

—— (1985), 'Children's Television: The Germination of Ideology', in Lusted, David, and Drummond, Phillip (eds.), *TV and Schooling* (London: British Film Institute).

FISKE, JOHN (1987), *Television Culture* (London: Methuen).

FRANCIS, SUE (1984), 'Housing the Family', in Matrix (ed.), Making *Space: Women and the Man-Made Environment* (London: Pluto Press).

FORGACS, DAVID (1992), 'Disney Animation and the Business of Childhood', *Screen*, 33(4).

FORTY, ADRIAN (1986), *Objects of Desire: Design and Society, 1750–1980* (London: Thames and Hudson).

FOUCAULT, MICHEL (1977), *Discipline and Punish* (London: Allen Lane).

—— (1979), *The History of Sexuality*, vol. 1 (London: Allen Lane).

—— (1980), 'The Eye of Power', in Gordon, Colin (ed.), *Michel Foucault: Power/Knowledge* (Brighton: Harvester Press).

FRASER, SIR ROBERT (1957), 'What Children Should See', *The Times*, 7 December.

FRITH, SIMON (1983), 'The Pleasures of the Hearth', in *Formations of Pleasure* (London: Routledge).

FURU, T. (1962), *Television and Children's Lives: A Before-After Study* (Tokyo: Japan Broadcasting Corporation).

GARNHAM, NICHOLAS (1990), *Capitalism and Communication: Global Culture and the Economics of Information* (London: Sage).

GORDON, M. (1951), 'Report on a Survey by the Coventry University Tutorial Class on the Adolescent and Television', unpublished manuscript, Coventry.

GRAHAM, ANDREW (1999), 'Broadcasting Policy in the Multimedia Age', in Graham, Andrew *et al.*, *Public Purpose in Broadcasting: Funding the BBC* (Luton: University of Luton Press).

GRIFFIN, SEAN (1999), 'Kings of the Wild Backyard: Davy Crockett and Children's Space', in Kinder, Marsha (ed.), *Kids Media Culture* (Durham and London: Duke University Press).

HALL, STUART, and SCHWARZ, BILL (1985), 'State and Society, 1880–1930', in Langan, Mary, and Schwarz, Bill (eds.), *Crises in the British State, 1880–1930* (London: Hutchinson).

—— and JACQUES, MARTIN (eds.) (1989), *New Times: The Changing Face of Politics in the 1990s* (London: Lawrence and Wishart).

HARALOVICH, MARY BETH (1988), 'Suburban Family Sitcoms and Consumer Product Design: Addressing the Social Subjectivity of Homemakers in the 1950s', in Drummond, Phillip, and Paterson, Richard (eds.), *Television and Its Audiences* (London: British Film Institute Press).

HARAWAY, DONNA (1997), *Modest_Witness@Second_Millennium. FemaleMan_Meets_OncoMouse* (New York: Routledge).

HARTLEY, IAN (1983), *Goodnight Children Everywhere* (London: Weidenfeld).

HARTLEY, JOHN (1987), 'Television Audiences, Paedocracy and Pleasure', *Textual Practice*, 1(2).

HENDERSHOT, HEATHER (1998), *Saturday Morning Censors: Television Regulation before the V-Chip* (Durham, NC: Duke University Press).

HENDRICK, HARRY (1990), 'Constructions and Reconstructions of British Childhood: An Interpretative Survey, 1800 to the Present', in James, Alison, and Prout, Alan (eds.), *Constructing and Reconstructing Childhood* (London: Falmer Press).

HILL, JOHN (1991), 'Television and Pop: the Case of the 1950s', in Corner, John (ed.), *Popular Television in Britain: Studies in Cultural History* (London: British Film Institute).

HILLMAN, SAUL, and OSWELL, DAVID (1998), *Children's Television Broadcasting: Backgrounds and Perceptions of Broadcasters in Children's Television in the 1990s* (London: Brunel University).

HIMMELWEIT, H., OPPENHEIM, A. N., and VINCE, P. (1958), *Television and the Child* (Oxford: Oxford University Press).

HIRST, PAUL (1981), 'The Genesis of the Social', *Politics and Power*, 3 (London: Routledge Kegan Paul).

—— , and ZEITLIN, J. (1991), 'Flexible Specialisation versus Post-Fordism', *Economy and Society*, 20(1).

HOGGART, RICHARD (1957), *The Uses of Literacy* (London: Chatto and Windus).

HOLLAND, PATRICIA (1992), *What is a Child? Popular Images of Childhood* (London: Virago).

—— (1996), ' "I've just seen a hole in the reality barrier!": Children, Childishness and the Media in the Ruins of the Twentieth Century', in Pilcher, J., and Wagg, S. (eds.), *Thatcher's Children* (London: Falmer Press).

HOLT, JOHN (1975), *Escape from Childhood: The Needs and Rights of Children* (Harmondsworth: Penguin).

HOME, ANNA (1993), *Into the Box of Delights* (London: British Broadcasting Corporation).

HOSKINS, COLIN, MCFADYEN, STUART, and FINN, ADAM (1997), *Global Television and Film: An Introduction to the Economics of the Business* (Oxford: Oxford University Press).

JAMES, ALISON, and PROUT, ALAN (eds.) (1990), *Constructing and Reconstructing Childhood* (London: Falmer Press).

JENNINGS, HILDA, and GILL, WINIFRED (1939), *Broadcasting in Everyday Life: A Survey of the Social Effects of the Coming of Broadcasting* (London: British Broadcasting Corporation).

JORDAN, AMY (1999), *The Three-Hour Rule: Insiders' Reactions* (Pennsylvania: Annenberg Public Policy Centre, University of Annenberg).

KAPUR, JYOTSNA (1999), 'Out of Control: Television and the Transformation of Childhood in Late Capitalism', in Kinder, Marsha (ed.), *Kids Media Culture* (Durham and London: Duke University Press).

KEANE, JOHN (1991), *The Media and Democracy* (London: Polity Press).

KINDER, MARSHA (1991), *Playing with Power in Movies, Television and Video Games: From Muppet Babies to Teenage Mutant Ninja Turtles* (Berkeley: University of California Press).

—— (ed.) (1999), *Kids Media Culture* (Durham and London: Duke University Press).

—— (1995), 'Home Alone in the 90s: Generational War and Transgenerational Address in American Movies, Television and Presidential Politics', in Bazalgette, Cary, and Buckingham, David (eds.), *In Front of the Children: Screen Entertainment and Young Andiences* (London: British Film Institute).

KLINE, STEPHEN (1993), *Out of the Garden: Toys, TV, and Children's Culture in the Age of Marketing* (London: Verso).

KUHN, ANNETTE (1984), 'Women's Genres', *Screen* 25(1).

KUMAR, KRISHAN (1995), *From Post-Industrial to Post-Modern: New Theories of the Contemporary World* (Oxford: Blackwell).

LACEY, KATE (1994), 'From *Plauderei* to Propaganda: On Women's Radio in Germany, 1924– 35', *Media, Culture and Society*, 16.

LATOUR, BRUNO (1987), *Science in Action: How to Follow Scientists and Engineers through Society* (Milton Keynes: Open University Press).

—— (1990), 'Drawing Things Together', in Lynch, Michael, and Woolgar, Steve (eds.), *Representation in Scientific Practice* (Cambridge, Mass.: MIT Press).

LEBEAU, VICKY (1997), 'The Worst of All Possible Worlds', in Silverstone, Roger (ed.), *Visions of Suburbia* (London: Routledge).

LIGHT, ALISON (1991), *Forever England: Femininity, Literature and Conservatism between the Wars* (London: Routledge).

LINGSTROM, FREDA (1953), 'Children and Television', *BBC Quarterly*, 8, April.

LIVINGSTONE, SONIA, and BOVILL, MOIRA 1999, *Young People, New Media* (London: London School of Economics and Political Science).

LUKE, CARMEN (1990), *Constructing the Child Viewer: A History of the American Discourse on Television and Children, 1950–1980* (New York: Praeger).

MACCOBY, ELEANOR (1951), 'Television: Its Impact on School Children', *Public Opinion Quarterly*, 15(3).

—— (1954), 'Why Do Children Watch Television?', *Public Opinion Quarterly*, 18.

MACDONALD, KEITH (1995), *The Sociology of the Professions* (London: Sage).

MADDEN, CECIL (1952), 'Television for the Younger Viewer', *BBC Yearbook*.

MATTELART, ARMAND, and DORFMAN, ARIEL (1975), *How to Read Donald Duck: Imperialist Ideology in the Disney Comic* (New York: International General).

MATTHESON, HILDE (1933), *Broadcasting* (London: Thornton Butterworth).

MAY, JOHN (1937), 'Radio Magic', *Woman*, 14 August.

MAYNE, JUDITH (1993), *Cinema and Spectatorship* (London: Routledge).

MCCARTHY, ANNA (1995), ' "The front row is reserved for scotch drinkers": Early Television's Tavern Audience', *Cinema Journal*, 34(4).

MCCULLOCH, DEREK (1946), 'Entertaining the Young Listener', *BBC Quarterly*, 1(1).

MEADEL, CECILE (1994), 'Between Corporatism and Representation: The Birth of a Public Radio Service in France', *Media, Culture and Society*, 16.

MERCER, COLIN (1986), 'That's Entertainment: The Resilience of Popular Forms', in Bennett, Tony, *et al.* (eds.), *Popular Culture and Social Relations* (Milton Keynes: Open University Press).

MILLER, PETER V. (1994), 'Made-to-Order and Standardized Audiences: Forms of Reality in Audience Measurement', in Ettema, James S., and Whitney, D. Charles (eds.), *Audiencemaking: How the Media Create the Audience* (London: Sage).

MONTGOMERY, KATHRYN (1989), *Target: Prime Time, Advocacy Groups and the Struggle over Entertainment Television* (New York: Oxford University Press).

MOORES, SHAUN (1988), 'The Box in the Dresser: Memories of Early Radio', *Media, Culture and Society*, 10(1).

—— (1993), *Interpreting Audiences: The Ethnography of Media Consumption* (London: Sage).

MORLEY, DAVID (1990), 'Behind the Ratings: The Politics of Audience Research', in Wollen, Tana, and Willis, Janet (eds.), *The Neglected Audience* (London: British Film Institute).

—— (1997), 'Theoretical Orthodoxies: Textualism, Constructivism and the "New Ethnography" in Cultural Studies', in Ferguson, Marjorie, and Golding, Peter (eds.), *Cultural Studies in Question* (London: Sage).

MURRAY, ROBIN (1989), 'Fordism and Post-Fordism', in Hall, Stuart, and Jacques, Martin (eds.), *New Times: The Changing Face of Politics in the 1990s* (London: Lawrence and Wishart).

NEWBURN, TIM (1992), *Permission and Regulation: Law and Morals in Post-War Britain* (London: Routledge).

NEWCOMB, HORACE, and ALLEY, ROBERT (1983), *The Producer's Medium* (New York: Oxford University Press).

OLIVER, MARK (1990), 'Deregulation and Organisation of ITV Companies', in Paterson, Richard (ed.), *Organising for Change* (London: British Film Institute).

OSBORNE, THOMAS (1998), *Aspects of Enlightenment: Social Theory and the Ethics of Truth* (London: UCL Press).

O'SULLIVAN, TIM (1991), 'Television Memories and Cultures of Viewing, 1950–65', in Corner, John (ed.), *Popular Television in Britain: Studies in Cultural History* (London: British Film Institute).

OSWELL, DAVID (2000), 'Professionalism and Children's Television: Governing the Ethics of the Public Servant?' in Lees, Tim, Ralph, Sue, and Langham Brown, Jo (eds.), *Is Regulation Still an Option in a Digital Universe?* (Luton: University of Luton Press).

PATERSON, RICHARD (1987), 'Family Perspectives in Broadcasting Policy', paper delivered at British Film Institute summer school.

PEAR, T. H. (1949), 'Psychology and the Listener', *BBC Quarterly*, 4(3).

PEARSON, GEOFFREY (1983), *Hooligan: A History of Respectable Fears* (London: Macmillan).

PERKINS, HAROLD (1989), *The Rise of the Professional Society: England since 1800* (London: Routledge).

PIORE, M. J., and SABEL, CHARLES (1984), *The Second Industrial Divide: Possibilities for Prosperity* (New York: Basic Books).

PROUT, ALAN, and JAMES, ALISON (1990), 'A New Paradigm for the Sociology of Childhood', in James, Alison, and Prout, Alan (eds.), *Constructing and Reconstructing Childhood* (London: Falmer Press).

REITH, J. C. W. (1924), *Broadcast Over Britain* (London: Hodder and Stoughton).

—— (1928), 'Introduction', *BBC Yearbook*.

—— (1949), *Into the Wind* (London: Hodder and Stoughton).

RILEY, DENISE (1983), *War in the Nursery: Theories of the Child and Mother* (London: Virago).

ROBERTSON, HOWARD (1947), *Reconstruction and the Home* (London: The Studio).

ROBINS, KEVIN (1992), 'What is "Flexible" about Independent Producers?', *Screen*, 33(2).

ROSE, JACQUELINE (1984), *The Case of Peter Pan or the Impossibility of Children's Fiction* (London: Macmillan).

ROSE, NIKOLAS (1985), *The Psychological Complex* (London: Routledge & Kegan Paul).

—— (1989), *Governing the Soul: The Shaping of the Private Self* (London: Routledge).

—— (1990), 'Psychology as a "Social" Science', in Parker, Ian, and Shotter, John (eds.), *Deconstructing Social Psychology* (London: Routledge).

ROWNTREE, B. SEEBOHM (1941), *Poverty and Progress* (London: Longmans, Green and Co.).

RUSSELL, R. D. (1946), 'Gramophones, Radio and Television', in Council of Industrial Design, *Design '46: A Survey of British Industrial Design* (London: HMSO).

SAID, EDWARD (1979), *Orientalism* (Harmondsworth: Penguin).

SCANNELL, PADDY (1988a), 'Radio Times: The Temporal Arrangements of Broadcasting in the Modern World', in Drummond, Phillip, and Paterson, Richard (eds.), *Television and Its Audiences* (London: British Film Institute Press).

—— (1988b), 'The Communicative Ethos of Broadcasting', paper presented to the *International Television Studies Conference* (London: British Film Institute).

—— (1991), 'Introduction: The Relevance of Talk', in Scannell, Paddy (ed.), *Broadcast Talk* (London: Sage).

—— and CARDIFF, DAVID (1982), 'Serving the Nation: Public Service Broadcasting before the War', in Waites, B., Bennett, T., and Martin, G. (eds.), *Popular Culture: Past and Present* (London: Open University Press).

—— —— (1991), *A Social History of Broadcasting* (London: Blackwell).

SCHRAMM, WILBUR, LYLE, JACK, and PARKER, EDWIN B. 1961, *Television in the Lives of Children* (Stanford, Calif.: Stanford University Press).

SENDALL, BERNARD (1982), *Independent Television in Britain*, vol. 1: *Origin and Foundation, 1946–62* (London: Macmillan).

—— (1983), *Independent Television in Britain*, vol. 2 (London: Macmillan).

SHAPIN, STEVEN, and SCHAFFER, SIMON (1985), *Leviathan and the Air-Pump: Hobbes, Boyle and the Experimental Life* (Princeton: Princeton University Press).

SILVERSTONE, ROGER (1994), *Television and Everyday Life* (London: Routledge).

—— and HADDON, LESLIE (1996), 'Design and the Domestication of Information and Communication Technologies: Technical Change and Everyday Life', in Mansell, Robin, and Silverstone, Roger (eds.), *Communication by Design: The Politics of Information and Communication Technologies* (Oxford: Oxford University Press).

SILVEY, ROBERT (1974), *Who's Listening? The Story of BBC Audience Research* (London: Allen Unwin).

SINCLAIR, JOHN, JACKA, ELIZABETH, and CUNNINGHAM, STUART (eds.) (1996), *New Patterns in Global Television: Peripheral Vision* (Oxford: Oxford University Press).

SMYTHE, DALLAS (1977), 'Communications: Blindspot of Western Marxism', *Canadian Journal of Political and Social Theory*, 1(3).

SPARKS, COLIN (1994), 'Independent Production', in Hood, Stuart (ed.), *Behind the Screens: The Structure of British Television in the Nineties* (London: Lawrence and Wishart).

SPIGEL, LYNN (1992), *Make Room for TV* (Chicago: University of Chicago Press).

—— (1999), 'Innocence Abroad: The Geopolitics of Childhood in Postwar Kid Strips', in Kinder, Marsha (ed.), *Kids Media Culture* (Durham and London: Duke University Press).

STAPLES, TERRY (1997), *All Pals Together: The Story of Children's Cinema* (Edinburgh: Edinburgh University Press).

STAIGER, JANET (1986), ' "The Handmaiden of Villainy": Methods and Problems in Studying the Historical Reception of a Film', *Wide Angle*, 8(1).

STEINBERG, SHIRLEY R., and KINCHELOE, JOE L. (1997a), 'Introduction: No More Secrets—Kinderculture, Information Saturation and the Postmodern Childhood', in Steinberg, Shirly R., and Kincheloe, Joe L. (eds.), *Kinder Culture: The Corporate Construction of Childhood* (Oxford: Westview Press).

—— —— (eds.) (1997b) *Kinder Culture: The Corporate Construction of Childhood* (Oxford: Westview Press).

STOWELL, GORDON (1940), 'The Listener Takes Part', *BBC Yearbook* (London: British Broadcasting Corporation).

STREATFIELD, NOEL (1951), 'Magic for Children', *BBC Yearbook* (London: British Broadcasting Corporation).

STROUT, RICHARD (1949), 'Every Cellar a Cinema', *New Statesman and Nation*, 28 May.

THORNBORROW, JOANNA (1998), 'Children's Participation in the Discourse of Children's Television', in Hutchby, Ian, and Moran-Ellis, Jo (eds.), *Children and Social Competence: Arenas of Action* (London: Falmer Press).

THUMIN, JANET (1995), ' "A Live Commercial for Icing Sugar": Researching the Historical Audience—Gender and Broadcast Television in the 1950s', *Screen* 36(1).

TRACEY, MICHAEL, and MORRISION, DAVID (1979), *Whitehouse* (London: Macmillan).

TUNSTALL, JEREMY (1993), *Television Producers* (London: Routledge).

UNGER, R. M. (1987), *False Necessity* (Cambridge: Cambridge University Press).

URWIN, CATHY (1985), 'Constructing Motherhood: The Persuasion of Normal Development', in Steedman, Carolyn, Urwin, Cathy, and Walkerdine, Valerie (eds.), *Language, Gender and Childhood* (London: Routledge & Kegan Paul).

VOLOSINOV, V. N. (1973), *Marxism and the Philosophy of Language* (London: Seminar Press).

WAGG, STEPHEN (1992), ' "One I made earlier": Media, Popular Culture and the Politics of Childhood', in Strinati, Dominic, and Wagg, Stephen (eds.), *Come on Down? Popular Media Culture in Post-War Britain* (London: Routledge).

WALKERDINE, VALERIE (1984), 'Developmental Psychology and the Child-Centred Pedagogy: The Insertion of Piaget into Early Education', in Julian Henriques, Wendy Hollway, Cathy Urwin, Couze Venn, and Valerie Walkerdine (eds.), *Changing the Subject: Psychology, Social Regulation and Subjectivity* (London: Cambridge University Press).

—— (1988), *The Mastery of Reason: Cognitive Development and the Production of Rationality* (London: Routledge).

—— and LUCEY, HELEN (1989), *Democracy in the Kitchen: Regulating Mothers and Socialising Daughters* (London: Virago).

WARTELLA, ELLEN (1994), 'Producing Children's Television Programs', in Ettema, James S., and Whitney, D. Charles (eds.), *Audiencemaking: How the Media Create the Audience* (London: Sage).

WEBSTER, JAMES G., and PHALEN, PATRICIA F. (1994). 'Victim, Consumer, or Commodity? Audience Models in Communication Policy', in Ettema, James S., and Whitney, D. Charles (eds.), *Audiencemaking: How the Media Create the Audience* (London: Sage).

WEEKS, JEFFREY (1981), *Sex, Politics and Society: The Regulation of Sexuality since 1800* (London: Longman).

WHITEHOUSE, MARY (1967), *Cleaning Up TV: From Protest to Participation* (London: Blandford Press).

WILSON, ELISABETH (1980, *Only Halfway to Paradise: Women in Post-War Britain, 1945–68* (London: Tavistock).

WOODARD, EMORY (1999), *The 1999 State of Children's Television Report* (Pennsylvania: Annenberg Public Policy Centre, University of Annenberg).

YOUNG, KIMBERLY (1998), *Caught in the Net: How to Recognise the Signs of Internet Addiction and a Winning Strategy for Recovery* (New York: John Wiley and Sons).

Index